DATE DUE

DEMCO 13829810

D1226405

Collector's Encyclopedia of

NIPPON
PORCELAIN

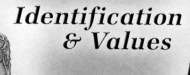

Identification
& Values

Seventh Series

Joan F. Van Patten

COLLECTOR BOOKS
A Division of Schroeder Publishing Co., Inc.

Dedication

This book is dedicated to all my wonderful friends who gave me so much support and help with it. Thanks so much for being there.

About the Author

Joan Van Patten is the author of *Collector's Encyclopedia of Nippon Porcelain, First through Sixth Series, Nippon Price Guide, Collector's Encyclopedia of Noritake, First and Second Series, Celluloid Treasures of the Victorian Era,* and *Nippon Dolls and Playthings,* all published by Collector Books.

She has written hundreds of trade paper and magazine articles and is a contributor to *Schroeder's Antiques Price Guide.*

Joan has been on the board of the INCC (International Nippon Collectors Club) since its inception. A co-founder of INCC, she also served as its first president and was a director of the club for many years. Joan edited and published the *Nippon Notebook* and the *INCC Newsletter* for five years. She has lectured on the subjects of Nippon, Noritake, and celluloid throughout the United States.

The research of antiques and collectibles, travel, and volunteer work are other major interests of the author.

The current values in this book should be used only as a guide. They are not intended to set prices, which vary from one section of the country to another. Auction prices as well as dealer prices vary greatly and are affected by condition and demand. Neither the author nor the publisher assumes responsibility for any losses which might be incurred as a result of consulting this guide.

Front cover: Vase with moriage bird decoration, Plate #4463, 13" tall, blue #52, $1,400.00 – 1,600.00. Coralene vase, Plate #4374, 7" tall, mark #242, $1,000.00 – 1,200.00.

Back cover: Wall plaque, Plate #4573, 8¾" wide, green #47, $500.00 – 600.00. Moriage man on a camel vase, Plate #4546, 14" tall, green #47, $1,500.00 – 1,800.00. Vase, Plate #4768, 7¾" tall, blue #52, $700.00 – 800.00.

Cover design: Terri Hunter
Book design: Karen Geary
Book layout: Mary Ann Hudson

Searching for a Publisher?

We are always looking for people knowledgeable within their fields. If you feel that there is a real need for a book on your collectible subject and have a large comprehensive collection, contact Collector Books.

Collector Books
P.O. Box 3009
Paducah, KY 42002-3009

www.collectorbooks.com

Copyright © 2002 by Joan Van Patten

❖ *Contents* ❖

Acknowledgments

So many people helped with this book that it's impossible to give adequate thanks to these contributors.

These books are not possible without the approval of my publisher, Billy Schroeder, and I want to thank him for having faith in my projects. He and his staff do a super job on all of my books. My editor, Lisa Stroup and her assistant Amy Hopper continue to make these books look so wonderful. The staff at Collector Books is first rate, and I am always so pleased with what they accomplish.

My good friend and co-author of *Nippon Dolls and Playthings*, Linda Lau, sent me many, many photos and wrote five chapters for this book! She is an extremely knowledgeable collector and is always willing to share her expertise with others. She has an exceptional collection of dolls and all kinds of wonderful Nippon, and I appreciate her guidance and prices she gave me for the dolls that are featured. Her thirst for research is unquenchable, and she is always finding something new and surprising to investigate. Thanks, Linda, for all your help.

As always, Mark Griffin and Earl Smith have provided me with numerous photos for this book, more than 160! How they keep finding so many new and wonderful pieces of Nippon is amazing to me. Their photographer, Clement Photographic Services, Inc. in Ft. Myers, Florida always does a superb job. These two people have a fantastic collection and in my estimation, the finest in existence. They are always eager to help with all of my books and without their help, it would not be possible to have such wonderful photos. Earl and Mark also helped with pricing items, which is an almost impossible task. Thank you both.

Judy Boyd also sent photos and wrote two chapters for this series. Judy is always there to help in any way necessary, and this project was no exception. Judy and I have been friends for nearly 20 years, and she is known as a very knowledgeable collector of Nippon. She loves to dig and delve into Nippon projects and will do a lot of research just to gain a little knowledge. Thanks, Judy, for all your help but most of all for being my special friend.

Jeffrey Mattison contributed the chapter on Anton Mauve and did an exceptional job with his research. For the help they gave to Jeffrey, I would like to thank William Rappard at the Netherlands Institute of Art History, Monica Verona at the Metropolitan Museum of Art, Patrick Sheehan at Sotheby's, Ed Roberts at Edward's Studio of Photography, Toledo Museum of Art, and Lawrence and Patricia Goan. Thank you, Jeffrey, for sharing your information with readers of this Series.

Lewis and BJ Longest sent me many wonderful photos for this book and also took photos for other collectors that are included. Lewis and BJ are two of the sweetest people you could ever hope to meet and are always ready when I request help. Lewis is a professional photographer and naturally, his photos are outstanding. Thanks to both of you.

Bob and Maggie Schoenherr are a special couple who also pitch in every time I'm looking for photos. This time was no exception. They have sent me photos of some wonderful Nippon pieces that they have in their collection, and I am so happy to include them in this Series. Thanks, Maggie and Bob.

Bob and Janet Bing — You told me that you wanted no special mention — but they provided me with many photos and descriptions, and I must tell them how much I appreciate their help. Thanks, Janet and Bob, for your contribution.

My sister-in-law, Marie Young boxed up many, many items and brought them to my house to be photographed. We spent several hours unpacking, photographing, and repacking Nippon. She is a long-time collector and started her "addiction" when she was still in her teens! She is a great sister as well as being a big help to me with the addition of her pieces in this book.

Jess Berry and Gary Graves have always been two of my favorite people. Jess had written many chapters in previous books, and he and Gary sent me some great photos for this Series. They have a wonderful collection and are always happy to share their new finds with others. My thanks go to these two great guys.

Dawn Fisher has a very large collection of dolls and other Nippon items. She invited me to her house and let me photograph anything and everything I wanted to — now that's friendship. Dawn, thanks so much for allowing me to include so many of your wonderful pieces.

Cheryl and Joe Meese also heeded the call for photos, and I have used many of theirs in this Series. Thanks to both of you for sharing your collection with the readers of this book.

Ken Landgraf sent me many photos of Nippon porcelain, and I am very pleased to include them in this Series. Ken is a knowledgeable collector who wanted to share his *finds* with others. Thanks, Ken, for all your help.

Ken Schirm is noted for his fantastic collection of wall plaques, but he also collects other quality pieces of Nippon. I am pleased to be able to include a number of his items in this book. Thanks, Ken, for the great photos.

My friend Walt Maytan has managed to collect some exceptional pieces of Nippon over the years and sent me some wonderful photos of several of these items. Walt is a longtime collector and extremely knowledgeable on this subject. Thanks for your help.

Jack and Lisa Landrum also sent photos of some of their special Nippon items. Jack takes great photos, and they make a wonderful addition to this book. Jack and Lisa are a special couple, and anyone who has ever been around them knows just how warm hearted and caring they both are. Thanks to both of you.

Frank and Ruth Reid are another special husband and wife team. It's always such a pleasure to be in their company. They too sent me numerous photos, some are in the Sixth Series and some are featured in this book. Thanks for sharing your items.

Nat Goldstein is "Mr. Personality" and is a very enthusiastic Nippon collector. He was one of the first to send me photos of some of his items, and I appreciate all the time he spent photographing and writing descriptions. Thanks, Nat.

My friend Valerie Herts is both a collector and dealer and has managed to locate some exceptional pieces of Nippon over the years. She was kind enough to photograph a number of these items so that I could include them in this book. Thanks, Val.

Lee and Donna Call are longtime friends and always manage to help with my books. They sent photos of some very special Nippon and I appreciate all that they have done. Thank you, Lee and Donna.

Others who have helped with this project are Shirley and Don Bakley, William and Irma Lusson, Ken and Sharee Pakula, Arnold and Stephanie Burt, Pat Selman, Todd Lawrence, Kathy and David McElrea, Lee Smith, David Lucas, Thomas and Barbara Ewanich, Elaine Lunde, Ed Wheat, Yvonne and Brian Hurst, Bill and Sylvia Beckerly, Gloria Addison, Doris and George Myers, Bernadette Knotts, Duke Ward, Scott Morrison, Jean Andress, Dave Prezch, Bernie Burlew, and Charles and Rosmond Sweeting.

I know that a few people are going to be disappointed that some of their photos were not used in this book. Some may have been duplicates of another collector's piece or perhaps had appeared in a previous book, and some may be appearing in (hopefully) another book in the future. I received many more photos than I could use — now that's a problem!

My heartfelt thanks to everyone who helped with this book. It would not have been possible without you.

Introduction

If you invest in beauty, it will remain with you all the days of your life.
Frank Lloyd Wright

Nippon era items were manufactured in Japan during the years of 1891 – 1921 and readers should refer to earlier volumes of this series for more information about their manufacture. So many items were produced and exported from Japan during these years that it is taking numerous books to cover the subject. Little did I know when the first book was published that so many more would follow.

Collecting Nippon wares is not only enjoyable but also educational. As we study the designs and scenes portrayed on the pieces, we learn more about our past. Collectors should question reliable dealers and other collectors and gain from their knowledge. They should study the books, visit antique shows and malls, and view as many items as they can. The International Nippon Collectors Club (INCC) provides members with a chat line, newsletters, yearly convention, a website, and help from fellow members. Click on their website http://www.nipponcollectorsclub.com for membership information.

A good collection requires a considerable amount of self-discipline and common sense, and my one rule about collecting is to buy quality but be sure to buy what you really like. It is much better to purchase one really good piece than four or five mediocre ones. Be selective in what you buy and collect. Do not purchase items that are cracked, chipped, have hairlines or repairs unless they are definitely lower in price. Worn gold also detracts from the beauty of the article. Condition should be of prime consideration. Well-executed pieces in MINT condition always hold their value. Collecting fads will also push up prices but remember that what is hot today may not be a year from now, and prices could drop.

Collectors love to find items in original boxes and with original price tags on them. It's amazing to think that some of these old stickers survived over the years. Evidently, the items were not even washed, and some of them may be over 100 years old! A few of the old children's tea sets and dolls have been found in their boxes, and collectors are thrilled when they locate them.

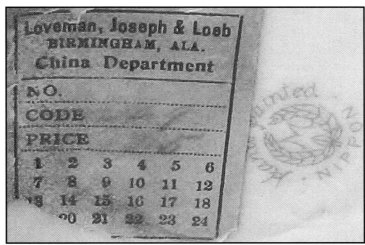

The Nippon market has remained strong, and many pieces are soaring to unprecedented levels. Buyers are more selective and knowledgeable in their purchases. Choice items are becoming harder to find, and anyone who buys items on the Internet knows how quickly items can go up in price. What might have sold for $1,700 two or three years ago may now be selling for $5,000 or more. We now have instant access to thousands of Nippon items each week and no longer have to go to the local mall to get our *fix*. And any serious collector knows just how addictive this hobby can be. All we have to do is click on our computer and voilá, all kinds of items are offered for sale. Of course, there are many complaints about these types of purchases as well. It would be the rare collector who has not received an item that was not as it was described. I know that I have gotten numerous cracked, chipped, and even repaired items. They were returned, but I was very disappointed that I did not end up with the pieces I had hoped to own.

Sellers also have problems as buyers don't always send in payment for their purchase or they retract their bids. Moreover, there are people who bid on an item that is identical to one they have. The only problem is that there is something wrong with their piece and once the new item arrives, they send back their not-so-perfect piece to the seller. In retaliation, some dealers have resorted to using invisible ink on their items. It is actually called swimmers ink that has been used in discos, private clubs, bars, and other admission places for years. You need a special pen that is usually sold with the kit. You can write something on the bottom of the item or you can use your own fingerprints for identification instead of writing because someone might be able to forge what you wrote but not your fingerprint. You simply pour a few drops of the invisible ink on a new clean stamp pad, press your finger on the pad and then on the piece you wish to mark. You can check the mark by using a black light that is usually sold with these kits. In this way, the pieces are marked without devaluing them in any way. The mark is not readily seen, and pieces cannot be switched.

This Seventh Series is loaded with hundreds of photos of items not featured in the earlier books and many chapters of information to aid collectors. It is my hope that collectors will be as excited about this new book as they have been the previous ones.

Historical Information

Several old news articles give us information about Japan and its pottery and porcelain industries. In the October 22, 1881, issue of the *Scientific American Supplement, No. 303,* I found the following: "Japanese chronicle claim that the first pottery was made in the year 660 B.C.; it was not, however, until the Christian era that the art made any considerable advances. In the year 1223 A.D., great improvements were made in manufacture and decoration of the ware. From that date to the sixteenth century the great potteries of Owari, Hizen, Mino, Kioto, Kaga, and Satsuma were established. The Rahn-Yaki, or crackled ware, was first made at Kioto, at the commencement of the sixteenth century. The best old Hizen ware, that which is still the most admired, was made at Arita Hizen, in 1580 to 1585; the old Satsuma dates from 1592. Consul-General Van Buren states that porcelain clays are found in nearly all parts of the country, and the different kinds are usually found in close proximity, and close to canals and rivers, which is of considerable advantage, as affording a means of transport. In all cases every variety of clay used in the manufacture of pottery is found in a natural state; there is no necessity to manufacture the quartzose or fusible clays as is done in others parts of the world, and which adds considerably to the cost of the ware. One of the peculiarities in the clay found in Japan is that it contains both the fusible and infusible materials in such proportions as to make a light, beautiful, translucent, and durable porcelain. At Arita, in Hizen, there is a clay found which contains 78¾ percent of silica, and 17¾ percent of alumina; from this clay is made the delicate, translucent egg-shell ware, without the addition of any other matter. From an adjoining bluff a clay is taken which has 50 percent of silica, and 38 percent of alumina; from this the common porcelain is made.

"Potter's clay is found in very large quantities in the provinces of Yamashiro, Hoki, Turoo Iyo, Hizen, Higo, Owari, Mikaera, Idyn, Musahi, and Mino. In the whole of Japan there are 283 localities where the clay is deposited; many of these only furnish inferior clay but they are all fitted for use in some of the various kinds of pottery. These clays are thoroughly powdered by means of what is called balance pounders, worked in some localities by water-power, but the work is often done by hand. The powder is then dried and stored on boards or flat boxes. This dough does not go through the process of fermentation. The shaping is almost exclusively done on the potter's wheel, which is set on a pivot working in a porcelain eye. As a rule, the wheel is turned by the potter himself, but in Hizen it is kept in motion by means of a band connected with its pivot and another wheel turned by a boy. In making dishes of other shape than round, a crude mould is sometimes used. After the clay has been shaped on the wheel, it is set away for drying, and usually in two or three days it is considered sufficiently dry for smoothing, which is done on the wheel with a sharp curved knife. The material is now made into bisque, or biscuit, by a preliminary baking in small ovens, when it is ready for painting, if it is to be painted on the biscuit; if not, it is ready for the glazing. In either event it will then go to the large furnace for the final baking. The kilns for this purpose are always built on hill sides and are joined together, increasing in size from the lower to the higher ones, and in number from four to twenty-five; these kilns are so constructed that the draught is from the lowest one, in addition to which each kiln has its own firing place. The result of this construction is that the upper ones are by far the most heated, and the ware is arranged accordingly; that which requires the least baking, in the lower kiln, and that which requires the greatest heat, in the upper. These connecting kilns have the merit of being heat saving, but they are usually small and badly constructed, and the heat in none of them is uniform.

"The glaze is made from the silicious clay and potash extracted from wood ashes. The potash is not a pure white, and this accounts for the dirty color usually to be observed in unpainted Japanese ware. In different districts the painting varies. For instance, in Owari, the greater part of the ware is painted a cobalt blue — the cobalt ore being found in the bluffs near the clay deposits, and is used for painting the cheaper wares, and for this purpose German cobalt is also employed. The painting with cobalt is generally done on the biscuit before glazing. In several districts a very handsome ware is made, and painted on the glaze. For this kind of painting the colors are mixed with a silicate of lead and potash, and baked the third time in a small furnace at a low temperature. The coloring oxides in use are those of copper, cobalt, iron, antimony, manganese, and gold. Japanese porcelain painting may be divided into two categories, decorative and graphic; the first is used to improve the vessel upon which it is placed, and this class includes all the ware except that of the province of Kaga, which would come under the head of graphic, as it delineates all the trades, occupations, sports, customs, and costumes of the people, as well as the scenery, flora, and fauna of the country. Owari ware is made in the province of that name; it is not as translucent, but stronger and more tenacious than some of the Hizen manufacture.

"The principal potteries are at a village called Seto, twelve miles from the sea; in this village there are more than 200 kilns. The ware is mostly painted a cobalt blue, and is merely of a decorative kind, consisting of branches of trees, grass, flowers, birds, and insects, all these being copied by the artist from nature. All the Owari ware is true hard porcelain, and is strong and durable. In Hizen, a number of wares are manufactured, the best known kind being the Eurari, which is made at Arita, but painted at Eurari. The colors in use are red, blue, green, and gold; these are combined in various proportions, but, as a rule, the red predominates. Generally the surface of the vessel is divided into medallions of figures, which alternately have red, blue, or white background, with figures in green or blue and gold.

"In Kioto, the ware manufactured is very similar to that produced in Satsuma, but it is lighter and more porous; the decorations are also nearly the same, being of birds and flowers. There is a description of ware made in Kioto, called Eraku, the whole body of which is covered with a red oxide of iron, and over this mythical figures of gild are traced. That produced in Kaga is faience, and in the style of painting is unlike any other in Japan, the predominating color being a light red, used with green and gold. The designs with which it is profusely decorated are trees, grasses, flowers, birds, and figures of all classes of people, with their costumes, occupations, and pastimes. The Banko ware is made at the head of the Owari Bay; it is an unglazed stone-ware, very light and durable, made on moulds in irregular shapes, and decorated

with figures in relief. On the island of Awadji, a delicate, creamy, crackled, soft paste porcelain is made. The figures used in decoration are birds and flowers, but outlined by heavy, dark lines.

"Consul Van Buren is of opinion that, at no distant day, Japan will be one of the foremost competitors in the pottery markets of the world, on account of the great variety and excellence of the clays, their proximity to the sea, the cheapness of labor, and the beauty and originality of the decorations. Already this important industry has been greatly stimulated by the foreign demand, and by the success of Japanese exhibitions at the Exhibitions of Vienna, Philadelphia, and Paris."

On August 6 of 1881 the following article appeared in the New York Times entitled Fine Japanese Ware. "Consul-General Van Buren's report on the pottery and porcelain industries of Japan is an able resume of the knowledge we at present possess on the subject, and contains at the same time much that is both original and interesting. The writer justly dwells on the very great natural advantages Japan enjoys in the matter of ceramic manufacture. The potter has only to dig. Excellent porcelain clays are found everywhere, and often near "water transportation." No doubt much of Japan's success as a porcelain producing country is attributable to this cause. We know that in China the discovery of real fine pure clay was regarded as the result of divine intervention, and the memory of the "inspired," who showed the people where they might find boccaro earth is gratefully remembered to this day. In Europe, too, those who have studied the subjects are familiar with the troubles that beset the potter of the Boboli gardens and the family of the Chiccanean. Nevertheless, to the artificial clay of those times we owe the exquisite pate tender of the old Sevres ware; a biscuit so much superior in many respects to that obtained from the natural kaolin, that 45 years after the latter had come into general use, a neglected store of the artificial material made the fortune of its finder, Ebelman. It is not a mere freak that induces people to give 500 guineas for a saucer of old Sevres.

"But even in Japan certain districts are more favored by nature than others. The Comparative table which the Consul-General gives is most interesting in this respect, for it shows how largely local advantages have influenced the development of the ceramic art in the various Provinces. Mikawa, now better known as Aichi-ken, stands first on the list, but much of the clay found there is not of the best quality. Hizen, as might be expected, comes next, and after it Mino, where the best egg-shell porcelain in Japan has been manufactured; a fact which the author, we observe, does not note. Kaga finds no place on the list at all, and this may perhaps surprise the very numerous lovers of that brilliant red and gold ware so largely exported to Europe at present. But the fact is that, despite the celebrity of the Kutanyaki, the Province of Kashiu possesses neither kaolin nor petuntse of first class quality. The potters of Daishoji have always been obliged to import their materials, and hence it happens that the amateur is often sadly puzzled by the specimen decorated after the Kutani style, but made of Hizen or Owari clay.

"Apropos of this Kagayaki, the author seems inclined to agree with the idea that it is representative of the graphic style in Japan. No doubt this dictum is true at present, but it is well to remember that delineation of "trades, occupations, sports, customs and costumes" are never found on the Kutani ware of former times. Something similar may be said of the nature of the ware. The Consul-General describes it as faience, which is true of the Kagayaki proper, i.e. the ware made entirely with materials found in the Providence, but the best pieces produced there in the past, and indeed much of the workshops' present outcome, must be described as fine porcelain."

Old stereograph cards also give us an insight into the pottery and porcelain world in Japan in the early 1900s. The cards shown here are all marked with a 1904 copyright and were sold by Underwood and Underwood, Publishers, New York, London, Toronto, Canada, and Ottawa, Kansas. The cards also tell us that the Works and Studios are in Arlington, New Jersey and Westwood, New Jersey. Stereograph cards and stereoscopes were very popular during this time period in history. These cards were both instructive and entertaining. An old book entitled *The World War Through the Stereoscope* accompanying a set of cards I own gives us the following insight to these items. The following information was written by Oliver Wendell Holmes, "A stereograph is an instrument which makes surfaces look solid. All pictures in which perspective and light and shade are properly managed have more or less of the effect of solidity; but by this instrument that effect is so heightened as to produce an appearance of reality which cheats the sense with its seeming truth.

Stereoscope

"We see something with the second eye which we did not see with the first; in other words, the two eyes see different pictures of the same thing, for the obvious reason that they look from points two or three inches apart.

"The stereograph, as we have called the double picture designed for the stereoscope, is to be the card of introduction to make all mankind acquaintances.

"The first effect of looking at a good photograph through the stereoscope is a surprise such as no painting ever produced.

The mind feels its way into the very depths of the picture."

We are told that the stereograph is a true window to the world of nature and the activities of man. It is also the only means possible of obtaining just what the mere picture lacks — the third dimension — producing perfect space with all objects shown accurately in their three natural dimensions.

The book's introduction goes on to tell us more about stereographs. "The stereograph is fundamentally different from the ordinary photograph because it is made on the principle of two-eye vision. That is, the ordinary photograph is made by a camera with a single lens, like a person with one eye, while the stereograph is made by a camera having two lenses set about as far apart as our two eyes. This camera, therefore, gives two somewhat dissimilar photographs, and this difference between them is of great importance, for when looked at through a stereoscope it produces these remarkable results.

"First, we get perfect space for eye and mind — not merely a suggestion of space as in ordinary pictures; objects stand out in all three dimensions, or as solids, as in nature.

"Second, we see objects and places life size — that is, in natural size and at a natural distance; the stereograph card serves as a window through which we look out at the object or place beyond.

"Third, while looking at these objects and places through the instrument, it is not only possible but it is easy and natural for one to lose all consciousness of immediate bodily surroundings and to gain real experience of seeing, of being present in the places themselves.

"It is positively true that not one of these three results can be obtained by any other illustrative means. In accomplishing these results the stereograph renders a service as an instructive medium that is absolutely unique and the importance of which cannot be overestimated nor its significance overstated. It means that we can now be as directly connected with the world outside through sight as our homes and offices are now connected with distant people by means of the telephone. The stereograph gives one the mental impressions of seeing the actual objects."

The first card shown (Photos 1 & 2) is titled, "A potter and his wheel fashioning a vase; Kinkosan works, Kyoto, Japan." On the back of the card is information about what is shown on the front of the card. Some of the words are missing, evidently due to some kind of sticker once being on the card. Some of what is written is as follows, "This is one of the most famous potteries in the world; if this spectacled and wise-looking person at the wheel were allowed to follow his own inspiration in respect to form instead of catering to European and American taste, he would probably produce something thoroughly good; Japanese craftsmen have instinctive good taste and good judgment in matters aesthetic.

"The wheel revolves on a vertical axis below. The potter sets it whirling every little while with a dexterous touch of those lean hands and his manipulations of the soft grayish clay soon produce from the shapeless lump with which he started a vase of perfect symmetry and more or less elaborate

Photo 1

design. His only tools are a few sticks of different shapes and sizes. The big bowl holds water with which to wet and soften the clay if it dries too fast to be manageable.

"The work here is all specialized. This man does modeling and nothing else, all day long. Other men are kept at work grinding and washing the crude clay to prepare it for his hands; still others prepare and apply the glazes, tend the kilns, decorate the ware with mineral paints, and add touches of gilding. Women and girls do some of the simpler and less remunerative kinds of work, like burnishing the gilt figures and bands for final effect."

The second stereograph card (Photo 3) is titled, "Workmen watching kilns full of Awata porcelain, Kyoto, Japan." The back of this card gives the following information, "This factory is in the eastern part of the city, in the neighborhood of the famous cloisonné works and some of the famous old temples. No. 67 of this series took you into a room where a potter was at work with his wheel, shaping a vase of soft clay. Now a number of just such vases and jars are being baked in the intense heat of ovens inside these kilns. Each oven is now sealed up tightly with a mask of clay, and these men stay here to keep up the fires (here is wood stacked conveniently at hand) and make sure that the temperature is maintained at the desired degree.

"On those racks overhead you see similar ware waiting for the next process it has to go through. Some pieces are simply glazed and refired, coming out a beautiful cream-color or buff, their transparent glaze all a mass of delicate 'crackle' — the fine network of microscopic breaks which gives so beauti-

ful a variation of the body color.

"It is a matter of regret to everybody who has studied the Japanese pottery of a century or two ago that foreign influence should be so demoralizing in the matter of aesthetics. The shapes designed by Japanese workmen before the days of European and American trade were vastly better than they are now, when the Japanese producer tries to please the poorer taste of western people.

"These men work for less the wages of errand-boys in American factories, but they can live comfortably — according to their ideals

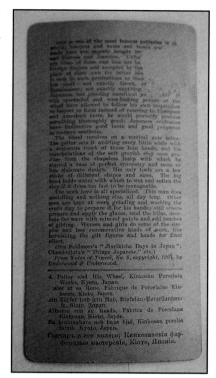

Photo 2

— on a small fraction of the sum necessary in America. Their food is chiefly rice, tea, and fish, their clothing and bedding, cheap cotton stuff. The exceedingly light costume of the elderly man yonder is occasioned partly by the heat of the furnaces, but it is not uncommon in many occupations."

The third stereograph card (Photo 4) is titled, "Pretty factory girls decorating cheap pottery for the foreign market, Kyoto, Japan" and gives the following information, "This is one of the many rooms in a porcelain factory in the eastern part of the city. All the ware you see here is cheap and intended exclusively for foreign sale. In fact, it would not sell here in Japan, for the designs in form and color, while they please the uncultivated taste of the average European or American purchaser, would never satisfy the more critical and discriminating judgment of the Japanese public!

"In other departments really beautiful ware is produced, long hours of patient labor by expert craftsmen being given to the shaping and decorating of genuine works of art. Girls are employed here because their labor is cheaper. A dollar a week seems a large sum to these little maids so solemnly absorbed in painting with their long-handled brushes. Notice how closely they are crowded together as they sit here on their heels before the low work-benches. They are gentle, demure, well-behaved girls, without any trace of the bold forwardness which girls of similarly humble origin are apt to acquire under Western factory conditions. Their gay-colored kimonos are of cheap cotton but worn with the grace of silken brocade; notice that the damsel at the end of the second row wears a broad sash tied behind.

Photo 3

"Some of the girls have been to public schools of elementary grade and learned to read and write — possibly some have not, for the schools are not absolutely free and it is sometimes difficult for a father with a large family to pay the fee of one yen (50 cts.) annually. Amusements all the girls have, for this is a land of holidays, processions, and street shows. They find their simple pleasures in walking about the flowery temple gardens and mingling with the chattering crowds about the booths of fakirs and venders of sweets. No such thing as flirtation is known to them — they have no boy friends and their marriages will be arranged by their elders."

Photo 4

The Monastic Series

To drink like a Capuchin is to drink poorly;
To drink like a Benedictine is to drink deeply;
To drink like a Dominican is pot after pot;
But to drink like a Franciscan is to drink the cellar dry.
Old French drinking song

Occasionally, collectors will find an item in the so-called monastic or monk series. These pieces are difficult to locate and generally expensive to purchase. Six scenes have been found, and some of these very same designs have been found on European and American wares that were made around that same time. I have found these very same scenes on Laughlin Art China, Morris Willmore Co. pieces, La Francaise Porcelain, and those bearing the beehive mark, to mention a few.

Backstamped, Morris Wellmore Co., Trenton, N.J.

Three of the monks are what we might call monastic tipplers, and the other three are smelling flowers, playing the violin or reading a newspaper. The bibulous monks are all drinking wine. One has a wine glass in his hand, another a wine bottle in one hand and a basket with grapes in the other, and the third has a blue and white covered stein. There are four known backgrounds, green with moriage trim, mustard color background with moriage trim, off-white, and off-white with enameled grapes and leaves. The following designs and backgrounds have been combined:

1. Monk wearing a brown habit with blue and white stein in his hand. The background on these pieces is that of enameled grapes and a brick wall.

2. Monk wearing a brown and white habit, holding a wine glass in his hand and having a background of enameled grapes, leaves, and a brick wall.

3. Monk with a basket in one hand and a wine bottle in the other. This has been found with three backgrounds, off-white, green with moriage trim, and mustard color with moriage trim.

4. Monk smelling flowers. This one also comes with an off-white background, green or mustard color background with moriage trim.

5. Monk playing a violin having a green background with moriage trim.

6. Monk reading a newspaper. This too comes with an off-white background and green with moriage trim.

Seventy-five percent of these items have been found bearing a maple leaf backstamp, and the remainder have the later M in wreath mark.

There is a very real and important link between wine and

monks. Records show that St. Benedict allowed his monks to have a half-pint of wine every day. Monks grew their own food in the monastery garden, and no doubt most had vineyards as well. In fact, one of monasticism's greatest services to Western civilization has been its contribution to wine making. For nearly 1,300 years, almost all the biggest and best vineyards were owned and operated by religious houses.

Monks have been devoted teachers for many centuries; they have taught reading, writing, farming, wine making, bread making, and other skills. During the Middle Ages many were religious scholars who helped keep learning alive, and before the invention of printing, the monks copied books by hand. The word "monk" comes from the Greek "monos" which means solitary man. Most lived and worked in a monastery, and this word comes from a Greek word meaning living alone. The chosen leader of the monks is called the abbot from the Hebrew word "abba" meaning father, and the monks called each other brother. Monasticism is a mode of life practiced by persons who have abandoned the world for religious reasons and devote their lives, either separately or in a community, to spiritual perfection. They take vows of celibacy, poverty, and obedience under which

they live. A novice takes his vows and receives his monk's habit and supposedly, the devil leaves him at this point. When one became a monk, he receives the tonsure, which is a monastic haircut from the Abbot.

Life was not easy for monks, and years ago they were not even allowed to show bare legs. Shoes were intended to last a whole year. Monks were allowed only one meal a day in the winter and a snack of bread and wine mid-morning. In the summer two meals were provided at midday and evening, and in the Middle Ages no meat eating was allowed.

Today, there is not a complete medieval monastery surviving in England. Henry VIII took away the entire monks' land and buildings when he disbanded the monasteries in the sixteenth century.

Monk designs have been found only on wine jugs, mugs, steins, humidors, and vases to date. Recently, an old Noritake Company salesman's page was offered for sale which featured the monk with basket and wine bottle. The watercolor is 7½" tall and 6" wide and in one corner has the numbers 1689/1. What a find! Readers should refer to the chapter "Matching Salesman's Pages with Nippon Items" for a photo of this page.

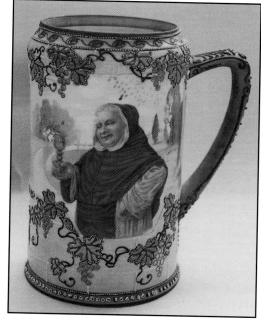

5½", green 52, $550.00 – 600.00 each.

9½", blue 52, $1,800.00 – 2,200.00 each.

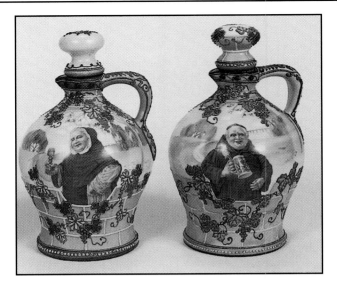

9½", green 47, $1,800.00 – 2,200.00 each.

9½", green 52, $1,900.00 – 2,300.00 each.

Woodland Nippon

There is little known about many of the Nippon patterns, and sometimes it takes a lot of researching and supposition as to how or why they were used. Very often, the discovery process merely consists of looking at what everybody has seen and thinking what nobody has thought. The Woodland pattern is just such a design.

The woodland scene found on Nippon items is evidently an adaptation of one originally used on Royal Doulton wares. This scene first appeared on the Doulton pieces in 1908.

The Nippon design features trees, cottages, clouds, and heraldry. Larger pieces have more cottages and trees, and the smaller items naturally have less. Four different heraldry shields have been found on the woodland items. There is a cross, an X, a \ (called a bend), and a type of stylized flower. Some of the flowers have four petals and four dots while others have three petals and three dots for decoration. Eighty percent of the Nippon items found with the woodland scene either have an X or cross in the shield.

Heraldry is like picture writing. It became fully developed about the end of the twelfth and the beginning of the thirteenth century. Through heraldry, we can trace the origins of many noble families and distinguish the different branch of each and the relations between families.

Heraldry had strong military associations and could be extremely useful when soldiers were going hand-to-hand combat. When everyone on the battlefield was in a suit of armor, it made it easier to tell who was who if a shield was on the helmet. Followers could distinguish their knights and each other by looking at the heraldry on the helmets.

Six backstamps have been found on woodland pieces. They are #4 the cherry blossom; #45 LFH with a crown; #47 M in wreath; #50 MM Nippon; #52 maple leaf; and #119 C.G.N. Nippon. A few have been found without a backstamp, and later wares are found with a Made in Japan backstamp. Research indicates that the majority of the backstamps are #47 (57%) and #52 (39%).

Most of the pieces marked with the M in wreath backstamp have a shield with an X, and the majority of the maple leaf marked items have the shield with a cross.

The woodland scene has been found on all types of items including after dinner coffee sets, bowls, cake sets, candlesticks, chambersticks, chocolate sets, compotes, condensed milk containers, cracker jars, creamers and sugar bowls, dresser items including trays, hatpin holders, powder boxes, hair receiver and small compotes, ewers, humidors, ladles, match holder ashtray combinations, matchbox holders with attached ashtrays, mustard pots, nappies, pitchers, relish dishes, salt and pepper sets, steins, tankard and mug sets, tea sets, trays, vases, wall plaques, whiskey, and wine jugs.

Left: x in shield; right: four petals in shield and three petals in shield at base.

+ in shield, \ (bend) in shield.

More Salesman's Pages

Many of the old Noritake Company salesman's pages have been featured in the Third, Fifth and Sixth Series of *Collector's Encyclopedia of Nippon Porcelain.* These sketches are actual paintings of items that were for sale by the company and were shown to prospective customers. Each is hand painted and some even have penciled marks on them, indicating just what the customer had ordered. It is safe to assume that these paintings vary slightly from the finished work, as each artist would paint with different skill. Color variations have also been noted. In this chapter, I am pleased to be able to show more of these wonderful pieces of art. They are extremely difficult to find, and when one is located, it may cost considerably more than the item it portrays.

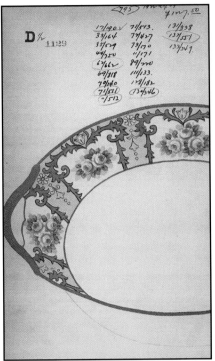

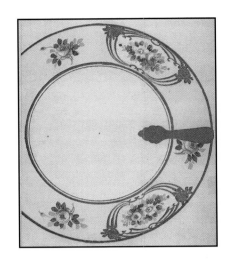

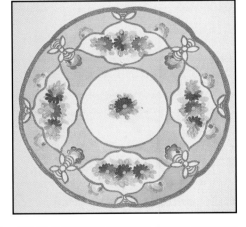

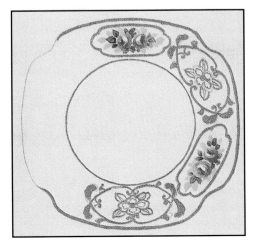

07-25-18 02:50PM

The item below is now available for pickup at designated location.

Monroe County Library System
zv231 Monroe Co Lib BEDFORD

Clarkston Independence DL
CALL NO: 738.209 VANPATT
AUTHOR: Van Patten, Joan F.
Collector's encyclopedia of Nippon
BARCODE: 34633001359304
REC NO: i51856864
PICKUP AT: Bedford Branch

847-9845 E-MAIL

JUDITH A PAUL
Bedford

7:2

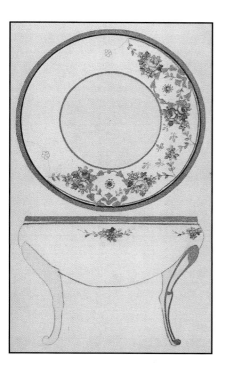

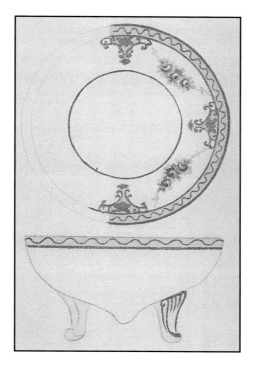

2211/5-8   2263/2
2286/2
4   690
2308/3
4
2332/3
4
2379/3
4
2422/2
4
2452/2

NOT FOR SALE.
SALESMANS USE
MADE IN JAPAN.

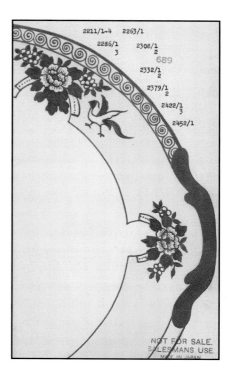

2211/1-4   2263/1
2286/1   2308/1
3   2
689
2332/1
2
2379/1
2
2422/1
3
2452/1

NOT FOR SALE.
SALESMANS USE
MADE IN JAPAN.

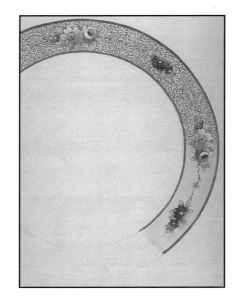

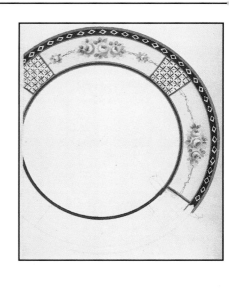

2280/6

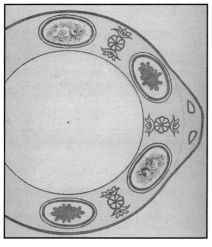

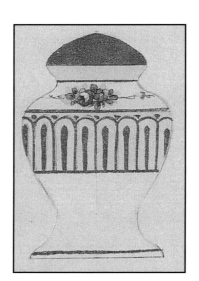

2280/2

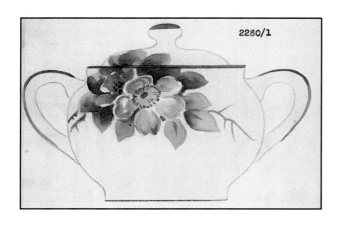

2280/1

Matching Salesman's Pages with Nippon Items

It is difficult enough to find an old Noritake Company salesman's page, but to locate the actual item it portrays just doubles the excitement.

Four of the following items are exact matches and the other two bear the same pattern as the one shown on the old page.

 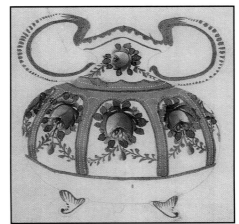

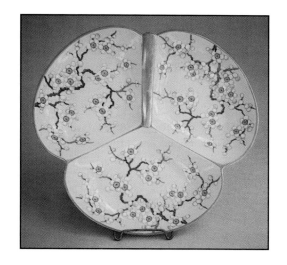

Flowers Featured on Nippon
By Judith Boyd

A Rose is a Rose is...

In the language of flowers, roses are the symbol of love and purity. In the language of Nippon, roses are a prized decoration, often lush and always lovely.

Because the rose is a flower that was frequently portrayed on the European china decorations and because the Nippon designers frequently copied European china patterns to appeal to the American market, we find a large variety of roses on our Nippon. Tiny gold roses border many patterns of tableware, lush red, yellow, pink, and white roses bloom on every sort of vase, and finely painted roses enhance the beauty of many cobalt items.

The classic form of the rose that we know today has only existed for the last 200 years. The rose was originally cultivated in China over 2,000 years ago, but not the plant we are familiar with today. It was not as lush, and its life span was short. About 1760, the first recurrent flowering rose plants were discovered in China and sent to Europe. These plants produced blooms repeatedly through the summer and into autumn. No longer would the "last rose of autumn" have such a melancholy tone. The Chinese plants were crossbred with European varieties which had been developed for their beauty; and by the end of the eighteenth century, the rose as we know it had emerged.

The history of the rose plant is long and varied. Egyptians used the rose for medicinal purposes. Even now, rose hips are an important source of vitamin C. The Egyptians also used roses in their religious ceremonies.

"Sub rosa" is an expression meaning secretive. In a Greek myth, Eros bribed the god of silence with a rose to hush up stories about Aphrodite, the goddess of Love, and her scandalous carrying-on with mortal men.

Another Greek legend recounts the secret meetings "under the roses" (sub rosa). When they were being defeated on land, the Greek generals retreated to a rose bower to discuss how Xerxes was beating them. There they secretly planned a new strategy which led to their victorious sea battle.

The Romans liked the "sub rosa" idea so much they improved upon it. Thanks to Eros, they translated it to mean "off the record" and hung garlands of roses over the banquet tables at all the Roman orgies. Nothing that was said or done there could be discussed outside.

During medieval times, the church adopted the symbol of the rose. They felt the beauty of the flower symbolized purity. A thirteenth century rose window can be seen in Notre Dame in Paris.

The famous War of the Roses took place in England during the late 1400s, between the House of York and the House of Lancaster. According to legend, men from both sides were walking in the King's rose garden and arguing about politics. The leader of the House of York plucked a white rose and said, "Everyone who is with me, wear this for your badge." The House of Lancaster then chose a red rose as their symbol. Thus, the bloody conflict was named. The House of York eventually won and adopted both a red and a white rose as a symbol of unity.

From these historical beginnings, the rose gradually evolved into a symbol of beauty and love. The Empress Josephine, wife of Napoleon, grew an extraordinary collection

of rose plants in her gardens at Malmaison.

In present times, there are about 150 varieties of genus Rosa. Perfume is made from the attar of roses. Rose petals that are picked early in the morning contain the highest concentrations of essential oil for perfume. Potpourri has been used for centuries to freshen the air in rooms, made with dried rose petals combined with other dried flowers.

Rose hip wine continues to be popular today and of course, a beautiful bouquet of roses still conveys the language of love.

Nippon roses are frequently found in combination with cobalt and gold. The strength and lushness of the flower stands up well to the richness of the cobalt color.

Roses are found on tapestry pieces, both in the main design and as border flowers. On moriage pieces, we find roses outlined in moriage and, rarely, full moriage roses. Roses, heavily outlined in black, are often found on pieces with a burnished gold-type background. The Nippon gold and white pieces often feature tiny roses in the gold garlands of leaves. Lines of colored roses serve as a border for various pieces of tableware.

Although real roses need to be watered, fed, and pruned often, Nippon roses require only a little water now and then to keep them fresh and beautiful. Take a closer look at the florals in your collection through rose-colored glasses. Do they give off a rosy glow?

Mum's the Word

The chrysanthemum is considered the Imperial flower of Japan.

When Joan Van Patten and I were on a visit to Japan, we were fortunate enough to view a chrysanthemum festival at the Nagoya Palace. Seeing the way that these magnificent flowers were treated, trained, and admired left no doubt in our minds of the reverence the Japanese people felt for these blooms.

The chrysanthemum originated in China, probably sometime before 500 BCE. During the fourth century, a poet named T'ao Yuan Ming refused a high government post and returned to his chrysanthemum garden. He said, rather than work for the government, he preferred to pick chrysanthemums, entertain his friends, and get drunk. Thus, the flower has come to symbolize a scholar in retirement.

Also, beginning in ancient China, they used the petals and leaves to make wine and medicine. The early morning dew collected from the flower was thought to help with longevity.

Zen Buddhist monks brought the chrysanthemum to Japan about 400 AD. The Japanese were instantly captivated by the beautiful flower and heaped honors upon it. Although the Chinese mum had tight, incurved petals, the Japanese gardeners over time developed their own distinctive plant. The Japanese plant had looser petals and a shaggier look.

The Japanese people designated the chrysanthemum an Imperial emblem in 797 and have honored it through the ages. The Imperial standard, stylized version of the flower has 16 petals. The throne of the Mikado was known as the "Chrysanthemum Throne." Ki-Ku, also known as the "Queen of the East," is the personal emblem of the Emperor.

When chrysanthemum plants reached Europe about the seventeenth century, the Europeans crossbred the Chinese and the Japanese types. The botanists gave it the name chrysanthemum, which comes from the Greek for golden flower, "chrysos" meaning gold, and "anthos" meaning flower. Over 700 varieties of chrysanthemums are in existence today.

They are prized blooms in most of Europe and in America. In Italy, perhaps because they bloom late in the autumn, mums are associated with the dead.

Chrysanthemums are found on many extensively decorated Nippon pieces. Among the most popular are cobalt and gold pieces with the flowers in gold-framed medallions. Two beautiful examples are shown below.

Another very collectible use of the Imperial Flower is on pieces with a gold background, covered with beads as seen in the handled urn and its detail shown below. The blooms on these pieces are large and exotic. In addition, mums are incorporated into many other Nippon floral designs. It is even thought that the "rising sun" symbol is a stylized version of the chrysanthemum.

Even though many Nippon patterns were adapted from Western designs, the Imperial Flower truly belongs to Nippon.

Many flowers grace our Nippon wares, and some of the most popular are the bleeding heart, lily of the valley, daffodil, iris, orchid, violet, poppies, pansy, wisteria, poinsettia, calla lily, sunflower, water lily, plum blossom, narcissus, tiger lily, and white daylily. We take so many of the hand-painted decorations for granted, and maybe it is time that we really take a closer look at these pieces.

Nippon Tricks or Treats
By Linda Lau

> *From ghoulies and ghosties and long-legged beasties and things that go bump in the night, Good Lord, deliver us!*
> **Old Cornish prayer**

What conjures up Halloween in your mind? Is it dark nights? Spooky owls? Menacing black cats? Smirking jack-o'-lanterns? Or maybe it is just the tricks or treats that interest you. If it is any of these things, then some Nippon items should appeal to your Halloween "spirit."

Halloween stems from the ancient Celtic harvest festival of Samhaim which was held on October 31, the last autumn night before the onset of winter. During this festival, the souls of the dead returned to visit their former homes. Other supernatural creatures such as phantoms, fairies, witches, and devils supposedly conjured up magic spells on any humans they would encounter.

In order to frighten these spirits away, the Celts would light huge bonfires and wear animal skins. These animal skins were the forerunners of Halloween costumes. Little children who had to walk the dark roads would carry lanterns carved from turnips. The turnips held hot coal so the children could see their way.

As centuries passed, Samhaim was incorporated into Christianity. October 31 became All Hallow's Eve, or Halloween, which was celebrated before All Saint's Day on November 1. "Hallow" is the Old English word for "saint" meaning the night before a holy day. On All Hallow's Eve, clowns disguised as the dead would demand treats from people as insurance against their pranks.

During the nineteenth century when the Irish immigrated to America, they brought their Halloween customs with them. Over time the carved turnip became a jack-o'-lantern carved out of a pumpkin. In the Victorian era, Halloween parties featured elaborate costumes and whimsical fortune telling. Bobbing for apples, a Celtic tradition where the first person to bite an apple was believed to be the first to marry in the coming year, was revived as a party game. By the way, I tested this last year and found it not to be true!

It was during the early 1900s that Halloween die cut decorations, candy containers, papier mache jack-o'-lanterns, noise makers, and party favors became popular. These items featured all of the classic Halloween images — owls, bats, cats, witches, ghosts, and devils. By the 1930s, beggar nights with children "trick or treating" was practiced nationwide.

The celebration of Halloween was extremely popular in the early 1900s. So it should come as no surprise that there are Nippon items available that, while not necessarily made for Halloween, evoke the spirit and feel of the holiday.

In order for our Halloween to have a ghost of a chance, we must first set the mood, and the scene on this "Halloween" plaque in photo 1 would certainly do that. The moon was believed to be a symbol of mysteries, but it is no mystery that this item would make a bewitching addition to any Nippon collection.

Photo 1

As you enter the dark, forbidding woods, you are certain to see an owl or two as in photos 2 and 3. Owls have long been associated with Halloween, and just maybe they are warning you to stay out of the witch's haunted forest.

Photo 2

Photo 3

This owl pictured in photo 4 looks particularly sinister as he flies right toward you. Be careful, who knows what goblins and ghouls lurk there!

Cats are the favorite pets of witches, and a black cat crossing your path is considered bad luck. However, most Nippon collectors would feel extremely lucky if this black cat in photo 5 crossed their path.

Photo 4

Speaking of witches, did you know that witches wear black to be like the night? Perhaps on this dark Halloween night you might like to partake of some witches' brew. Well, this child-size pumpkin tea set in photo 6 will do the trick. But beware, like collecting Nippon, the brew just might become addictive!

Photo 5

Photo 6

Photo 7

A day's outing to search for the perfect Halloween pumpkin is a tradition for many families. The pumpkin eventually replaced the carved turnip lanterns, and it is more readily available in the United States. This little boy in photo 7 has found himself a rare Nippon pumpkin, and it looks like he is not going to let anyone else take it!

The jack-o'-lantern is based on an old Irish legend about a drunk, Jack, who tricked Satan into a tree. Once Satan was in the tree, Jack carved a cross in the trunk and only allowed Satan down after he promised not to claim Jack's soul once he died. When Jack died, he was not allowed into heaven, and Satan would not take him either. Satan threw Jack an ember to light his way through eternal darkness where he now found himself. Jack put the ember into a carved turnip lantern.

This Nippon era jack-o'-lantern in photo 8, while made of cardboard and crepe paper rather than porcelain, would surely light up the faces of many a Halloween collector. He is definitely one rare pumpkin. And, with his laughing smirk, he apparently knows it!

It is almost the witching hour and time for tricks or treats. But first, we must be

Photo 8

properly dressed for the occasion. These dolls in photos 9 and 10, dressed in their best black and orange, were likely used as party favors or decorations.

Photo 10

Photo 9

At last, it is time for Nippon collectors to be tricked or treated. The origin of trick or treat may have begun in ninth century England with an event called "souling." On All Souls Day, Christians would go from village to village begging for soul cakes. In return for the soul cakes, the beggars would promise to pray for the dead.

With these Nippon era candy containers in photo 11, you certainly will not be tricked. Made of cardboard, crepe paper, and papier mache, these candy containers are rare treats for Halloween collectors. The bottoms open to reveal the candy.

Our costumes are ready, the moon is out, the wind is howling, there is frost in the air, and the apple cider is warming on the stove, so let's all go trick or treating.

Photo 11

The Other Nippon
A Look at Non-Porcelain Nippon Items
By Linda Lau

One area of collecting that many Nippon collectors ignore is those items that are made from materials other than porcelain. In fact, some collectors don't even realize that during the Nippon era the Japanese were producing items made from a variety of materials including metal, wood, papier mache, celluloid, glass, ebony, bone, pottery, and cardboard. These items, while not of the decorative quality of the porcelain products, were usually handmade and sometimes hand painted. The photo below shows a Nippon paper and wood fan that is hand painted with roses and gold much like the porcelain vase that is shown in front of it. Notice that the left medallion on the fan pictures a basket of flowers similar to those on the front of the vase. The variety of items that

Paper and wood fan, hand-painted design similar to vase shown with it.

can be found ranges from household goods like nut bowls, baskets, candlesticks, flower frogs, incense burners, and buttons to children's items such as dolls, toys, and holiday candy containers. Like the porcelain, many of the items were utilitarian so they were used and discarded when broken, worn out, or no longer needed.

During the Nippon era, the Japanese found themselves with an over-abundance of labor. There were approximately 40 million people living in Japan in 1891, and by 1909 this figure had risen to 50 million. Therefore, it was necessary for the Japanese to expand into as many markets as practical. Low wages were paid to almost all of the workers, enabling the Japanese to compete more effectively with other more established countries. Japan's low prices allowed her to sell all types of goods all over the world.

On the non-porcelain items, the Japanese utilized many of the skills they already possessed such as basketry, woodworking, and pottery making. Therefore, it is only natural that many of the non-porcelain Nippon items found today are made utilizing those techniques. Another area that the Japanese excelled in was the manufacture of celluloid items, especially dolls and rattles. A main component of celluloid is camphor, and the Japanese had ready access to large supplies

of camphor since it is a product of Taiwan. In fact, there are reports that Japan had a monopoly on the world's supply of camphor, and they controlled the market price of camphor thereby putting some American celluloid companies out of business.

Collection of celluloid dolls and toys.

World War I also helped the Japanese expand into American markets since prior to that time, Germany and France accounted for the largest share of dolls, toys, and holiday items being imported into the United States. In fact, at the beginning of World War I, it was estimated that as much as 90% of the dolls and toys sold at Christmas came from Germany and France. The war allowed Japan, at least for a few years, to take over these markets.

So, if you are a Nippon collector, why should you be interested in these other items? First of all, they give us another perspective into the wares and products that Americans were using and wanted during that time. It is interesting to combine and display the porcelain items with their non-porcelain counterparts. For instance, it is fun to display a box of Made in Nippon matches with a

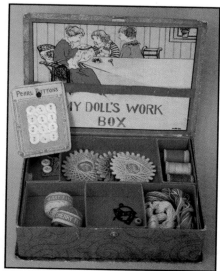

Child's sewing set and Nippon pearl buttons.

porcelain ashtray. You will see that both the matches and ashtray pictured at the top of the next page have an aviation theme.

Another perhaps more important reason for knowing about these items is that many are highly collectible in their own right. This is especially true for the holiday candy containers and celluloid dolls and rattles. The holiday candy containers are very much sought after. These candy containers are usually made of cardboard and crepe paper with cotton or papier mache decorations. Nippon-marked examples are rare, and holiday collectors are willing to pay top dollar for them since the Nippon marking means they were definitely made before 1922. Celluloid collectors seek out the dolls and rattles, and today it is not unusual to see some examples in the hundred-dollar range. Of course, if you want a Nippon celluloid Kewpie, Santa Claus or Charlie Chaplin, you can expect to pay more than that.

Whatever the reason for collecting them, non-porcelain Nippon items can be a fun addition to your porcelain collection and who knows, you might even find a real treasure or two.

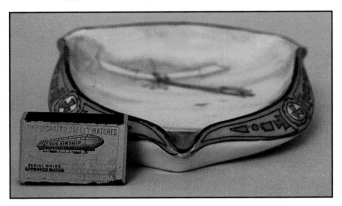

Made in Nippon matches.

Collection of Easter and Halloween candy containers.

Metal stork incense set.

Wood with lacquer buckets.

Paper label on wooden nutbowl.

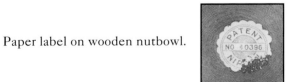

Wooden nutbowl.

The Desert Song
By Judith Boyd

The romance of the desert has long been a subject of song, story, and even painting on porcelain. From Biblical times, the hot winds and blowing sands, the always-distant sight of a palm tree, the mysterious mirage, and the sudden wonderful relief of an oasis have been the object of many real or imagined adventures. Thus, our beloved Nippon Arab rides into our collections astride his patient camel.

Our Nippon sheik of the desert, often faceless, is wrapped in his jalabiyya, a long white robe with a hood, to protect him from the heat and the blowing sands. Upon his head, he usually wears a kufiyya with an agal rope around it. The agal is the symbol of his ability to uphold the obligations and responsibilities of manhood. He has been wearing these clothes for generations, for they provide both protection and meaning for him.

Although the majority of our Nippon pieces picture the Arab on his camel, some rare pieces have him speaking by a wall or walking near an oasis. The life of our Arab was very difficult — not at all as romantic as we would like to picture it. They traveled with their herds from one barely fertile area to another, stayed for a time and then moved on.

The reliable camel is his beast of burden and means of transportation. Although horses were often ridden, the camel has always been known as the reliable "ship of the desert." His familiar hump is a storage area for fat which enables him to go great distances without food or drink. This is very useful in an area where the main crop is sand. When he does feed, the camel is a plant eater. Those funny-looking feet are especially useful for walking on the desert sands. On each foot, he has two large toes, connected by webbing. This makes a larger surface area, so he will not sink into the sand as walks. The camel's beautiful long eyelashes are the envy of many a Nippon collector. He uses them to protect his eyes from the sand.

One of the unusual things about our Arab on a camel pieces is the two distinct ways they have been painted. Some

are done in a realistic style and others in almost a cartoon fashion. Both versions are usually very colorful. Some of the pieces have heavy moriage palm trees and fancy moriage border decorations. You will often find that the background scene has a matte finish, while the man's white robe is done in shiny enamel.

In the background, there are usually a few standard objects. A pyramid is often seen in the distance. Perhaps the artist who devised these paintings thought that this would be a certain symbol of the Middle East, even though many of the Bedouin that are pictured were found in the Sinai Desert or the Negev. The pyramid is a vague, suggested shape — the excitement of the opening of King Tut's tomb did not come until after the Nippon period had concluded.

The tent is a fairly standard feature of this painting. The low-

slung Bedouin tent was often divided into two sections by a curtain, the ma'nad. One half of the tent was for the men and was used for guests. This was called the "sitting place" or mag'ad. The other half was for the women and was called the mahara-

The "Arab on a Camel" scene has always been popular with Nippon collectors and may form a sub-collection unto itself. The harsh desert climate certainly appears more romantic from the vantage point of your living room sofa.

ma. The tents were not elaborate affairs because they had to be moved many times. Palm trees are always shown and sometimes a friend, also on a camel, accompanies our Nippon sheik.

Nippon pieces that show other obvious desert scenes can be found. Sometimes the empty oasis is pictured. Perhaps it is only a mirage from the mind of our Arab wandering through the desert. There are also paintings of a mosque or other build-

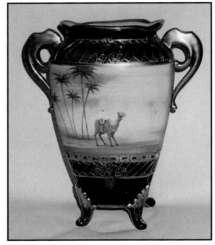

ings surrounded by the palm trees and desert sands.

It is impossible to distance oneself from the insect world. Bugs live all around us, although most of the time we are not even aware of them. We speculate about the possibility of life forms on other planets, and yet we are so ignorant about the most numerous class of animals on earth. Insects are the most successful group of animals in the world today. Of the world's species, they collectively outweigh every other form of life on the planet, and in fact, some termite colonies and locust swarms can contain up to a billion individuals!

The ancestry of insects stretches back at least 400 million years. Insects are agriculturists, architects, paper makers, potters, web spinners, herders, and even undertakers. They are the undisputed champions of evolutionary success, and some zoologists believe that the social life of some forms of insects rivals that of man.

Bugs and insects can be both extremely intrusive and beneficial in our lives. They have a far longer pedigree than man and can impose severe physiological and ecological restrictions on us. Some insects number many millions to the acre!

Ever notice how many insects have been featured on pieces of Nippon porcelain? One day when I was admiring a beautiful coralene piece decorated with a dragonfly, I started to wonder just how many different kinds might be found on these collectibles.

First, I went through the books, then checked with some collector friends and discovered nine; the butterfly, dragonfly, hornet, honeybee, praying mantis, scarab or beetle, grasshopper, housefly, and even a spider.

Many techniques were utilized in the decorating process; some items are hand painted, others have a cloisonné effect, some are coralene, others moriage, and some even gold etched. A number of them are presented as relief decoration.

Many Japanese keep crickets, beetles, and fireflies as pets, and they hold a special place in their hearts. They are said to remind the nature-loving Japanese of a simpler, less hectic age. In fact, a favorite pastime for Japanese children is searching for grasshoppers and butterflies.

An August 1999 headline in my local newspaper said, "Bug-eyed businessman pays $90,000 for beetle in Japan." Giant stag beetles are extremely popular in Japan and are often called "black diamonds" because of their shiny black exoskeletons. The one that sold for $90,000 was a 3" bug and was considered unusually large. The buyer remained unidentified, but supposedly the beetle was for his own collection. This purchase makes buying Nippon seem like an inexpensive hobby!

Scarabs are bright-colored large beetles that can be up to 6" in length. They have two pairs of wings, and the hard front wings cover the hind wings when they are folded. They have layered antennae that are used as sense organs. They also have distinctive horns or protuberances growing on their head or thorax. One of the best-known species of scarab is the Japanese beetle.

There are over 300,000 kinds of beetles, and the scarab played a role in the spiritual lives of ancient Egyptians. In ancient Egyptian beliefs, the scarab amulet, which represents the dung beetle, was symbolic of regeneration and new life and was used as funerary jewelry. The scarab was placed on a mummy to give it amuletic protection during passage to the underworld. Some funerary scarabs were made with separate wings and then were sewn to the mummy wrappings over the chest area. Certain funerary chants were said as the scarab was laid on the chest area where the heart would ordinarily be. This act was performed for the dead as part of the mummification ritual and was called the "Opening of the Mouth." Once the custom of burying scarabs with the bodies of the dead became a recognized ritual, the habit of wearing them as ornaments by the living came into fashion.

Since beetles fly only during the hottest part of the day, they were associated with the sun and thus with life and regeneration. Since time immemorial in Egypt, the idea of "life" has been associated with the scarab. Even in recent times in the Eastern Sudan area, the insect is dried, pounded, and mixed with water. Women who believe it to be an unfailing aid for the production of large families then drink this liquid.

The particular beetle the ancient Egyptians chose to copy for the scarab amulet belongs to a family of dung feeding beetles that live in tropical countries. The species are generally of black color but among them are found some with the richest metallic shadings. Dung beetles are relatively large and conspicuous. A peculiarity exists in the structure and location of their hind legs. They are placed near the extremity of the body, so far from each other that they give the insect a peculiar appearance when walking. These extraordinary legs are of course used for rolling the dung balls which they use for food and on which they lay their eggs. While the beetle's body is rather fat and rounded, the front edge of the head is thin, like the blade of a shovel.

A beetle only 1½" long can build up and roll a ball of dung into the size of a small apple. The males and females work in pairs collecting and rolling dung into a compact ball. These balls are then carted off and buried in holes in the ground. If the ball is formed into a pear-shaped pellet, it is used as food for the young beetles after they hatch. Dung is also a rich food source for the mature beetle and if the beetles roll round feeding balls, they are used for consumption later on.

The Egyptians likened the rolling of a dung ball to the daily passage of the sun across the sky. They knew that the beetle buried its ball, and that later more beetles would appear crawling out of the ground. Thus, the scarab became the symbol of rebirth after death.

Grasshoppers date from 225 to 300 million years ago and are among the oldest forms of insect life. Grasshoppers are voracious leaf-chewers; they tear off plant leaf tissue and swallow it. They are generally small and unimpressive in appearance. They have strongly developed enlarged back legs, which are good for jumping; in fact, some can jump as far as three feet. Grasshoppers are noted for jumping to escape predators and for singing to attract potential mates. The hind leg in the male usually has a row of protruding joints that produce the characteristic chirping sounds when rubbed against the hard wing veins. The singing plays an important role in the courtship of many species.

They have large compound eyes which are high on each side of the head, well placed to monitor the surrounding environment and to give early warning of any danger. Their antennae are much shorter than their bodies, and most have keen eyesight and hearing.

They burrow in the soil or live in rotting wood or beneath bark or stones. Most camouflage themselves to resemble part of their surroundings. Their eggs are laid in a small hole in the ground, and the young are tiny replicas of the parents.

Hornets as well as their nests are also featured on Nippon pieces. Each spring young females make nests by chewing tiny pieces of wood and mixing it with their saliva. The nests are usually found suspended from the limb of a tree, in crevices in rocks, in the hollows of trees or artificial sheltered places. Each has a small doorway at the bottom which is always guarded. The typical mature nest is the size and

shape of a football, and some even get to be nearly two feet in diameter. The nest may have as many as forty layers of paper that provide insulation against excessive heat or cold.

Hornets average in length from about 1" to 1¼" and they have a very powerful, painful sting! They feed on other insects, their own larvae, and ripe fruit. Hornets hunt spiders, and one kind even fills up their cells with helpless paralyzed spiders. They lay an egg and close the cell, and when the egg hatches, the hornet grub has a supply of fresh food! The fertilized eggs produce female workers; unfertilized eggs produce males that have no stinger. The bulk of the colony dies off at the end of autumn, and only young mated females survive the winter.

Around 3100 BCE, King Menes chose the hornet as a symbol for his kingdom due to its fierce and dangerous nature. Hornets are found among the earliest Egyptian hieroglyphs.

Butterflies are found on more pieces of Nippon than any of the other insects. They have slender bodies with four broad wings and have been called "flying flowers." In the wild they are usually brightly colored, ½" to 11" wide, and male butterflies are usually brighter in color than females. They have two big round eyes and six legs. Most feed on nectar from flowers and thrive in the sunlight. Their hair-like clubbed antennae are used for both smelling and hearing. When the butterfly rests, it folds its wings together above its head. The butterfly cannot fly if its body temperature is less than 86 degrees Fahrenheit. If temperatures are colder, the butterfly sits in the

sun or flutters its wings to warm itself up. As summer draws to end, butterflies become more sluggish, and only a small number survive and hibernate through the winter. They have to find a sheltered spot to await the arrival of spring. Most butterflies fly during the day, whereas moths fly at dusk or night.

Butterflies are graceful and pretty, but some are also destructive. Caterpillars depend on plants for food and in turn destroy food plants. When caterpillars have grown to full size, their behavior changes, and they stop eating and begin wandering.

Butterflies look like "flying jewels," and their scales can take on every color of the rainbow. Many of them have different color patterns

at different seasons, and butterflies in northern areas often have darker wings than their southerly cousins. The scales on their wings help them find mating partners by both smell and sight. Butterflies have exoskeletons, which means that their skeleton is on the outside of the body.

Butterflies are among the most compellingly beautiful of insects, and there are about 20,000 known species. Butterflies emerge from caterpillars which is truly a Cinderella story if I ever heard one.

Dragonflies are considered the tigers of the insect world because of their superb hunting skills. They begin their life as an egg in the water, and after hatching, young dragonfly

larvae can eat hundreds of mosquito larvae a day. They are also called devil's darning needles, mosquito hawks, and horse stingers.

Dragonflies have strong jaws and are skillful and

powerful fliers despite their low wing beat frequency. They are large and swift but do not sting. Their ability to fly is unmatched; in fact, they can fly at speeds of 40 – 60 mph and hunt other insects by sight. They can hover with ease and even fly backward. They have elongated, transparent paired wings which are unlinked in flight. Each delicate pair flaps independently; the forewings create a downbeat, the underwings beat upwards, and the procedure reverses. They can also glide, locking the four wings into an immovable whole to conserve energy.

Dragonflies have large heads which rotate and allow for a 360-degree field of view that gives them excellent eyesight. They have powerful toothed mouthparts and very large compound eyes. They measure from 1" to 5" long, and their slender bodies can be red, green, brown or black. They form their legs into a kind of basket and scoop their prey (mostly mosquitoes and bees) out of the air and transfer it to their mouth. An adult dragonfly can catch and eat its own weight in 30 minutes.

Unlike many other insects, dragonflies do not spread disease or damage crops. Although they may be intimidating in size, they are harmless to humans.

Dragonflies can be traced back to the beginning of the insect fossil world and are one of the most primitive insect flyers. The dragonfly fossil shown in the photo was found in China and is evidently many millions of years old.

Honeybees are social animals that live and work together as a group. They can survive only as a member of a community. They are resident aliens from Europe and not natives of the United States. Honeybees pollinate flowers that will produce seeds and fruits. They live in colonies of 35,000 to 50,000 members.

There are three classes of bees: the queen, the workers, and the drones. The drones do no work; their only task is to

mate with the queen. The queen's only function is to lay eggs, up to 1,500 a day, one at a time. Twenty-one days later adult worker bees emerge. The queen is the center of the honeybee hive, and a queen bee can produce up to 600,000 fertile eggs in her lifetime.

The workers collect the pollen and make honey from the nectar found in a myriad of flowers. Honeybees are vegetarians and the chief pollinators of many vegetables, fruits, and forage crops. Their whole economy centers on the gathering of nectar and pollen which is carried in small baskets on the outer sides of the worker's hind legs, brought back to the hive, and placed directly into the cells. Bees must store enough honey to last throughout the winter. If a bee has to go just one day without food, it will starve.

Honeybees have two antennae that are used for feeling and smelling. Their stinger is covered with pointy barbs, and the bee usually only stings in self-defense. However, when it does, the stinger sticks in the victim, and the bee dies.

Bees are also capable of transmitting detailed information by a dance pattern, a very sophisticated system of communication and navigation. They perform both the round dance and the waggle dance to tell the distance to and direction of the source of food. They do the circle dance when food is within 80 feet of the hive. When the food is between 80 and 380 feet, bees do the waggle or figure-eight dance.

Although bees produce beeswax and honey, their greatest benefit to man is in the pollination of the many crops.

Praying mantises are long, slender, stick-like, winged insects capable of turning their triangular heads from side to side. Their flexible necks allow them to "look over their shoulders" even though they do not have shoulders. Some mantises even have a single ear behind their hind legs. Their closest relatives are cockroaches. They are found in green and brown colors and are also called soothsayers or devil's riding horse. Mantises are found in warm temperature and tropical regions throughout the world. They move with lightning speed, and their arms become fierce weapons that grip and tear. The mantis lies patiently waiting for prey; they do not chase their food. In fact, the strike takes only milliseconds to complete. The praying mantis is a cannibal, and its first meal is usually a sibling. While mating,

the female often chews off her partner's head, while he continues without interruption at his task. They use their front legs to trap prey, but these are essentially useless for walking. Their legs are equipped with sharp spines so that they can grasp and hold their intended victim.

There are about 2,000 known species of mantis. They are insectivores, eating flies, bees, moths, and butterflies. Some of the larger species can capture small lizards, frogs, and even hummingbirds. They hunt by ambush and employ their vision, not sense of smell, to capture their prey. A hinged mechanism at the leg joint enables them to spring forward and impale other insects.

Mantises often sit back on their rear appendages and hold their front pair of appendages together. Some people think this gives them the appearance of praying, hence the name. In actuality, when they are in this position, they are really preying as they wait to catch insects.

In the autumn, female mantises make egg cases called oothecae and attach them to twigs, branches of trees, and even to the sides of houses. The female mantis uses a foam from her body to make this egg case. Most of these survive the winter. In the spring, the eggs develop into young mantises; one egg case can release around 200 to 400 nymphs that immediately begin preying on other insects or each other. They themselves are easy prey for birds, frogs, lizards and toads.

True flies have two wings, one on each side of their bodies. They are so lightweight that it would take almost 2,000 flies to equal one ounce. Flies have two large compound eyes that enable them to see in many directions at one time which is why it is hard to sneak up on one. They may even be able to detect colors humans cannot see. Flies are called "spongers" because everything they eat must be liquid. They suck it up!

After the female mates, she is ready to lay 100 – 150 eggs four to eight days later. Fly eggs require only eight to twelve hours to hatch. Three days after the female lays her eggs, she is ready to mate again. If she lives long enough, she may lay two to six batches of eggs. Flies have a relatively short life span of two weeks to three months, but the average is about 21 days.

Houseflies die when the temperature falls below 32 degrees or rises above 115 degrees. Sometimes the fly shuts down temporarily which is called diapause, a state similar to hibernation. This shut-down protects it from extreme temperatures or lack of moisture or food.

Flies have claws and pads on their feet that enable them to walk on any surface. The fly examines everything with its mouthpart. It goes from item to item, contaminates food, and poses potential danger by transmitting diseases. There are nearly 100,000 known species in the world.

An interesting story about the fly is that it is alleged that the Declaration of Independence was signed on July 4, 1776 without anyone changing the wording because of the terrible fly population in Philadelphia at the time. The signers wanted to avoid the discomfort of the flies and possible fly bites so they just signed and left.

I have not seen an actual **spider** on a piece of Nippon but spider webs are found on a few, so there must be a spider lurking somewhere.

Spiders can survive in many environments, and there are over 30,000 different kinds and all sizes of spiders known to man. They probably first evolved around 400 million years ago. All spiders make silk which they use for a number of things from transportation to communication, from capturing prey to avoiding predators. Just inside and around your home are probably a dozen or more kinds of spiders!

Spiders have eight legs, with the foremost pair acting as

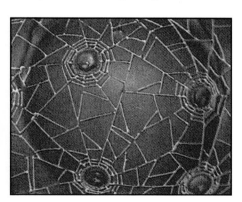

feelers. Most have eight eyes and an acute sense of hearing and touch. Males are usually more brightly colored and smaller than the females. Their bodies are made up of two parts, and the back part has the organs that produce the silk threads. Spiders may have two to four pairs of spinnerets from which a viscid fluid oozes which hardens into silken threads. They have no wings and no antennae.

Spiders are predacious and feed on insects. They are cannibals and are the worst enemies of other spiders. They entangle their victims with their snares and webs, or they stalk and catch their prey after patient lurking. Not all spiders have poison glands, but most do. There are two groups of spiders, web builders and wanderers. Female orb weavers construct lacy, circular webs, similar to a cartwheel design. Some of the strands are dry and some are sticky. The orb web is generally constructed at night and is used to capture mostly airborne prey. Spider silk is extremely strong which makes the web the ultimate prey-capturing device.

Many webs are transparent and not easily seen unless covered with dewdrops. When an insect is caught in a weaver's web, it struggles and thrashes which jerks the web line. During this struggle, a vibration in the web is created and this essentially sends the message, "Dinner is served."

Once an insect is caught in the spider web, the spider then releases a stream of sticky threads through its spinnerets, quickly wrapping the prey in thick bandages of silk that immobilize it and prevent it from escaping or damaging the web. As the trapped insect struggles, the spider injects paralyzing poison into it. Spiders live on a liquid diet; after injecting its poison, the spider releases digestive enzymes which reduces its prey to liquid. It only takes about five seconds to bite and begin wrapping up a housefly.

Bugs live all around us, and yet most of the time we are not even aware of them. There are millions of different bugs and spiders, and they live all over the world. It is impossible to distance oneself from the insect world. For one thing, they intrude by force of sheer numbers. Of the world's species, 80 percent are insects. Estimates place their total at 10 quintillion. They are found everywhere. The combined weight of all insects in the world is more than that of all other terrestrial animals! Insects are part of where we have come from, what we are now, and what we will be.

Even on Nippon pieces, it is a bug's life after all!

Source Discovered: Anton Mauve
Dutch Landscape Painter
By Jeffrey Mattison

The morning after — you know how it is. We have all experienced it, the disappointment that results from being outbid in the last moment for that special Nippon item on eBay the night before. Off and on for an entire week, I had been studying the photograph of a 10" scenic wall plaque featuring a shepherd with a dog at his side, watching over a flock of sheep (see Series 1, Plate 357). My bid sat unchallenged for days, but at the end, I was outbid, and the reserve had not been met. That was just the beginning!

The image of the shepherd scene had become quite fixed in my mind (I suppose staring at something for a week will do that to you!). So it was rather shocking when the very next morning, I stumbled upon a print in an antique shop and found myself asking, "Where have I seen this before?" Of course, I knew immediately that I was looking at the subject our Nippon artist had copied on the shepherd plaque. Having read Joan Van Patten's Sources Discovered chapters in Series 4 and 5, I became eager to pursue my discovery. After contacting the seller, I was pleased to acquire the plaque from an individual in Canada. The next steps were to purchase the print, attempt to identify the artist, and learn as much as possible about both the artist and the painting.

A friend loaned me a book that identifies artists by their signatures. Quickly I learned that the artist responsible for the shepherd painting was Anton Mauve, Dutch, 1838 – 1888. A fair amount of biographical information was available on the Internet and at public libraries, but coming up with the name of the painting proved a formidable task. Many inquiries eventually led me to The Netherlands and the Rijksbureau Voor Kunsthistorische Documentatie, the Netherlands Institute for Art History. There, Mr. Willem Rappart was extremely helpful in providing biographical data and specific facts that led me to a great deal of information about the painting.

Anton Mauve executed the painting around 1886 – 1887. It is entitled "Spring" and is an oil on canvas that measures 22⅜" x 35⅞". The painting was a gift from Mr. George I. Seney to the Metropolitan Museum of Art in 1887. Parke-Bernet Galleries, New York City, sold the painting at auction on March 27, 1956, for the sum of $750.00. The auction catalog refers to the painting as Item Number 42 and provides a small reproduction of it, together with a brief description. The catalog also makes reference to another of Mauve's shepherd paintings, which was sold at the same auction.

An illustration of "Spring" and a single-page biographical article on Anton Mauve appeared in a 1915 issue of *The Mentor* magazine. A portion of the article reads, "The landscapes and sheep of Anton Mauve are more than mere pictures of sheep in the meadow. They are creations of a tender, dreamy, and poetic nature. For this reason the paintings of Mauve are not only popular today, but hold a peculiar place of their own.... While his pastoral scenes are pitched in a somewhat sad and minor key, they have a peaceful and soothing effect on the mind." Is it possible that a copy of this publication made its way into the hands of someone at Morimura Brothers around 1915?

Anton Mauve was born on September 18, 1838, at Zaandam, a small shipbuilding town in North Holland. His father, a minister, objected to Anton's desire to become an artist. Nevertheless, at the age of 16, Mauve became the pupil of Frederik van Os, an artist best known for his landscape paintings of cattle. He studied in the following years under the guidance of several artists, including Josef Israels and Willem Maris, spending winters in Amsterdam and summers in The Hague. He made regular visits to Osterbeek, where he worked from 1858 to 1868. In the early 1870s, he moved to a studio in The Hague where he first met his wife, Ariette Sophia Jeannette ("Jet") Carbentus, a cousin of Vincent van Gogh. Anton Mauve and his wife lived in The Hague until 1885, when they decided to move to Laren. There they resided in a home that he named "Ariette," after his wife.

In 1876, the Museum Boymans in Rotterdam purchased Mauve's painting entitled "Cows in the Shade" and thus became the first Dutch gallery to acquire one of his paintings. In the same year, he founded the Hollandsche Teeken-Maatschappij (Dutch Drawing Society) with Maris and Hendrik Mesdag. Anton Mauve became a prominent member of "The Hague School," a group of painters who sought to portray everyday life in a direct and realistic manner. The majority of Mauve's paintings and drawings were landscapes and portraits of common, working people. His landscapes most often featured farms and fields with sheep, cattle or horse-drawn wagons, together with the shepherds and farmers that tended to them. Mauve was especially skilled in rendering light and its effects on the figures that appeared in the scenes he sketched and painted.

The works of Anton Mauve influenced many artists — most notably Vincent van Gogh. Late in 1881 and early in 1882, van Gogh spent several weeks with Mauve, who gave Vincent drawing and painting lessons at his studio in The Hague. In a letter dated December 21, 1881, van Gogh wrote that Mauve had "initiated me...into the mysteries of the palette." One source suggests that van Gogh completed his first painting in oil while studying with Mauve. Even long before he became an artist, Vincent van Gogh admired Mauve's paintings. In a letter dated October 30, 1877, he praised "a very fine one — a shepherd with a flock of sheep crossing the dunes."

Like van Gogh, Mauve was known to experience periods of moodiness and irritability, suffering occasionally from fits of dejection. The following is an excerpt from an article by John W. Keefe that was published in the Winter, 1966 issue of *Museum News*, a publication of the Toledo Museum of Art: "Modern psychiatry would have called Mauve a manic-depressive, for he would periodically sink into fits of depression which would last for months and robbed him of the ability to paint. During these periods, he would walk along the canals or dunes with his sketchbook making brief drawings that sometimes became finished watercolors or paintings. As quickly as this depression appeared, it would lift and Mauve would be filled with energy and worked long hours, as if to compensate for lost time. The depressed quality of mind was important in his work for it caused the lingering feeling of melancholy that can be detected in many pictures. In much of his artistic production, there was a gentle sadness and a sympathetic understanding of the bare and humble lives of his peasant subjects." The article also describes how Mauve would capture the intensity of a particular scene by cutting a small hole in a piece of paper and looking through the hole at a concentrated subject, without distraction from the surrounding area. As a result, many of his works reflect an intense observation of nature.

Anton Mauve died of a heart attack at age 49 while visiting his brother in Arnhem, Holland, on February 5, 1888. Upon learning of Mauve's death, Vincent van Gogh sent his widowed cousin a picture of a blossoming peach tree that he named "Souvenir de Mauve." The Art Institute of Chicago exhibited 15 of Anton Mauve's oil paintings in the summer and fall of 1894. Earlier that same year, a lengthy article appeared in an issue of *The Art Journal* that describes a meeting of the painter's fellow artists and friends on February 5, 1889, the first anniversary of his death. They met at Mauve's graveside to erect a monument in his honor. The informative article contains a tremendous amount of insight into the artist's family, education, and personality. It also features his portrait and illustrations of six paintings and drawings — all featuring a shepherd with a flock of sheep. At the conclusion of the article, the author writes, "The beloved and admired artist is not dead. As we walk in the rural lanes beneath the slender birches wrapped in their mantle of silver-gray haze, or watch the chequered sunlight dancing into the secluded nooks of some emerald meadow, when we hear the echoes of the tinkling sheep bells on the moors, we think, There lives Mauve!"

With the discovery of another subject of our Nippon artist's work, Nippon collectors more than a century later can also exclaim, "There lives Mauve!"

At left, the print which appeared in Sept. 1924 issue of *Pictorial Review* magazine. The painting, at the right, hung in the Metropolitan Museum of Art which owned the painting until 1956.

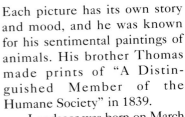

A copy of Sir Edwin Landseer's Newfoundland dog is featured on a number of Nippon items. It is from the original painting titled "A Distinguished Member of the Humane Society" which was painted in 1838 and is considered one of his finest works. This painting is presently at the National Gallery. It is the portrait of a dog named Paul Pry, sitting proudly and nobly by the water's edge. Landseer had seen the faithful pet carrying a basket of flowers in his teeth, and this awakened his admiration for the animal. The dog belonged to Mrs. Newman Smith, and the original painting sold for 50 guineas.

The Newfoundland is a breed of working dogs that originated in Newfoundland, Canada. Males are about 28" high at the shoulders while the female stands about 26" tall. Males are large, weighing about 150 lbs.; females weigh about 110 to 120 lbs. They have deep chests, a broad, massive head, small dark brown eyes, a flat, oily coat, small ears that are close to the head, a strong neck and a fairly moderate length tail which is covered with lots of long hair.

They are known for their intelligence, loyalty, and tractability, and these dogs make ideal pets for children. Newfoundland dogs are powerful swimmers and have been known to rescue people from drowning. They are in demand principally as watchdogs and companions.

The copy shown in this chapter was taken from the *New Practical Reference Library*, Rosch-Fowler Publishing Co., 1913. It depicts a beautiful black and white Newfoundland dog waiting on a wharf. This print has been found on both Nippon rectangular and round wall plaques and on humidors. The rectangular plaque looks as though it has a frame around it, as do all the rectangular plaques.

Landseer's dog paintings of the 1830s constitute one of the high points of his art.

also her pets and gamekeepers. He enjoyed considerable royal patronage and recognition, and the Queen knighted him in 1850.

It is said that Landseer was drawing as early as five years old, and at the age of 16 he was an actual exhibitor at the Royal Academy. He began to draw animals when he was very young, and some of the sketches he made when he was five, seven, and 10 years of age are preserved at the South Kensington Museum.

Edwin's father John was an engraver and author, and Thomas, his elder brother was also the engraver of many of Edwin's other works as well as this one. In 1866, Landseer completed the four bronze lions for the Nelson monument in Trafalgar Square. He was the most famous English artist of his generation, and he is buried at the Cathedral of St. Paul's in London.

Many prints of this famous Newfoundland dog were printed by the Perry Pictures Company in the latter part of the nineteenth and into the twentieth century. This company produced high quality artwork that collectors could buy for just pennies. The Perry Pictures was a production of *The Perry Magazine*, founded by Eugene Ashton Perry (1864 – 1948) in Boston, Massachusetts. From the years of 1898 to 1906, this publication included a catalog of reproduction art that could be purchased by collectors.

This picture of Sir Edwin Landseer is from an antique engraving from the *Illustrated News*, dated October 11, 1873. It was published to mark the death of the famous artist 10 days before.

Each picture has its own story and mood, and he was known for his sentimental paintings of animals. His brother Thomas made prints of "A Distinguished Member of the Humane Society" in 1839.

Landseer was born on March 7, 1802 and died in October of 1873. He frequently painted Queen Victoria and her children,

The J. & P. Coats Sewing Set
By Linda Lau

If you collect long enough, every now and then you will come across something totally unique and undocumented. Such is the case with the child's sewing set pictured here. This set, with its Nippon doll, was probably marketed sometime between 1915 and 1920. It is an advertising item for the J. P. Coats Company (who later became the company we know as Coats & Clark). It is very rare and may even be one of the few left in existence. After all, these types of sets were meant to be played with and then discarded. To find one with the dressed doll, sewing thread, and instructions still intact is remarkable. Even the historian at the Coats and Clark Company has never seen or heard of one.

The kit included a 10½" doll, sewing supplies such as needle and thread, and a pattern for both a girl's and a boy's sailor-style outfits. It is assumed that the cloth for the clothes was provided with the kit. Due to the style of the clothes and because the hat has 'U S A' embroidered on it, one is led to believe that it was designed to play upon the patriotism of World War I when even children were encouraged to support the war effort. Since it is an advertising item, there are a number of references to J. & P. Coats cottons and the instructions note that the outfits are "To be made with J. & P. Coats Cottons."

The kit also gives us an insight into the "education" of a young girl in the early 1900s and the company's advertising techniques:

"No child's education is complete without a fair knowledge of sewing and to encourage young people to sew at home the manufacturers of J. & P. Coats Cottons have prepared some complete outfits for girl dolls and for boy dolls…"

Even back then companies wanted to appeal to and put their products before those that someday would grow up and buy their products.

The Nippon doll in this set is a rather commonly found one with a bisque head and shoulderplate, a red cloth body, and bisque arms and legs. The doll is marked PATENT NO./30441/NIPPON. We do not know what company made these dolls or how J. & P. Coats obtained them. We do know this: even with a commonly found doll, there is nothing common about "a good girl's complete sewing set."

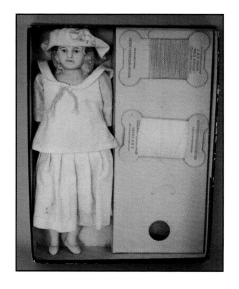

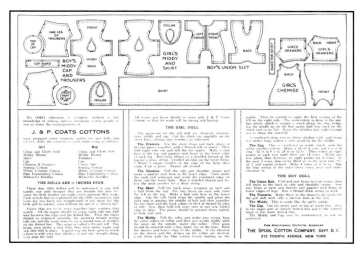

Endangered Species
Animals on Nippon
By Linda Lau

Take a quick look at Nippon porcelain and you will see that animals play a major role in the designs and scenes depicted whether the animal is at the centerpiece of the decoration or merely part of an overall scene.

Dog design on a Victorian silverplate castor frame; similar dog found on Nippon plaque below.

Many of the animal decorations utilized on Nippon have their beginnings in the Victorian era. The Victorians loved animals and nature and wherever possible used animals in their decorating. One example of the Victorian's fascination with wildlife is their use of taxidermy and animal skins in their decorating schemes. In those days it was not unusual to go into the proper Victorian

Nippon dog plaque.

parlor and see a tiger skin rug on the floor or small taxidermy animals displayed under a glass dome. Household items such as furniture, silverplate, Majolica pottery, and needlepoint lambrequins and footstools were often decorated with images of animals. Victorian-era artists such as Sir Edwin Landseer (deer, elk, dogs, and horses), Anton Mauve (sheep), and Adolph Schreyer (Arabian horses) relied heavily on animals in their paintings and drawings. Their artwork was so popular

Majolica pitchers with molded in relief animal designs.

Animal	Decorating Technique
Bat	HP, Moriage
Bear	HP (Polar Bear), MIR, Figural
Buffalo/Bison	HP, MIR
Camel	HP, MIR, Coralene
Cat	HP, Decal, Figural
Cow	HP
Deer	HP, Decal, MIR, Coralene
Dog	HP, Decal, MIR, Figural
Elephant	HP, MIR, Figural
Elk	HP, Decal, MIR
Fox	Figural
Goat	Decal
Horse	HP, Decal, MIR, tapestry
Kangaroo	HP
Lion	HP, Decal, MIR, Figural
Mice	HP
Monkey	Figural
Moose	Decal, MIR
Mule	HP
Rabbit	HP, MIR, Figural
Raccoon	MIR
Seal	Figural
Sheep/Ram	HP, Figural (handles)
Squirrel	HP, MIR, Figural
Tiger	MIR, Figural
Oxen	HP, MIR

HP stands for hand painted, MIR stands for molded in relief.

that almost no home was complete without one of their prints or engravings hanging on the wall. These paintings often showed animals as the Victorians knew them, on the farm or in natural surroundings. Still lifes featuring game and hunt scenes such as dogs tracking rabbits and deer were also in vogue, although many decorators of the day felt that these subjects were inappropriate for the dining room.

Deer scene plaque.

The Victorians also had a fascination with exotic places and things including wildlife. In 1868, Chicago's Lincoln Park Zoo, the first zoo in the United States, opened to the public. The opening of zoos in America led to an interest in

Victorian figural squirrel nutbowl.

many of those animals that today we tend to take for granted — lions, elephants, tigers, camels, and monkeys. Remember, most Victorians had only seen the animals they tended on the farm or hunted for dinner. To see an elephant or lion in person for the first time must have truly been extraordinary. P.T. Barnum would also have a major impact on the public's desire for these exotic animals with the opening of his museum in New York City. Not only

Nippon figural squirrel nutbowl.

did the museum house curiosities but also every type of exotic animal P.T. could locate and buy. Perhaps the best-known animal that P.T. brought to the United States was Jumbo, the world's largest elephant, which he bought from the London Zoo in 1882. Jumbo's arrival in the United States caused an immediate sensation, and likenesses of elephants would soon appear on prints, pottery, glassware, and advertising items.

It should come as no surprise then that the Japanese utilized many of these same animals on their porcelain. Not only did they copy the paintings of the popular artists but also utilized a variety of decorating techniques (such as figurals and molded in relief) that had been used on furniture, silverplate, and Majolica.

To date, we have identified 26 different animals that can be

Child's bowl decorated with decals of two rare Nippon animals, a goat and cats, shown dressed, with dogs around the edge. Elite B Nippon mark.

found on Nippon porcelain. In addition, this figure does not even include the myriad of birds, reptiles, insects, and amphibians that can be found.

Child's tea set with hand-painted rabbits.

Animals on tapestry, portrait, and coralene pieces are rare and, other than the bat (yes, it is a mammal), animals on moriage seem to be nonexistent. Recently a deer and a camel decorated with coralene beading have been found so who knows what other animals may be out there.

Two of the more unusual animals found on Nippon are the polar bear and kangaroo; items depicting these animals are rarely found. The polar bear vase may have

been decorated to commemorate Admiral Peary's expedition to the North Pole, which he reached in April 1909. So why a kangaroo? Perhaps to appeal to the Australian market.

The Victorians loved their pets and often immortalized them in their artwork and needlework. Cats may be the most popular household pets today but in the Victorian era, dogs were more popular. Only a few Nippon items have been found with cats making them a rare Nippon animal. Dog prints were an especial favorite of the Victorians, and the Newfoundland was one of the most popular as it was the Victorian symbol of protectiveness and dependability. The Victorians' love of dogs explains why there are a number of different Nippon dog items including plaques, ashtrays, and humidors. It would appear that many of these dog items were designed to appeal to the male population.

Other animals that turn up regularly on Nippon are deer, moose, and elk. This is primarily due to the popu-

larity of Sir Edwin Landseer's paintings and prints featuring these animals in their natural habitats. Indeed, a home was considered out of touch with the time if it did not display one of his prints such as "Monarch of the Glen," a proud stag

majestically sniffing the air, or "The Stag at Bay."

Today, it is getting harder and harder to find Nippon animals, making them our own "endangered species."

Rare set of Nippon figural animals. The lion, elephant, and reposing tiger are marked Nippon stamped in purple ink; four of the animals have their original price of 10¢ marked on them. Elephant is 3½" tall x 4¼" long.

Nippon's Music to My Ears

Did you ever notice that several musical instruments are featured on Nippon wares? So far, I have found nine different scenes and two figural items. There are three wall plaques; all have the same background, but each has a different man holding a musical instrument. One is playing a banjo, another a guitar, and the third an accordion. I have also found two shapes of humidors and ashtrays painted with these same patterns. The two figural musical items are a piano and RCA's Little Nipper. Two patterns feature Egyptian women playing the harp, two others have a violin-playing monk or a young girl with her friends, and the remaining two patterns feature horn-blowers, an "arrival of the coach" scene and a young girl herding geese.

The majority of these pieces bear the green M in wreath mark which indicates that they were manufactured between the years of 1911 to 1921. The others have the maple leaf mark, the crown mark, and the words "Hand Painted Nippon."

The figural piano is a two-piece item; the top lifts off the bottom. It was most likely used as a trinket box. It is extremely rare, and I have only seen one other. The molded in relief Egyptian decorated box is another two-piece item and rare piece. It features an Egyptian woman playing a

harp. At one end of the harp is the bust of a pharaoh wearing the crown of Lower Egypt. An Egyptian decorated vase shows a similar harp.

Before the harpist plucked the strings, she would purify her hands by washing them. It is said that many of the verses that these musicians played and sang were hymns to the gods. These old harps are similar to those found today; each one has many strings stretched on a large, upright frame.

Some Nippon pieces portray a man wearing a brown suit and tall hat and playing the guitar in a field of flowers. This musician is also found on a humidor, see Plate 90, also Plate 359 for a partial smoke set. The same background is used on a wall plaque featuring a banjo, but this one has a black man wearing a red and striped shirt and brown hat. The banjo, another stringed musical

instrument, has a long neck, a round body, and four or five strings that are plucked with the fingers or a pick. This design has also been found on a humidor and two different shaped ashtrays. The third scene featured on a wall plaque (with this very same background) is of a man

The two pieces depicting long horns are very popular with Nippon collectors. In the carriage scene a footman, riding on the back of the carriage is blowing a horn, perhaps as a warning or announcement to others that the coach is arriving. The little girl may be herding her geese with the

wearing a brown jacket and hat, playing the accordion. The accordion has keys, metal reeds, and a bellows. Pulling out and pressing together the bellows forces air through the reeds that are opened by fingering the

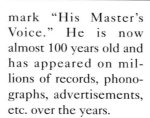

aid of a horn or she may just be playing it to amuse herself while she goes about her work. The sweet sound of music is in the air whenever a collector finds one of these special items.

Nipper is probably the most recognized dog in the world and is the main figure in the logo of the RCA Corp. trade-

keys. The man playing the accordion is also found on a humidor, Plate 1913.

A violin is shown in the hands of a monk on several Nippon items, a vase, a mug, and a wine jug. This scene is one of those featured in the monastic series. Other monks in

mark "His Master's Voice." He is now almost 100 years old and has appeared on millions of records, phonographs, advertisements, etc. over the years.

These items are small, measuring 3" in height, and the base is 4½" long. Most that are found are marked with Nippon as the country

the series are reading the newspaper, sniffing flowers, or drinking wine. These pieces are among the most desirable of any Nippon wares.

In addition, on a child's dish which is evidently part of a tea set, we find a little girl walking along with two friends, playing what appears to be a violin. The violin has four strings played with a bow.

of origin, but several have been located that are marked Germany. They all bear the names of cities all over the United States, such as Watertown, New York, Colorado Springs, Colorado, and even Burlington, Vermont. The wording often contains numbers, but so far these numbers pose a mystery as no data has been found as to what they mean.

When I was doing research for the Third Series of *Collector's Encyclopedia of Porcelain*, I wrote to the RCA Corp. in Indianapolis, and they gave me the following information:

Little Nipper was a real fox terrier owned originally by the brother of an English artist. When the dog's owner died, the little animal became the pet of the artist.

One day in the late 1800s, the artist, Francis Barraud, discovered the dog listening to an old-style horn-speaker phonograph with head cocked. The artist concluded the terrier thought he was hearing his original master's voice. Hence the painting and the title "His Master's Voice."

The painting became the property of the Victor Talking Machine Company in 1901, and the artist was permitted to paint a number of originals to supplement the annual royalty paid him by Victor to use the painting in various promotions.

An old 1906 ad for Victor machines states that one could be purchased on the Club Plan for a $1.00 deposit and payments of $1.50 a month. For this the buyer got a dozen records and a Victor Royal machine. The total cost of the package was $35.00. Another old ad featured in a British publication gave an account from the *New York Herald* of how the "Victor" (English name for gramophone) entertained and delighted the friends of the Queen. It went on to say that, "you can entertain your friends in the same manner as the Princess and Peers of England are entertained. The Victor Talking Machine is easily within your reach and its library of music is unlimited." The machines were popular in not only the United States but Britain as well, and some of this may have been due to the awards won at the St. Louis Exposition in 1904 by the company.

The Victrola was advertised in a December 1920 ad, and Nipper's logo appears in the bottom right corner of the ad. When the Victor Company was acquired by RCA in 1929, the picture became the property of RCA and was used for years as the company's trademark. About 30 years ago, the trademark with the fox terrier was phased out, however, Little Nipper has since been revived and is again used as part of the RCA logotype.

Items featuring musical instruments as their design are unusual to find and make a nice addition to any collection. Although they do not really play tunes, they have found their way into many collectors' hearts. If you want to hear more music, there are always the Nippon birds. But that could be another whole chapter!

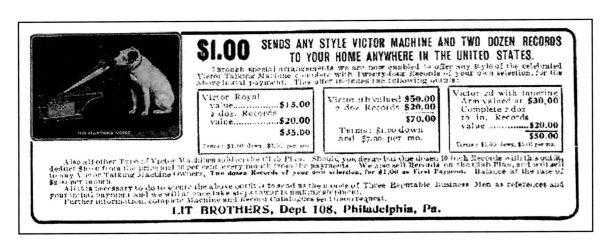

Cover of 1919 sheet music.

There are very few pieces of Nippon porcelain portraying the domestic cat. In fact, the number of items that I have found with a cat is very small. There are many pieces with dogs, horses, and camels, but why was the cat ignored? Being a cat lover, this omission is a "cat-astrophic" event! Cats have not been domesticated as long as dogs, but felines have inhabited five of our earth's seven present continents for at least 40 million years. Domestication most likely started in Egypt about 3,500 – 4,000 years ago. The Egyptians worshipped cats and mummified their dead cats along with other pets. They even risked punishment of death for killing a cat, even accidentally. They felt so strongly about their family cats that when one died, everyone went into mourning and shaved off their eyebrows.

During the Dark Ages in Europe, the Church savagely persecuted cats and of course, this continued even in America during the witch-hunting era. Thankfully, nineteenth century Victorians restored the cat to the role of a beloved household pet, and the first competitive cat show was at the Crystal Palace in 1871 in London.

The majority of items featuring a cat as their design is "a-meows-ing" and cater to children in the form of dolls, feeding dishes or play tea sets.

Friday's Child doll and figural child with cat

Ashtray.

Child's play teapot.

Wall plaque.

Child's feeding dish.

Child's plate with Elite B Nippon mark.

Stylized cat design found on 12" Royal Nishiki vase.

Morimura Brothers Dolls
By Linda Lau

Morimura Brothers was perhaps the largest of the Nippon doll manufacturers, and they were a leader in the development, manufacture, and export of Nippon dolls, being one of the first companies in Japan to realize the potential of the doll and toy market in the United States. They are also the best known of the Nippon doll manufacturers since they marked many of their bisque-head dolls with their distinctive "MB" and komaru symbol.

Before the outbreak of World War I, Germany was the leader in doll production, with France a distant second. The German dominance in the manufacture of bisque dolls would be curtailed in 1914 with the advent of World War I. With Germany at war and anti-German sentiment brewing here in the United States, many American doll importers sought out other manufacturers who could supply the vast amount of bisque dolls desired by the American public. Morimura Brothers took the initiative, and as this information from Mr. Ikuo Fukunaga provides, they established a factory for producing bisque dolls in Nagoya.

As a first step, Morimura Gumi set up a ceramic research laboratory for the production of ceramic toys on the site of Nippon Toki factory in March 1916. And, in 1917, Morimura Gumi established Nippon Gangu (Japan Toy) Company with a capital of 200,000 yen and constructed a factory for making Morimura bisque dolls at Sanbon Aze 1,616, Sakou-cho, Nishi-ku, Nagoya. Hirose Jikko was made president and Yamachi Toraturo general manager.

On this project, Morimura Gumi worked in concert with Froebel-Kan (Froebel House in English), a playthings shop in Kanda, Tokyo which still exists at Kanda Ogawa-cho 3-1, Chou-ku, Tokyo. Froebel House provided technical assistance and dispatched some personnel to Nippon Gangu. The Morimura bisque dolls were distributed by Morimura Brothers in the American market.

When World War I drew to a close in 1918, European producers returned to the American market. Although the quality of Morimura bisque dolls was on a par with that of European products, Morimura Brothers was forced to withdraw from the American market as they were unable to compete on price with the devaluation of European currencies. Nippon Gangu closed its door in 1921.

As we learned from the above information, Morimura Brothers' venture into the production of bisque dolls was relatively short lived. During that time, however, they manufactured a wide variety of all-bisque and bisque head dolls as shown in the following ad, and today many of these dolls are extremely popular with collectors.

Morimura's line of bisque-head character babies included their famous Baby Ella. Baby Ella, shown below with original box, was one of the first dolls produced by Morimura Brothers and was still in production in 1921; therefore, it is one of the more common Morimura Brothers dolls found today. It bears the mold number 2 and was produced in sizes 4/0 (7" tall) to 12 (23" tall). Baby Ella can be found with both sleeping glass eyes and painted eyes. It was also the mold Morimura Brothers used for their Crying Doll which they advertised in 1919.

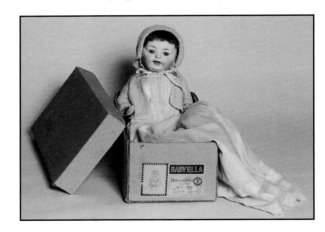

They also produced a solid dome head doll named My Darling. Collectors should be aware that the solid dome head baby does not have the typical Morimura Brothers mark on the back of the head. Instead, it has only the mold number 3 followed by a dash and then the size number. Because of this marking, collectors may mistake these dolls for German dolls. Since Morimura Brothers advertised their solid dome head dolls from 1917 through 1921 there are quite a few available. However, the only way to be sure it is a Morimura Brothers My Darling is to obtain one with its original box or tag.

Another Morimura Brothers doll commonly found is their Full Jointed Doll, shown below right, which is their line of girl dolls with ball-jointed bodies. These dolls use mold no. 1 and again were produced in sizes 4/0 (approximately 8" tall) through 11 (approximately 28" tall). In 1920 they would boast, "Our Full Jointed Doll is the finest finished Doll made. It cannot be surpassed." These dolls had glass eyes and came with either mohair or human hair wigs.

The other type of bisque-head doll produced by Morimura Brothers was their Kidolyn doll, shown below left, that was "Hip Jointed. Jointed Arms. Hips and Knee Jointed." As the name suggests, these dolls have shoulder plates with imitation kid bodies. They have a rather typical dolly-face, glass eyes, and are mold no. 5. They were not produced in the variety of sizes as the Full Jointed Doll but were produced from 1917 through 1921.

In addition to bisque-head dolls, Morimura Brothers also produced all-bisque dolls in "a complete line in staple and fancy designs." Some of their best-

known all-bisque dolls include Cho-Cho San, Baby Darling, Baby Belle, and Dolly. It is still possible to find some of these dolls with their original stickers, as shown above right, which is really the only way to be sure that Morimura Brothers produced the doll. In addition to the original sticker, some (but not all) Morimura Brothers dolls are also marked "Nippon" as the country of origin.

Morimura Brothers owned the rights to Queue San Baby that was patented in February 1916 by Hikozo Araki, and Dolly that was patented in October 1917 by Frederick Langfelder. Queue San Baby was produced in a number of different molds and several different sizes as shown in the

photo above. Today the most rare are perhaps the fully jointed and kneeling Queue San Babies.

During the years, Morimura Brothers advertised many types of dolls including "Standing character dolls with Buster Brown and Sailor suits assorted" and china limb dolls that repeated "our excellent line of 1919." Today, most of these dolls are hard to identify since Morimura

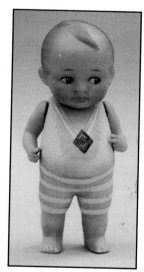

Brothers did not always mark or tag their dolls and, of course, on those dolls that did have tags, the tags have often times been removed.

However, even as varied and popular as the Morimura Brothers dolls were by 1920, there were growing problems in the production of dolls. Japan was facing increasing competition from the return of German dolls to the market as well as from the United States in the form of composition dolls. Additionally, Morimura Brothers was having problems meeting manufacturing goals "which are due to the constant increase in wage scales as well as almost prohibitive prices of raw materials." Morimura Brothers stopped producing dolls in 1921 when it closed Nippon Gangu (Japan Toy) and sold its Miscellaneous Import department to Langfelder, Homma, and Hayward, Inc. Therefore, even though Morimura Brothers bisque head dolls are marked "Japan," they were all produced during the Nippon era that ended in September 1921.

Nippon doll collecting is increasing by leaps and bounds and the prices are skyrocketing. This photo shows how one doll collector has some of her Nippon dolls and tea sets displayed in her house. In fact, she has devoted several rooms to her dolls. For collectors wanting to know more about this exciting field, check out *Nippon Dolls and Playthings* which is published by Collector Books and written by the author of this chapter, Linda Lau, and Joan Van Patten.

Rare, Unusual, and Just Plain Funny Nippon

I have been collecting Nippon porcelain for over 30 years, and it is amazing that new and wonderful things are still being found. After writing six books on Nippon featuring thousands and thousands of items, I am always surprised when I spot an item I have never seen before. Can you imagine all the different molds and designs that must have been used during the 1891 – 1921 period?

Numerous items have been found that appear to have been gifts given by the Morimura Brothers Company, and the 1903 Morimura Bros. porcelain calendar was most likely such a gift. It is a super piece and although unmarked is an item that any collector would love to add to their collection. It appears to have a mold shape identical to that of an RS Prussia item.

The thing that makes the "spare tire" ashtray shown in the two photos above right unique is the fact that it has a porcelain "rim" insert. The porcelain insert is just less than 4" in diameter and has no mark. When the

Ashtray showing wheel insert removed. Insert is just under 4" dia. and has no marking.

insert is placed on top of what looks like an ordinary ashtray, the piece is transformed. The ashtray is 5¾" wide and 2" high, and it bears the green M in wreath mark. It is a great find.

Flying swan decorated pieces are difficult to locate, but when they are found with a lavender colored background, it is truly time for rejoicing. Both vases are 6" tall and bear the green M in wreath mark.

Unusual items which are not rare are extra nice to add to our collections. They are not as difficult to locate

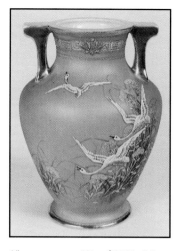

6", green 47, $750.00 – 850.00.

6", green 47, $750.00 – 850.00.

but are still seldom found. The vase shown below painted in patriotic colors and decorated in a moriage fashion is such a piece. It is 9½" tall and bears the M in wreath mark. Some collectors feel that the pattern resembles an Oriental rug motif.

Vase with moriage trim, front, 9½" tall, mark #47.

Back of vase at left.

Sugar, once called "white gold," has shaped a great deal of the history of the New World. It was very expensive, and in fact, in the sixteenth century sugar was so rare that a teaspoonful cost about the equivalent of five dollars today. It was still being shipped in crude wooden barrels in the late 1800s and was sold in bulk quantities, scooped out of the

barrels at the request of each customer. The advent of the sugar carton revolutionized packaging. In 1900 the American Sugar Refining Co. officially adopted the brand name "Domino" and another unusual Nippon find is the so-called "domino," set, shown below left, which includes a sugar cube tray and creamer. The tray is 6½" wide, and the creamer is 4¼" wide, including the handle. This set is the same shape as the glass ones shown in the background of the photo and bears the M in wreath mark as its backstamp.

A whiskey jug is not that unusual to find, but locating one with the name "E.M. Higgins Old Velvet" on it makes it all the more special. The writing appears to be fired on, and it must have been a special order by the Higgins Company years ago. It measures 6½" tall; the same item without any writing is shown in Plate 3593.

Blouse/shirt collar button boxes are not so expensive to purchase, but they are unusual to locate. Each of these boxes in the photo below shows the shirt collar as part of its design. These boxes are approximately 2½" in diameter. The one on the left is backstamped with mark #10 and the right one is #84, the Rising Sun mark.

Whiskey jug, 6½", advertising, green mark #47.

Knife rests look something like miniature sawhorses, and years ago there was one for every diner at table. Can you imagine washing all those dishes? Both knife rests shown at the bottom of the page are 3½" long and are marked with the green M in wreath.

Left: 2⅝" across, mark #10; right: 2⅜" across, Rising Sun mark.

Figural birds are not that plentiful, and for the bird lover they are the ultimate bird collectible. The first one shown is a napkin holder which makes it especially desirable. Perhaps it is part of a set as there is a similar item portraying a figural owl in Plate 1534. This yellow bird is 3¾" tall while the other four birds in the photo are 4¼" tall. All are backstamped with the green M in wreath mark.

Left to right: 3¾" tall, all others 4¼" tall; all green #47.

The egg-shaped trinket or candy box below is 4½" long and is decorated in what appears to be an Easter theme. It has moriage trim and features little yellow chickens as its decoration. Although it is unmarked, it is definitely from the Nippon era.

Top of moriage egg.

Egg-shaped trinket or candy box, moriage trim, unmarked, 4½" long.

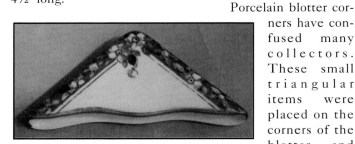

Porcelain blotter corners have confused many collectors. These small triangular items were placed on the corners of the blotter and were part of a desk set. There are two holes on the back side

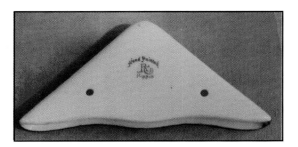

which were used to attach the corners to the blotter. A complete set consists of four corners. This particular set is backstamped with the RC mark.

Rare, unusual — and then there are the just plain funny pieces that make us laugh. In this category I have to include the pieces with animals engaging in human behavior. The frogs in the next four photos appear to be beating each other with sticks or perhaps they are dueling. There are several known items in this pattern, and it is a favorite with collectors. They all have a green background, and the frogs are found in moriage decoration. The back of each piece also has a single moriage frog on it. Most are backstamped with the maple leaf mark. Other cute items are the child's tea set and feeding dishes, one example of which is shown on the next

page, where the design is of dogs dressed in clothes and playing field hockey. There is even a child's tea set that is decorated with dogs playing tennis!

Moriage vase, frogs, unmarked, 5¼" tall.

Another clever piece and one also hard to find is the small figural sitting Indian which appeals to both doll and figural collectors. It is 3¼" tall and incised with the word Nippon.

I guess you could call the next item funny, but I call it ridiculous. It was advertised on the Internet as a "rare" sugar bowl with a sugar shaker as its cover. The photos were not too clear, so taking a chance, one collector bid on it and mailed off a check for this very "desirable" piece. Can you imagine her surprise when it turned out that the item was actually a coverless sugar bowl and the cover was one of the shakers from a salt and pepper set! That seems to be one of the problems of buying through the mail. We

cannot actually hold and see the item and very often, it arrives with hairlines, worn gold, and even mismatched pieces such as this one. Buying via mail is always a gamble, but we never know when a wonderful, rare piece may arrive in the mail, so we continue playing the game.

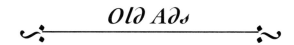

Old Ads

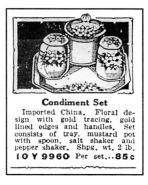
1920 Charles William Stores catalog.

Seven-Piece Salad or Berry Set

Made of very high grade American semi-porcelain, richly decorated in ivory finish, gold tracings and beautiful floral spray design. Set consists of one large salad or berry bowl, 10 inches in diameter, and six individual salad dishes, 5¼ inches in diameter. Shpg. wt., 7 lbs.
I O Y I I95 Price, per set.................. ....$3.75

Salad or Berry Set

Made of American porcelain with a wide enameled orange border, fancy gold festoon inner border and gold outlined center design of flowers in natural colors. Bowl, 9½ inches in diameter; dishes, 5¼ inches. Shpg. wt., 4½ lbs.
I O Y I I87 Price, per set. **$1.85**

Mayonnaise Set

Fine quality Japanese China. Assorted designs. Set consists of 1 bowl, 4½ in. diam., plate and a ladle. Shpg. wt., ¾ lb.
I O Y 9958
Price, per set..**89c**

Japanese China Tea Set

A uniquely "different" set; in blue underglaze, all-over decoration of Japanese "Bird of Paradise," known as the famous "Howo Bird" decoration. Set consists of tea pot (capacity, 6 cups) and 6 cups and saucers. Diameter of cup 4 inches, height of cup 2 inches, 6 tea plates, 7¼ inches in diameter, 1 sugar bowl and 1 cream pitcher. Sold in sets only. Shpg. wt., 8 lbs.
I O Y 5302
Price, per set...**$6.98**

Olive or Nut Set

Japanese China. Consists of 7 pieces — 1 large footed bowl and 6 footed individual bowls. Shpg. wt., 2 lb.
I O Y 9962
Per set ..**$1.25**

No. 12303G. Curry set of 5 individual porcelain dishes, shaped to fit a heavily lacquered box with pretty Oriental design in gilt on cover. Each dish hand-painted in bird design and striped around edge in gold. May also be filled with candy, making a most unique gift. Price prepaid $3.75

No. 12304G. Curry set similar to the above, but much larger and circular instead of square: contains seven individual dishes instead of five, in pretty black lacquer box. Price prepaid $6.50

In addition to the above the new Vantine Book shows hundreds of dainty tea table accessories, such as lacquered trays, unique china ware, Oriental delicacies, etc., etc., many of which are to be had only at Vantine's.

1916 Vantine catalog.

Japanese Tea Sets, consisting of tea pot, sugar bowl, cream pitcher, six cups and saucers. Each set packed in individual boxes—Japanese fashion—in our studios in Japan, and sent from our store in New York to the recipient in the same Oriental wrappings. Unique gift packages conveying an atmosphere of the Orient that is both original and attractive. Prices quoted include free delivery to any express office in the United States.

No. 7858G—Nagoya Tea Set	-	-	$6.50
No. 7613G—Fine Seto Tea Set	-	-	7.50
No. 7614G—Kobe Tea Set	-	-	9.00
No. 37924G—Kutani Tea Set	-	-	10.00
No. 7615G—Kobe Tea Set	-	-	12.00

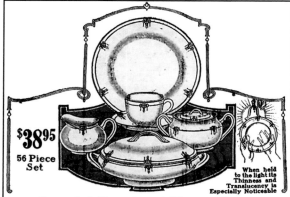

$38.95
56 Piece Set

When held to the light its Thinness and Translucency is Especially Noticeable

Imported Translucent Nippon China

The newest design in dinnerware, gold band around edge with a gold hair line broken by medallions of dull green, purple and gold on beautiful white translucent china.
150C370—56-Piece Set. Complete service for 12 persons. Includes the following pieces:

12 Tea Cups and Saucers.	1 Covered Vegetable Dish, 12 in. (2 Pcs.)
12 Dinner Plates, 10 in.	1 Oval Open Vegetable Dish, 9¾ in.
12 Fruit Dishes, 5¼ in.	1 Covered Sugar Bowl, 1 pt. (2 Pcs.)
1 Platter, 13¾ in.	1 Cream Pitcher, ¾ pt.
1 Sauce Boat, 1 pt.	Shipping weight, 70 pounds.

Price, set...**$38.95**

1920 Montgomery Ward catalog.

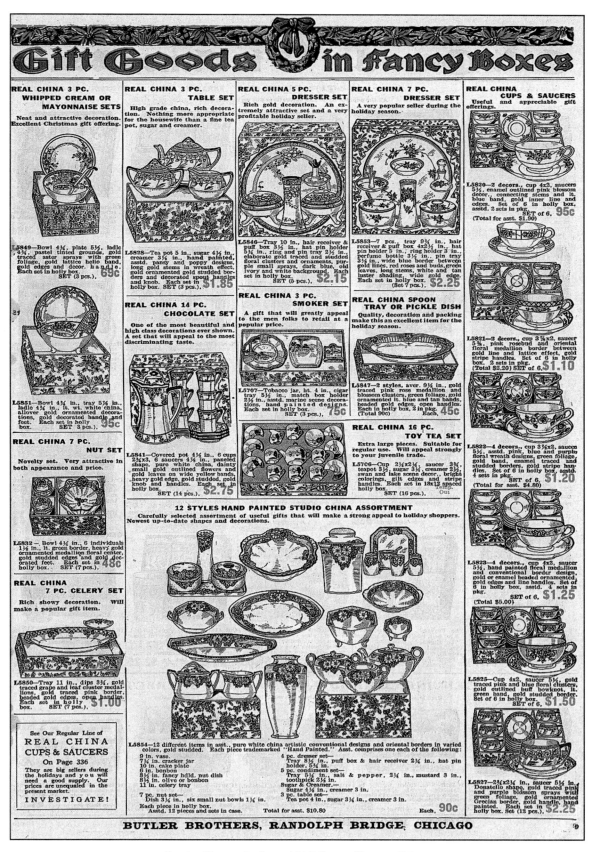

Butler Bros. ads from 1917 Santa Claus edition.

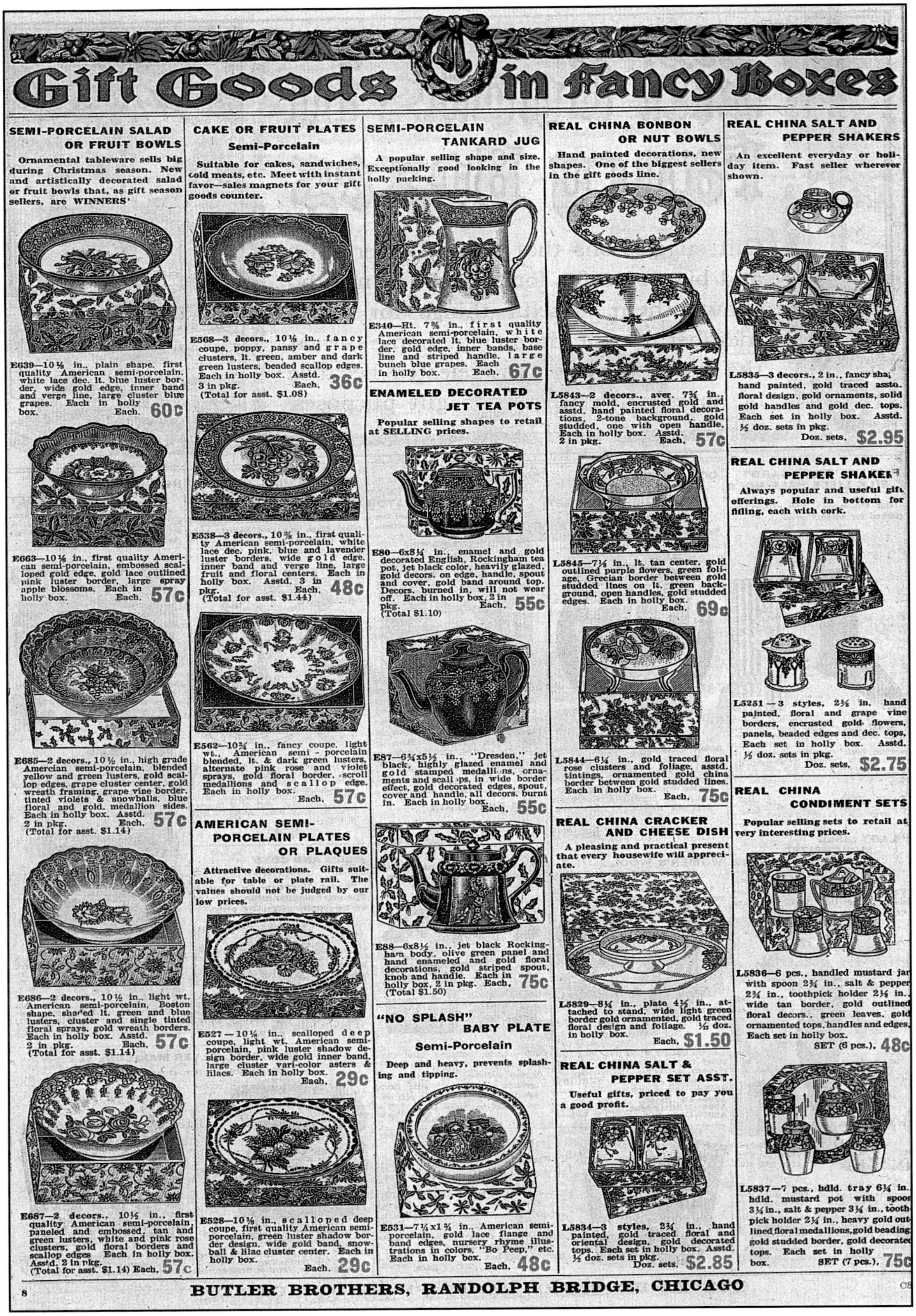
Gift Goods in Fancy Boxes
SEMI-PORCELAIN SALAD OR FRUIT BOWLS
Ornamental tableware sells big during Christmas season. New and artistically decorated salad or fruit bowls that, as gift season sellers, are WINNERS'
E639—10⅛ in., plain shape, first quality American semi-porcelain, white lace dec. lt. blue luster border, wide gold edge, inner band and verge line, large cluster blue grapes. Each in holly box. Each, 60c
E663—10⅛ in., first quality American semi-porcelain, embossed scalloped gold edge, gold lace outlined pink luster border, large spray apple blossoms. Each in holly box. Each, 57c
E685—2 decors., 10½ in., high grade Amercian semi-porcelain, blended yellow and green lusters, gold scallop edges, grape cluster center, gold wreath framing, grape vine border, tinted violets & snowballs, blue floral and gold medallion sides. Each in holly box. Asstd. 2 in pkg. Each, 57c (Total for asst. $1.14)
E686—2 decors., 10½ in., light wt. American semi-porcelain, Boston shape, shaded lt. green and blue lusters, cluster and single tinted floral sprays, gold wreath borders. Each in holly box. Asstd. 2 in pkg. Each, 57c (Total for asst. $1.14)
E687—2 decors., 10½ in., first quality American semi-porcelain, paneled and embossed, tan and green lusters, white and pink rose clusters, gold floral borders and scallop edges Each in holly box. Asstd. 2 in pkg. (Total for asst. $1.14) Each, 57c
CAKE OR FRUIT PLATES
Semi-Porcelain
Suitable for cakes, sandwiches, cold meats, etc. Meet with instant favor—sales magnets for your gift goods counter.
E568—3 decors., 10⅛ in., fancy coupe, poppy, pansy and grape clusters, lt. green, amber and dark green lusters, beaded scallop edges. Each in holly box. Asstd. 3 in pkg. Each, 36c (Total for asst. $1.08)
E538—3 decors., 10⅜ in., first quality American semi-porcelain, white lace dec. pink, blue and lavender luster borders, wide gold edge, inner band and verge line, large fruit and floral centers. Each in holly box. Asstd. 3 in pkg. Each, 48c (Total for asst. $1.44)
E562—10¾ in., fancy coupe, light wt., American semi-porcelain blended, lt. & dark green lusters, alternate pink rose and violet sprays, gold floral border, scroll medallions and scallop edge. Each in holly box. Each, 57c
AMERICAN SEMI-PORCELAIN PLATES OR PLAQUES
Attractive decorations. Gifts suitable for table or plate rail. The values should not be judged by our low prices.
E527—10⅛ in., scalloped deep coupe, light wt. American semi-porcelain, pink luster shadow design border, wide gold inner band, large cluster vari-color asters & lilacs. Each in holly box. Each, 29c
E528—10⅛ in., scalloped deep coupe, first quality American semi-porcelain, green luster shadow border design, wide gold band, snowball & lilac cluster center. Each in holly box. Each, 29c
SEMI-PORCELAIN TANKARD JUG
A popular selling shape and size. Exceptionally good looking in the holly packing.
E340—Ht. 7⅜ in., first quality American semi-porcelain, white lace decorated lt. blue luster border, gold edge, inner bands, base line and striped handle, large bunch blue grapes. Each in holly box. Each, 67c
ENAMELED DECORATED JET TEA POTS
Popular selling shapes to retail at SELLING prices.
E80—6x8¼ in., enamel and gold decorated English, Rockingham tea pot, jet black color, heavily glazed, gold decors. on edge, handle, spout and cover, gold band around top. Decors. burned in, will not wear off. Each in holly box, 2 in pkg. Each, 55c (Total $1.10)
E87—6¾x5½ in., "Dresden," jet black, highly glazed enamel and gold stamped medallions, ornaments and scallops, in wide border effect, gold decorated edges, spout, cover and handle, all decors. burnt in. Each in holly box. Each, 55c
E88—6x8½ in., jet black Rockingham body, olive green panel and hand enameled and gold floral decorations, gold striped spout, knob and handle. Each in holly box, 2 in pkg. Each, 75c (Total $1.50)
"NO SPLASH" BABY PLATE
Semi-Porcelain
Deep and heavy, prevents splashing and tipping.
E531—7¼x1¾ in., American semi-porcelain, gold lace flange and band edges, nursery rhyme illustrations in colors, "Bo Peep," etc. Each in holly box. Each, 48c
REAL CHINA BONBON OR NUT BOWLS
Hand painted decorations, new shapes. One of the biggest sellers in the gift goods line.
L5843—2 decors., aver. 7¾ in., fancy mold, encrusted gold and asstd. hand painted floral decorations, 2-tone background, gold studded, one with open handle, Each in holly box. Asstd. 2 in pkg. Each, 57c
L5845—7⅛ in., lt. tan center, gold outlined purple flowers, green foliage, Grecian border between gold studded lines on lt. green background, open handles, gold studded edges. Each in holly box. Each, 69c
L5844—6¼ in., gold traced floral rose clusters and foliage, asstd. tintings, ornamented gold china border between gold studded lines. Each in holly box. Each, 75c
REAL CHINA CRACKER AND CHEESE DISH
A pleasing and practical present that every housewife will appreciate.
L5829—8¼ in., plate 4½ in., attached to stand, wide light green border gold ornamented, gold traced floral design and foliage. ½ doz. in holly box. Each, $1.50
REAL CHINA SALT & PEPPER SET ASST.
Useful gifts, priced to pay you a good profit.
L5834—3 styles, 2¾ in., hand painted, gold traced floral and oriental design, gold decorated tops. Each set in holly box. Asstd. ½ doz. sets in pkg. Doz. sets, $2.85
REAL CHINA SALT AND PEPPER SHAKERS
An excellent everyday or holiday item. Fast seller wherever shown.
L5835—3 decors., 2 in., fancy sha[pe,] hand painted, gold traced assto. floral design, gold ornaments, solid gold handles and gold dec. tops. Each set in holly box. Asstd. ½ doz. sets in pkg. Doz. sets, $2.95
REAL CHINA SALT AND PEPPER SHAKERS
Always popular and useful gift offerings. Hole in bottom for filling, each with cork.
L5251—3 styles, 2⅝ in, hand painted, floral and grape vine borders, encrusted gold flowers, panels, beaded edges and dec. tops, Each set in holly box. Asstd. ½ doz. sets in pkg. Doz. sets, $2.75
REAL CHINA CONDIMENT SETS
Popular selling sets to retail at very interesting prices.
L5836—6 pcs., handled mustard jar with spoon 2¾ in., salt & pepper 2¾ in., toothpick holder 2⅛ in., wide tan border, gold outlined floral decors., green leaves, gold ornamented tops, handles and edges. Each set in holly box. SET (6 pcs.), 48c
L5837—7 pcs., hdld. tray 6¼ in., hdld. mustard pot with spoon 3¼ in., salt & pepper 3¼ in., toothpick holder 2¼ in., heavy gold outlined floral medallions, gold beading, gold studded border, gold decorated tops. Each set in holly box. SET (7 pcs.), 75c
8
BUTLER BROTHERS, RANDOLPH BRIDGE, CHICAGO

Butler Bros. ads for 1917 Santa Claus edition.

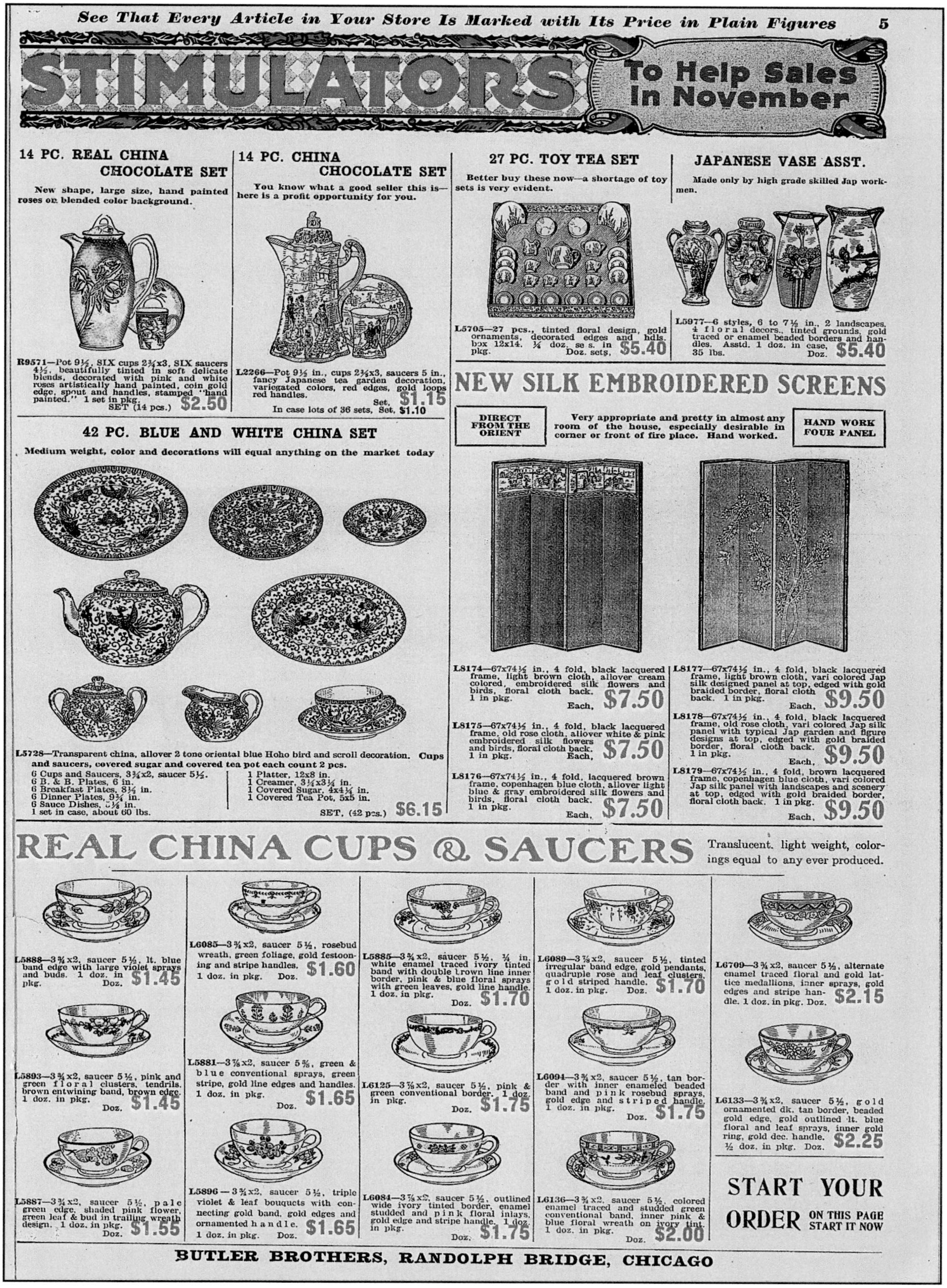

See That Every Article in Your Store Is Marked with Its Price in Plain Figures 5

STIMULATORS To Help Sales In November

14 PC. REAL CHINA CHOCOLATE SET

New shape, large size, hand painted roses on blended color background.

R9571—Pot 9½, SIX cups 2¾x3, SIX saucers 4½, beautifully tinted in soft delicate blends, decorated with pink and white roses artistically hand painted, coin gold edge, spout and handles, stamped "hand painted." 1 set in pkg. SET (14 pcs.) $2.50

14 PC. CHINA CHOCOLATE SET

You know what a good seller this is—here is a profit opportunity for you.

L2266—Pot 9½ in., cups 2⅜x3, saucers 5 in., fancy Japanese tea garden decoration, variegated colors, red edges, gold loops red handles. Set, $1.15

In case lots of 36 sets, Set, $1.10

27 PC. TOY TEA SET

Better buy these now—a shortage of toy sets is very evident.

L5705—27 pcs., tinted floral design, gold ornaments, decorated edges and hdls. box 12x14. ¼ doz. se s. in pkg. Doz. sets, $5.40

JAPANESE VASE ASST.

Made only by high grade skilled Jap workmen.

L5977—6 styles, 6 to 7½ in., 2 landscapes, 4 floral decors., tinted grounds, gold traced or enamel beaded borders and handles. Asstd. 1 doz. in case, 35 lbs. Doz. $5.40

42 PC. BLUE AND WHITE CHINA SET

Medium weight, color and decorations will equal anything on the market today

L5728—Transparent china, allover 2 tone oriental blue Hoho bird and scroll decoration. Cups and saucers, covered sugar and covered tea pot each count 2 pcs.

6 Cups and Saucers, 3¾x2, saucer 5½.
6 B. & B. Plates, 6 in.
6 Breakfast Plates, 8¼ in.
6 Dinner Plates, 9¾ in.
6 Sauce Dishes, 5⅛ in.
1 set in case, about 60 lbs.

1 Platter, 12x8 in.
1 Creamer, 3¼x3¼ in.
1 Covered Sugar, 4x4¼ in.
1 Covered Tea Pot, 5x5 in.

SET, (42 pcs.) $6.15

NEW SILK EMBROIDERED SCREENS

DIRECT FROM THE ORIENT

Very appropriate and pretty in almost any room of the house, especially desirable in corner or front of fire place. Hand worked.

HAND WORK FOUR PANEL

L8174—67x74½ in., 4 fold, black lacquered frame, light brown cloth, allover cream colored, embroidered silk flowers and birds, floral cloth back. 1 in pkg. Each, $7.50

L8175—67x74½ in., 4 fold, black lacquered frame, old rose cloth, allover white & pink embroidered silk flowers and birds, floral cloth back. 1 in pkg. Each, $7.50

L8176—67x74½ in., 4 fold, lacquered brown frame, copenhagen blue cloth, allover light blue & gray embroidered silk flowers and birds, floral cloth back. 1 in pkg. Each, $7.50

L8177—67x74½ in., 4 fold, black lacquered frame, light brown cloth, vari colored Jap silk designed panel at top, edged with gold braided border, floral cloth back. 1 in pkg. Each, $9.50

L8178—67x74½ in., 4 fold, black lacquered frame, old rose cloth, vari colored Jap silk panel with typical Jap garden and figure designs at top, edged with gold braided border, floral cloth back. 1 in pkg. Each, $9.50

L8179—67x74½ in., 4 fold, brown lacquered frame, copenhagen blue cloth, vari colored Jap silk panel with landscapes and scenery at top, edged with gold braided border, floral cloth back. 1 in pkg. Each, $9.50

REAL CHINA CUPS & SAUCERS

Translucent, light weight, colorings equal to any ever produced.

L5888—3¾x2, saucer 5½, lt. blue band edge with large violet sprays and buds. 1 doz. in pkg. Doz. $1.45

L5893—3¾x2, saucer 5½, pink and green floral clusters, tendrils, brown entwining band, brown edge. 1 doz. in pkg. Doz. $1.45

L5887—3¾x2, saucer 5½, pale green edge, shaded pink flower, green leaf & bud in trailing wreath design. 1 doz. in pkg. Doz. $1.55

L6085—3¾x2, saucer 5½, rosebud wreath, green foliage, gold festooning and stripe handles. 1 doz. in pkg. Doz. $1.60

L5881—3⅞x2, saucer 5⅜, green & blue conventional sprays, green stripe, gold line edges and handles. 1 doz. in pkg. Doz. $1.65

L5896—3¾x2, saucer 5½, triple violet & leaf bouquets with connecting gold band, gold edges and ornamented handle. 1 doz. in pkg. Doz. $1.65

L5885—3¾x2, saucer 5½, ¼ in. white enamel traced ivory tinted band with double brown line inner border, pink & blue floral sprays with green leaves, gold line handle. 1 doz. in pkg. Doz. $1.70

L6125—3⅞x2, saucer 5½, pink & green conventional border. 1 doz. in pkg. Doz. $1.75

L6084—3⅞x2, saucer 5½, outlined wide ivory tinted border, enamel studded and pink floral inlays, gold edge and stripe handle. 1 doz. in pkg. Doz. $1.75

L6089—3⅞x2, saucer 5½, tinted irregular band edge, gold pendants, quadruple rose and leaf clusters, gold striped handle. 1 doz. in pkg. Doz. $1.70

L6094—3¾x2, saucer 5½, tan border with inner enameled beaded band and pink rosebud sprays, gold edge and striped handle. 1 doz. in pkg. Doz. $1.75

L6136—3¾x2, saucer 5½, colored enamel traced and studded green conventional band, inner pink & blue floral wreath on ivory tint. 1 doz. in pkg. Doz. $2.00

L6709—3¾x2, saucer 5½, alternate enamel traced floral and gold lattice medallions, inner sprays, gold edges and stripe handle. 1 doz. in pkg. Doz. $2.15

L6133—3¾x2, saucer 5½, gold ornamented dk. tan border, beaded gold edge, gold outlined lt. blue floral and leaf sprays, inner gold ring, gold dec. handle. ½ doz. in pkg. Doz. $2.25

START YOUR ORDER ON THIS PAGE START IT NOW

BUTLER BROTHERS, RANDOLPH BRIDGE, CHICAGO

Butler Bros. ads from 1917 Santa Claus edition.

Choice Selections of Imported China

Hand Painted

The china shown here is the best hand painted Nippon Ware that can be had. The designs are remarkably pretty and the colors are of that soft harmonious blending typical of Oriental decorations. Light and durable.

5-Piece Hand Painted Dresser Set
Conventional border with Oriental Pheasant, flowers and leaves. 9-in. round gray, hatpin holder, ring tree, puff box and hair receiver. Shipping weight, 7 lbs.
50C928—Each Set........$4.98

$248 Four-Piece Dresser Set
Floral and gold line decorations. Hand Painted. Includes the four essential pieces. Ship.wt., about 3 lbs.
50C938—Per set.......$2.48

$2⁹⁵

$6²⁵

$9⁷⁵
7-Piece Berry Set
Rose border on black and gold stippled background, followed by conventional leaf design. Hand painted. Diameter of bowl, 9 in. Diameter of berry dishes, 5¼ inches. Shipping wt., about 15 pounds.
150C995—Price..$9.75

$9⁶⁵

Hand Painted 7-Piece Berry Set
A beautiful open handled 10-inch bowl and six 5¼-inch fruit saucers to match. Large sprays of wild roses. Gold edge and handles. A very good value. Ship. wt., about 15 lbs.
150C997—Price, set......$6.25

7-Piece Berry Set
Unusually attractive. Tinted background. Sprays of beautiful colored raspberries and gold decorated open handles. Diameter of bowl about 10 inches. Diameter of sauce dishes, 5¼ inches. Ship. wt., 15 lbs.
150C996—Price, set........$9.65

$5⁴⁵
7-Piece Lemonade Set
Large capacities. Pitcher and 6 handled lemonade Tumblers to match. All over assorted floral decorations. Hand Painted. A splendid value. Ship. wt., about 15 pounds.
150C930—Per set.......$5.45

Three-Piece Tea Set
Two-tone band, broken by full blown roses. Delicate ivory top laced with gold. Hand Painted. Unusually attractive. Ship. wt., 8 pounds.
50C937—Price, set.................$2.95

Our Handled Fruit Basket
Woven bamboo basket with hand painted china coupe plate bottom. Floral and blackberry decoration with tinted background. Makes a very attractive center piece. Ship. wts., 6, 8 and 10 lbs.

Article No.	Width of Basket	Price
50C1015	About 9 inches	$3.25
50C1016	About 10 inches	3.98
50C1017	About 11 inches	5.25

Hand painted with pheasant on scenic background. Ship. wt., 16 oz.
50C900—Price (cup and saucer)..33c
Set of three..92c

Assorted floral decorations. Tinted bands encircle cup and saucer. Studio hand painted. Ship. wt., 1 lb.
50C988—Price cup and saucer..85c

Dainty, artistic, conventional borders. Assorted decorations. Hand Painted. Gold trimmed handles. Ship. wt., abt. 1 lb.
50C1011—Price, cup and saucer..63c

Beautiful Oriental hand painted decorations. Gold-trimmed handles. Ship. wt., 16 oz.
50C1014—Price, cup and saucer..69c

Tinted background. Hand painted in assorted decorations of wild flowers. Shipping wt., 16 oz.
50C989—Price cup and saucer......89c

Neat hand painted conventional borders. Beautiful assorted decorations. Shipping weight, 16 oz.
50C1012—Price, cup and saucer..73c

$3.98 Sugar and Creamer
New and attractive shape. Japanese water lily with green leaves on blue tinted background. Hand Painted. Coin gold bands on edge and handles. Ship. wt., about 5 lbs.
50C994—Price Pair...$3.98

Bread and Butter Plates
American Ware. Printed decal Pansy decoration on tinted background. Gold edge. Diameter, 6½ in. Ship. wt., 2 lbs.
50C936—Price...69c

Utility Plate $1²⁵
Hand painted. Unique floral decorations on tinted background. Conventional green and gold border. Diam., 8 in. Ship. wt., about 3 lbs.
50C1007—Price...$1.25

Utility Plate $1¹⁵
Tinted background with beautiful floral sprays. Hand painted. Coin gold band. Diam., 8 in. Ship. wt., about 3 lbs.
50C1004—Price......$1.15

Fruit Plate 79c
All over Oriental decorations. Hand Painted. Assorted designs in natural colors. Diameter, 7½ in. Ship. wt., 18 oz.
50C1010—Price......79c

Utility Plate $1³⁵
Clusters of colored grapes overhanging beautiful tinted background. Gold band encircles edge. Hand Painted. Diam., 8 in. Ship. wt., abt. 3 lbs.
50C1006—Price......$1.35

Utility Plate $1²⁹
Nicely hand painted raspberry decorations on tinted background. Diam., 8 in. Gold band encircles edge. Ship. wt., abt. 3 lbs.
50C1005—Price......$1.29

$2.25 Sugar and Creamer
Hand painted conventional border broken by full blown rose. Ship. wt., 3 lbs.
50C890—Price of set......$2.25

Bon Bon Dish
Hand painted with black striped conventional border interspersed with pink flowers. Decorated in center with red and white roses and green leaves. Open handles. Diam., 7½ in. Ship. wt., 2 lbs.
50C907—Price...89c

$3.89 Sugar and Creamer
Oval shape. Conventional grape design and handles in dull coin gold. Green leaves and gold bands on wide ivory tinted band. Hand Painted. Ship. wt., about 5 lbs.
50C993—Price Pair......$3.89

Fancy Bon Bon Tray
Hand decorated with red poppy, narcissus and foliage, on a richly tinted background. Two-handled fancy shape. Length, 8¾ in. Ship. weight, 5 pounds.
50C906—Price...........$1.48

$1.89 Sugar and Creamer
Assorted Oriental decorations. Beautifully tinted. Gold trimmed handles. Hand Painted. Ship. wt., 3 lbs.
50C899—Price, set.......$1.89

Handled Cake Plate
Large spray of apple-blossoms on tinted background. Dull coin gold edge. Coin gold open work handles. Hand Painted. Diam., 10 in. Ship. wt., 3 lbs.
50C999—Price...$2.65

$2²⁵ Handled Cake Plate
Spring flowers with tinted backgrounds. Gold line encircles edge. Open work handles. Hand Painted. Diam., 10 in. Ship. wt., abt. 4 lbs.
50C1002—Price...$2.25

$2⁹⁸ Handled Cake Plate
Large clusters of grapes on all over tinted background. Coin gold open work handles. Hand Painted. Diam., 10 in. Ship. wt., 4 lbs.
50C1001—Price...$2.98

Handled Cake Plate
Hand painted. Tinted background with raspberry decorations in artistic colors. Coin gold open work handles. Diam., 10 in. Ship. wt., about 4 lbs.
50C1000—Price...$2.85

$4.25 Oval Shape Sugar and Creamer
Artistically hand painted. Raspberries, ivory and gold bands form the decorations. Dull coin gold handles. Hand Painted. Ship. wt., about 5 lbs.
50C992—Price, set.....$4.25

Four-Piece Condiment Set
Convention a l border of gold, ivory and blue with floral design. 6½-in. tray, salt and pepper shakers and mustard jar. Hand Painted. Ship. wt., 4 lbs.
50C924—Each Set........$1.45

1920 Montgomery Ward catalog.

54

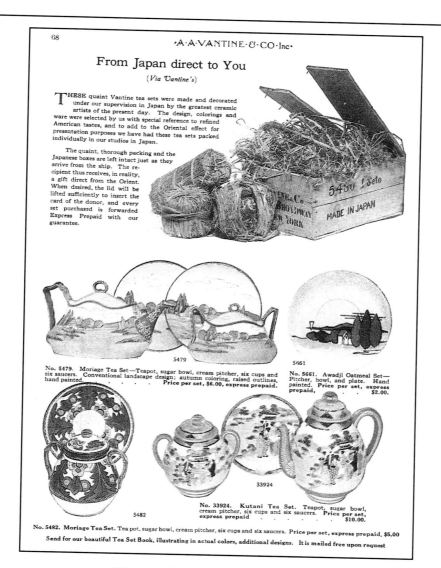

Old A.A. Vantene & Co. catalog ads.

JAPANESE VASES

Note the odd shapes, the exquisite, inimitable decorations that only the Japs can produce. Bigger sellers every year. Note the many assortments, big in variety and low in price. Compare these values.

JAPANESE SATSUMA VASES

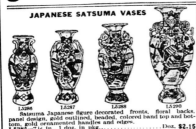

L5286 L5287 L5288 L5290

Satsuma Japanese figure decorated fronts, floral backs, panel design, gold outlined, beaded, colored band top and bottom, gold ornamented handles and edges.

			Doz. $2.15
L5286—7½ in., 1 doz. in pkg.			2.50
L5286—8½ " ½ "			3.75
L5287—9¾ " ½ "			
L5289—16 " ¼ "			9.75
L5290—18 " ¼ "			17.25

JAP HAND PAINTED PORCELAIN VASE ASSTS.

L5220—6 styles, 7¼x8¼ in. pastel tints, 2 water scenes, 2 landscapes, 2 floral decors, gold traced and beaded borders, edges and hdls. Asstd. 1 doz. in case, 44 lbs. Doz. **$5.25**

L5965—12 styles, 6½ to 8½ in., selected shapes, floral and scenic decors., enamel beaded and traced borders and hdls., some gold edges and hdls. Asstd. 2 doz. in case, 75 lbs. (Total for asst. $12.00) Doz. **$6.00**

L5966—9 styles, ht. 10 in., tinted or mottled bodies, profuse gold or enamel decorated floral and landscape designs, gold decorated tops and hdls. Asstd. 3 doz. in case, 174 lbs. (Total for asst. $18.00) Doz. **$6.00**

L5977—6 styles, 6 to 7½ in., 2 landscapes, 4 floral decors. tinted grounds, gold traced or enamel beaded borders and handles. Asstd. 1 doz. in case, 35 lbs. Doz. **$5.40**

L5976—6 styles, 7½ to 8¾ in., hard baked white chain body, in asstd. shapes. Pastel tints with full hand painted decors., 3 floral and 3 water scenes. Each with harmonizing enamel traced or gold decorated bands and handles. 1 doz. (6 pair) in case, 35 lbs. Doz. **$7.25**

JAP HAND PAINTED PORCELAIN VASE ASSORTMENTS—Continued

L5978—6 styles, aver. 7 to 8½ in., pastel tints, 4 scenic, 2 gold traced floral designs, conventional borders, enamel or gold traced and beaded. Asstd. 1 doz. in case, 35 lbs. Doz. **$8.50**

L5967—12 styles, ht. 12 in., floral bouquet, marine and landscape decors., enamel and gold frames, borders and hdls. Asstd. 1 doz. in case, 187 lbs. Doz. **$8.50** (Total for asst. $17.00)

L5979—6 styles, 9½ to 11¾ in., 3 landscape, 3 floral decors., pastel tinted grounds, enamel or gold traced and beaded mosaic borders and handles. Asstd. 1 doz. in case, 50 lbs. Doz. **$12.50**

L5971—6 styles, ht. 12 in., pastel tinted grounds, colored enamel floral and bird designs, enamel studded conventional borders and hdls. 1 doz. in case, 122 lbs. Doz. **$12.75**

L5227—6 styles, ht. 12 in., pastel tinted grounds, colored enamel floral and bird designs, enamel studded conventional borders and hdls. 1 doz. in case, 122 lbs. Doz. **$13.50**

L5969—6 styles, 15 in., Awata assortment, all-over assorted shaded tints, elaborate fruit, floral and landscape decors., richly trimmed in gold. half gold handles. 1 doz. (6 pair) in case. Doz. **$14.40**

L5968—6 styles, 15 in., 3 landscape and marine, 3 floral designs, enamel and gold outlining. frames and borders, gold dec. hdls. Asstd. 1 doz. in case, 170 lbs. Doz. **$12.00**

L5972—6 styles, ht. 12 in., tinted grounds, floral and scenic designs, profuse gold ornamentations, border tops, gold dec. edges and handles. Asstd. 1 doz. in case, 85 lbs. Doz. **T. O.**

L5230—6 styles, ht. 15 in., tinted bodies, floral sprays and landscape panels, gold and enamel tracings, gold edges and handles. Asstd. 1 doz. in case. Doz. **$14.00**

L4463—6 styles, aver. ht. 11½ in., 4 floral, 2 landscape designs, tinted grounds, embossed gold frame or border designs with beaded edges, gold hdls. and knobs. 1 doz. in case, 90 lbs. Doz. **Out**

L5225—6 styles, ht. 15 in., plain and shaded grounds, elaborate blossoms and marine scene decors., gold traced borders, frames, hdls. and edges. 1 doz. in case, 170 lbs. Doz. **$16.00**

L5232—6 styles, ht. 12 in., smooth tinted bodies, Jap floral and landscape panels, embossed or beaded gold framings, gold hdls. 1 doz. in case, about 150 lbs. Doz. **$18.00**

L5973—6 styles, ht. 12 in., 2 enameled conventional bird and scroll designs, 4 floral and scenic decors., profuse gold or enamel beaded borders and framing, gold bands, edges and handles. Asstd. 1 doz. in case, 100 lbs. Doz. **$18.00**

L5970—6 styles, ht. 18 in., pastel tinted grounds, large floral clusters and medallions, profuse gold and enamel ornamentations, edges and hdls. Asstd. 1 doz. in case, 275 lbs. Doz. **$20.00**

1917 Butler Bros. catalog.

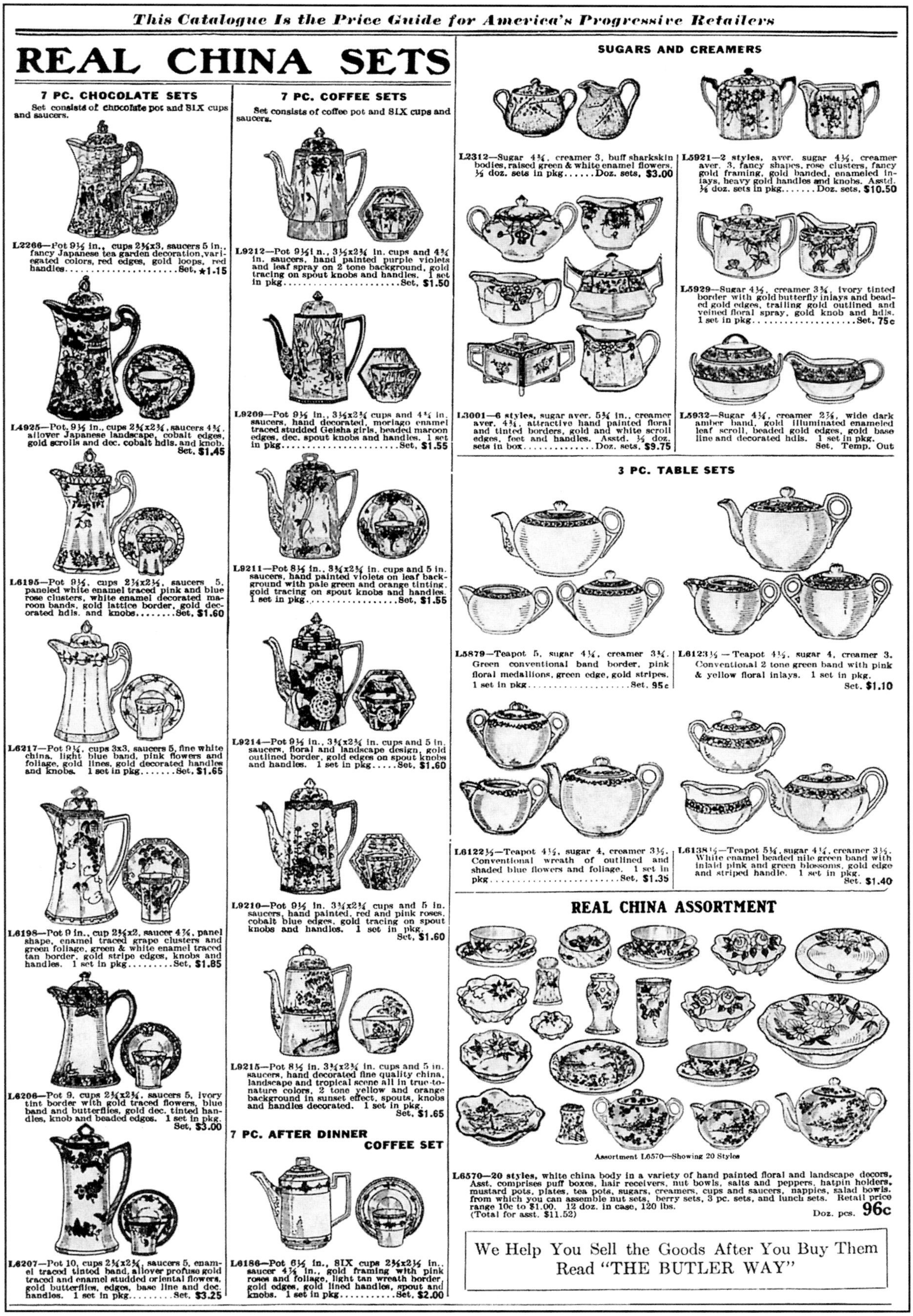
This Catalogue Is the Price Guide for America's Progressive Retailers

REAL CHINA SETS

7 PC. CHOCOLATE SETS

Set consists of chocolate pot and SIX cups and saucers.

L2266—Pot 9½ in., cups 2¾x3, saucers 5 in., fancy Japanese tea garden decoration, variegated colors, red edges, gold loops, red handles.....................Set, ★1.15

L4925—Pot, 9½ in., cups 2¾x2¾, saucers 4¾, allover Japanese landscape, cobalt edges, gold scrolls and dec. cobalt hdls. and knob. Set, **$1.45**

L6195—Pot 9½, cups 2¾x2½, saucers 5, paneled white enamel traced pink and blue rose clusters, white enamel decorated maroon bands, gold lattice border, gold decorated hdls. and knobs........Set, **$1.60**

L6217—Pot 9¼, cups 3x3, saucers 5, fine white china, light blue band, pink flowers and foliage, gold lines, gold decorated handles and knobs. 1 set in pkg.......Set, **$1.65**

L6198—Pot 9 in., cup 2¾x2, saucer 4⅞, panel shape, enamel traced grape clusters and green foliage, green & white enamel traced tan border, gold stripe edges, knobs and handles. 1 set in pkg.........Set, **$1.85**

L6206—Pot 9, cups 2¾x2¾, saucers 5, ivory tint border with gold traced flowers, blue band and butterflies, gold dec. tinted handles, knob and beaded edges. 1 set in pkg. Set, **$3.00**

L6207—Pot 10, cups 2¾x2¾, saucers 5, enamel traced tinted band, allover profuse gold traced and enamel studded oriental flowers, gold butterflies, edges, base line and dec. handles. 1 set in pkg.........Set, **$3.25**

7 PC. COFFEE SETS

Set consists of coffee pot and SIX cups and saucers.

L9212—Pot 9½i n., 3½x2¾ in. cups and 4¾ in. saucers, hand painted purple violets and leaf spray on 2 tone background, gold tracing on spout knobs and handles. 1 set in pkg.......................Set, **$1.50**

L9209—Pot 9½ in., 3¼x2¾ cups and 4¾ in. saucers, hand decorated, moriago enamel traced studded Geisha girls, beaded maroon edges, dec. spout knobs and handles. 1 set in pkg.......................Set, **$1.55**

L9211—Pot 8½ in., 3¾x2¾ in. cups and 5 in. saucers, hand painted violets on leaf background with pale green and orange tinting, gold tracing on spout knobs and handles. 1 set in pkg..................Set, **$1.55**

L9214—Pot 9½ in., 3¾x2¾ in. cups and 5 in. saucers, floral and landscape design, gold outlined border, gold edges on spout knobs and handles. 1 set in pkg.....Set, **$1.60**

L9210—Pot 9½ in. 3¾x2¾ cups and 5 in. saucers, hand painted, red and pink roses, cobalt blue edges, gold tracing on spout knobs and handles. 1 set in pkg. Set, **$1.60**

L9215—Pot 8½ in. 3¾x2¾ in. cups and 5 in. saucers, hand decorated fine quality china, landscape and tropical scene all in true-to-nature colors, 2 tone yellow and orange background in sunset effect, spouts, knobs and handles decorated. 1 set in pkg. Set, **$1.65**

7 PC. AFTER DINNER COFFEE SET

L6186—Pot 6½ in., SIX cups 2⅜x2½ in., saucer 4⅞ in., gold framing with pink roses and foliage, light tan wreath border, gold edges, gold lined handles, spout and knobs. 1 set in pkg...........Set, **$2.00**

SUGARS AND CREAMERS

L2312—Sugar 4¾, creamer 3, buff sharkskin bodies, raised green & white enamel flowers. ½ doz. sets in pkg......Doz. sets, **$3.00**

L5921—2 styles, aver. sugar 4½, creamer aver. 3, fancy shapes, rose clusters, fancy gold framing, gold banded, enameled inlays, heavy gold handles and knobs. Asstd. ⅙ doz. sets in pkg.......Doz. sets, **$10.50**

L3001—6 styles, sugar aver. 5¾ in., creamer aver. 4¾, attractive hand painted floral and tinted borders, gold and white scroll edges, feet and handles. Asstd. ½ doz. sets in box..............Doz. sets, **$9.75**

L5929—Sugar 4½, creamer 3¾, ivory tinted border with gold butterfly inlays and beaded gold edges, trailing gold outlined and veined floral spray, gold knob and hdls. 1 set in pkg...................Set, **75c**

L5932—Sugar 4¼, creamer 2⅞, wide dark amber band, gold illuminated enameled leaf scroll, beaded gold edges, gold base line and decorated hdls. 1 set in pkg. Set, Temp. Out

3 PC. TABLE SETS

L5879—Teapot 5, sugar 4¼, creamer 3¾. Green conventional band border, pink floral medallions, green edge, gold stripes. 1 set in pkg.........................Set, **95c**

L6123½—Teapot 4⅓, sugar 4, creamer 3. Conventional 2 tone green band with pink & yellow floral inlays. 1 set in pkg. Set, **$1.10**

L6122½—Teapot 4½, sugar 4, creamer 3½. Conventional wreath of outlined and shaded blue flowers and foliage. 1 set in pkg..........................Set, **$1.35**

L6138½—Teapot 5¼, sugar 4¼, creamer 3⅓. White enamel beaded nile green band with inlaid pink and green blossoms, gold edge and striped handle. 1 set in pkg. Set, **$1.40**

REAL CHINA ASSORTMENT

Assortment L6570—Showing 20 Styles

L6570—20 styles, white china body in a variety of hand painted floral and landscape decors. Asst. comprises puff boxes, hair receivers, nut bowls, salts and peppers, hatpin holders, mustard pots, plates, tea pots, sugars, creamers, cups and saucers, nappies, salad bowls, from which you can assemble nut sets, berry sets, 3 pc. sets, and lunch sets. Retail price range 10c to $1.00. 12 doz. in case, 120 lbs. (Total for asst. $11.52) Doz. pcs. **96c**

We Help You Sell the Goods After You Buy Them
Read "THE BUTLER WAY"

1917 Butler Bros. catalog.

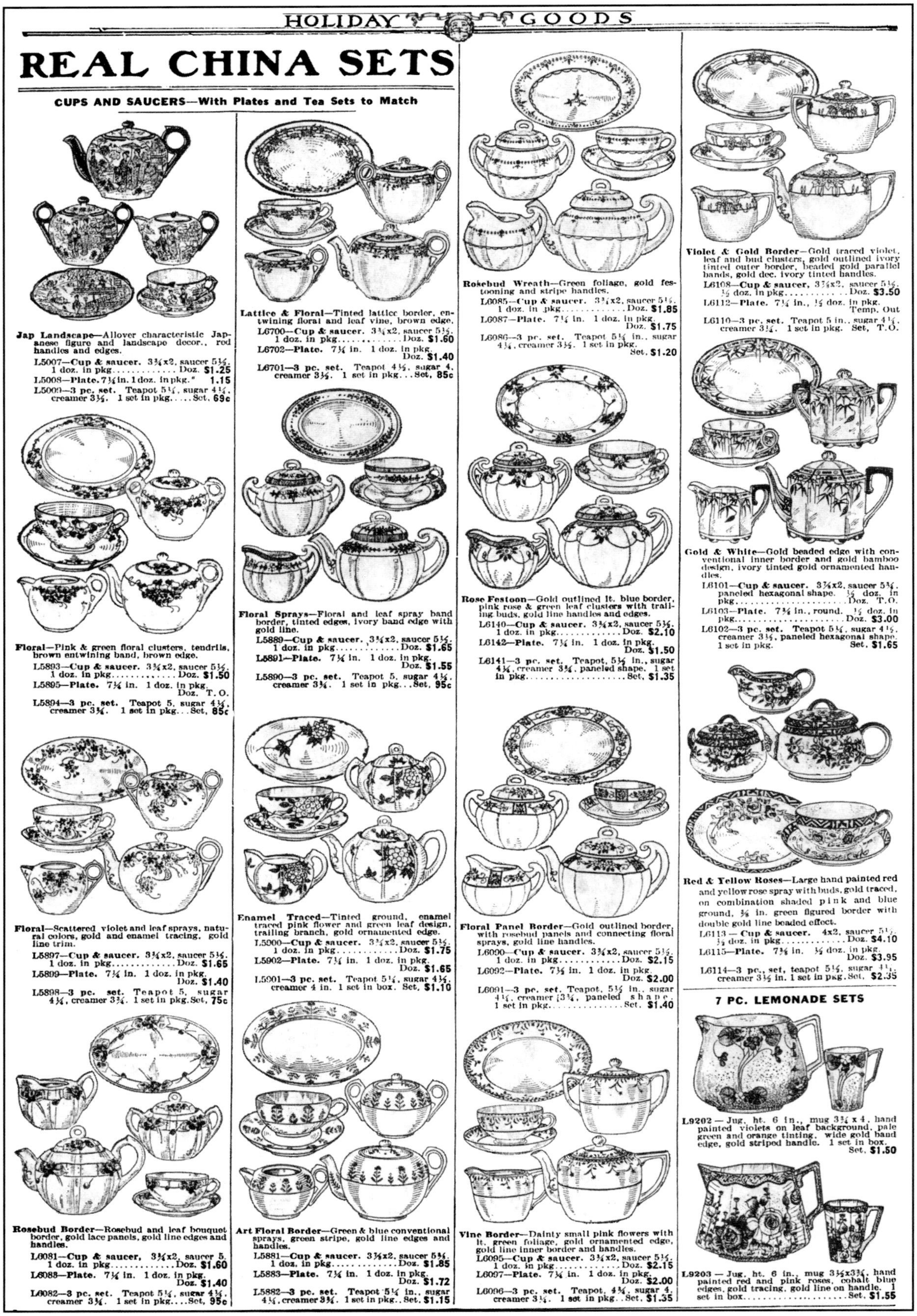

HOLIDAY GOODS

REAL CHINA SETS

CUPS AND SAUCERS—With Plates and Tea Sets to Match

Jap Landscape—Allover characteristic Japanese figure and landscape decor., red handles and edges.
L5007—**Cup & saucer.** 3¾x2, saucer 5½. 1 doz. in pkg............ Doz. **$1.25**
L5008—**Plate.** 7¼ in. 1 doz. in pkg." **1.15**
L5009—**3 pc. set.** Teapot 5¼, sugar 4¼, creamer 3½. 1 set in pkg.....Set, **69c**

Floral—Pink & green floral clusters, tendrils, brown entwining band, brown edge.
L5893—**Cup & saucer.** 3¾x2, saucer 5½. 1 doz. in pkg.............Doz. **$1.50**
L5895—**Plate.** 7¼ in. 1 doz. in pkg. Doz. T. O.
L5894—**3 pc. set.** Teapot 5, sugar 4¼, creamer 3¾. 1 set in pkg...Set, **85c**

Floral—Scattered violet and leaf sprays, natural colors, gold and enamel tracing, gold line trim.
L5897—**Cup & saucer.** 3¾x2, saucer 5½. 1 doz. in pkg............Doz. **$1.65**
L5899—**Plate.** 7¼ in. 1 doz. in pkg. Doz. **$1.40**
L5898—**3 pc. set.** Teapot 5, sugar 4¼, creamer 3¾. 1 set in pkg. Set, **75c**

Rosebud Border—Rosebud and leaf bouquet border, gold lace panels, gold line edges and handles.
L6081—**Cup & saucer,** 3¾x2, saucer 5. 1 doz. in pkg.............Doz. **$1.60**
L6088—**Plate.** 7¼ in. 1 doz. in pkg. Doz. **$1.40**
L6082—**3 pc. set.** Teapot 5¼, sugar 4¼, creamer 3¾. 1 set in pkg....Set, **95c**

Lattice & Floral—Tinted lattice border, entwining floral and leaf vine, brown edge.
L6700—**Cup & saucer.** 3¾x2, saucer 5½. 1 doz. in pkg.............Doz. **$1.60**
L6702—**Plate.** 7¼ in. 1 doz. in pkg. Doz. **$1.40**
L6701—**3 pc. set.** Teapot 4½, sugar 4, creamer 3½. 1 set in pkg...Set, **85c**

Floral Sprays—Floral and leaf spray band border, tinted edges, ivory band edge with gold line.
L5889—**Cup & saucer.** 3¾x2, saucer 5½. 1 doz. in pkg...............Doz. **$1.65**
L5891—**Plate.** 7¼ in. 1 doz. in pkg. Doz. **$1.55**
L5890—**3 pc. set.** Teapot 5, sugar 4½, creamer 3¾. 1 set in pkg...Set, **95c**

Enamel Traced—Tinted ground, enamel traced pink flower and green leaf design, trailing branch, gold ornamented edge.
L5900—**Cup & saucer.** 3¾x2, saucer 5½. 1 doz. in pkg...........Doz. **$1.75**
L5902—**Plate.** 7¼ in. 1 doz. in pkg. Doz. **$1.65**
L5901—**3 pc. set.** Teapot 5¼, sugar 4½, creamer 4 in. 1 set in box. Set, **$1.10**

Art Floral Border—Green & blue conventional sprays, green stripe, gold line edges and handles.
L5881—**Cup & saucer.** 3⅞x2, saucer 5¾. 1 doz. in pkg.............Doz. **$1.85**
L5883—**Plate.** 7¼ in. 1 doz. in pkg. Doz. **$1.72**
L5882—**3 pc. set.** Teapot 5¼ in., sugar 4¼, creamer 3¾. 1 set in pkg.. Set, **$1.15**

Rosebud Wreath—Green foliage, gold festooning and stripe handles.
L6085—**Cup & saucer.** 3¾x2, saucer 5½. 1 doz. in pkg.............Doz. **$1.85**
L6087—**Plate.** 7¼ in. 1 doz. in pkg. Doz. **$1.75**
L6086—**3 pc. set.** Teapot 5¼ in., sugar 4¼, creamer 3½. 1 set in pkg. Set, **$1.20**

Rose Festoon—Gold outlined lt. blue border, pink rose & green leaf clusters with trailing buds, gold line handles and edges.
L6140—**Cup & saucer.** 3¾x2, saucer 5½. 1 doz. in pkg.............Doz. **$2.10**
L6142—**Plate.** 7¼ in. 1 doz. in pkg. Doz. **$1.50**
L6141—**3 pc. set.** Teapot, 5½ in., sugar 4¼, creamer 3¾, paneled shape. 1 set in pkg....................Set, **$1.35**

Floral Panel Border—Gold outlined border, with rosebud panels and connecting floral sprays, gold line handles.
L6090—**Cup & saucer.** 3¾x2, saucer 5½. 1 doz. in pkg............Doz. **$2.15**
L6092—**Plate.** 7½ in. 1 doz. in pkg. Doz. **$2.00**
L6091—**3 pc. set.** Teapot, 5½ in., sugar 4¼, creamer 3¾, paneled shape. 1 set in pkg...............Set, **$1.40**

Vine Border—Dainty small pink flowers with lt. green foliage, gold ornamented edge, gold line inner border and handles.
L6095—**Cup & saucer.** 3¾x2, saucer 5½. 1 doz. in pkg............Doz. **$2.15**
L6097—**Plate.** 7¼ in. 1 doz. in pkg. Doz. **$2.00**
L6096—**3 pc. set.** Teapot, 4¾, sugar 4, creamer 3¼. 1 set in pkg..Set, **$1.35**

Violet & Gold Border—Gold traced violet, leaf and bud clusters, gold outlined ivory tinted outer border, beaded gold parallel bands, gold dec. ivory tinted handles.
L6108—**Cup & saucer,** 3¾x2, saucer 5½. ½ doz. in pkg............Doz. **$3.50**
L6112—**Plate.** 7¼ in., ½ doz. in pkg. Temp. Out
L6110—**3 pc. set.** Teapot 5 in., sugar 4¼, creamer 3¼. 1 set in pkg. Set, T.O.

Gold & White—Gold beaded edge with conventional inner border and gold bamboo design, ivory tinted gold ornamented handles.
L6101—**Cup & saucer.** 3⅞x2, saucer 5¾, paneled hexagonal shape. ½ doz. in pkg.......................Doz. T.O.
L6103—**Plate.** 7¾ in., round. ½ doz. in pkg.......................Doz. **$3.00**
L6102—**3 pc. set.** Teapot 5¼, sugar 4½, creamer 3½, paneled hexagonal shape. 1 set in pkg. Set, **$1.65**

Red & Yellow Roses—Large hand painted red and yellow rose spray with buds, gold traced, on combination shaded pink and blue ground, ⅜ in. green figured border with double gold line beaded effect.
L6113—**Cup & saucer.** 4x2, saucer 5½. ½ doz. in pkg.............Doz. **$4.10**
L6115—**Plate.** 7⅜ in. ½ doz. in pkg. Doz. **$3.95**
L6114—**3 pc., set,** teapot 5½, sugar 4¼, creamer 3½ in. 1 set in pkg. Set, **$2.35**

7 PC. LEMONADE SETS

L9202—Jug, ht. 6 in., mug 3¾ x 4, hand painted violets on leaf background, pale green and orange tinting, wide gold band edge, gold striped handle. 1 set in box. Set, **$1.50**

L9203—Jug, ht. 6 in., mug 3½x3¾, hand painted red and pink roses, cobalt blue edges, gold tracing, gold line on handle. 1 set in box.......................Set, **$1.55**

1917 Butler Bros. catalog.

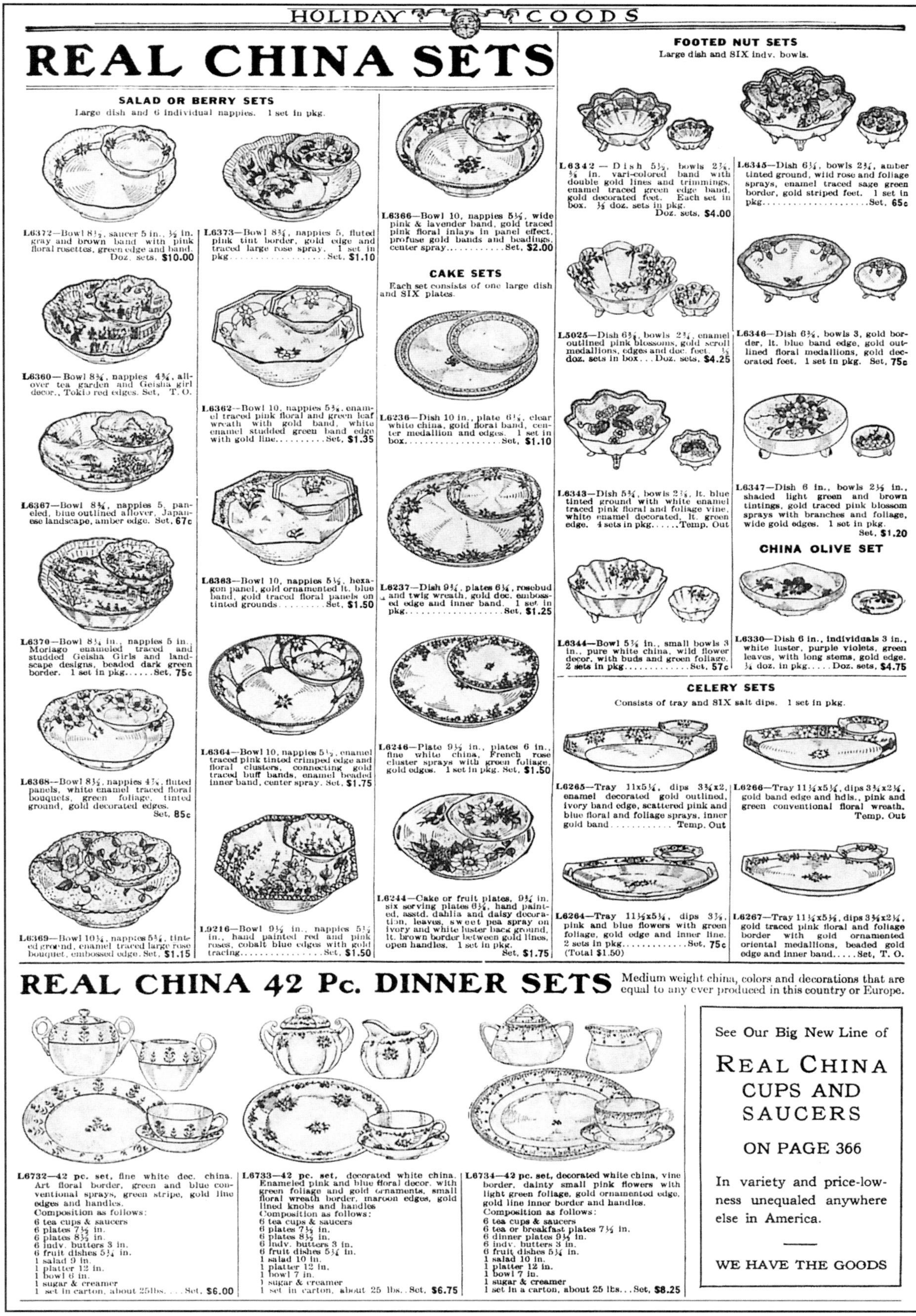

HOLIDAY GOODS

REAL CHINA SETS

SALAD OR BERRY SETS

Large dish and 6 individual nappies. 1 set in pkg.

L6372—Bowl 8½, saucer 5 in., ½ in. gray and brown band with pink floral rosettes, green edge and band. Doz. sets, **$10.00**

L6373—Bowl 8¾, nappies 5, fluted pink tint border, gold edge and traced large rose spray. 1 set in pkg. Set, **$1.10**

L6366—Bowl 10, nappies 5½, wide pink & lavender band, gold traced pink floral inlays in panel effect, profuse gold bands and beadings, center spray. Set, **$2.00**

L6360—Bowl 8¾, nappies 4¾, allover tea garden and Geisha girl decor., Tokio red edges. Set, T. O.

L6362—Bowl 10, nappies 5⅜, enamel traced pink floral and green leaf wreath with gold band, white enamel studded green band edge with gold line. Set, **$1.35**

L6367—Bowl 8¾, nappies 5, paneled, blue outlined allover, Japanese landscape, amber edge. Set, **67c**

L6363—Bowl 10, nappies 5½, hexagon panel, gold ornamented lt. blue band, gold traced floral panels on tinted grounds. Set, **$1.50**

L6370—Bowl 8¼ in., nappies 5 in., Moriago enameled traced and studded Geisha Girls and landscape designs, beaded dark green border. 1 set in pkg. Set, **75c**

L6364—Bowl 10, nappies 5½, enamel traced pink tinted crimped edge and floral clusters, connecting gold traced buff bands, enamel beaded inner band, center spray. Set, **$1.75**

L6368—Bowl 8½, nappies 4⅞, fluted panels, white enamel traced floral bouquets, green foliage, tinted ground, gold decorated edges. Set, **85c**

L6369—Bowl 10¼, nappies 5¾, tinted ground, enamel traced large rose bouquet, embossed edge. Set, **$1.15**

L9216—Bowl 9½ in., nappies 5½ in., hand painted red and pink roses, cobalt blue edges with gold tracing. Set, **$1.50**

CAKE SETS

Each set consists of one large dish and SIX plates.

L6236—Dish 10 in., plate 6⅛, clear white china, gold floral band, center medallion and edges. 1 set in box. Set, **$1.10**

L6237—Dish 9¼, plates 6¼, rosebud and twig wreath, gold dec. embossed edge and inner band. 1 set in pkg. Set, **$1.25**

L6246—Plate 9½ in., plates 6 in., fine white china, French rose cluster sprays with green foliage, gold edges. 1 set in pkg. Set, **$1.50**

L6244—Cake or fruit plates, 9¼ in. six serving plates 6½, hand painted, asstd. dahlia and daisy decoration, leaves, sweet pea spray on ivory and white luster back ground, lt. brown border between gold lines, open handles. 1 set in pkg. Set, **$1.75**

FOOTED NUT SETS

Large dish and SIX indv. bowls.

L6342—Dish 5½, bowls 2⅞, ⅝ in. vari-colored band with double gold lines and trimmings, enamel traced green edge band, gold decorated feet. Each set in box. ⅓ doz. sets in pkg. Doz. sets, **$4.00**

L6345—Dish 6¼, bowls 2¾, amber tinted ground, wild rose and foliage sprays, enamel traced sage green border, gold striped feet. 1 set in pkg. Set, **65c**

L5025—Dish 6¾, bowls 2¾, enamel outlined pink blossoms, gold scroll medallions, edges and dec. feet. ⅓ doz. sets in box. Doz. sets, **$4.25**

L6346—Dish 6⅜, bowls 3, gold border, lt. blue band edge, gold outlined floral medallions, gold decorated feet. 1 set in pkg. Set, **75c**

L6343—Dish 5¾, bowls 2⅞, lt. blue tinted ground with white enamel traced pink floral and foliage vine, white enamel decorated, lt. green edge. 4 sets in pkg. Temp. Out

L6347—Dish 6 in., bowls 2½ in., shaded light green and brown tintings, gold traced pink blossom sprays with branches and foliage, wide gold edges. 1 set in pkg. Set, **$1.20**

L6344—Bowl 5⅞ in., small bowls 3 in., pure white china, wild flower decor, with buds and green foliage. 2 sets in pkg. Set, **57c**

CHINA OLIVE SET

L6330—Dish 6 in., individuals 3 in., white luster, purple violets, green leaves, with long stems, gold edge. ¼ doz. in pkg. Doz. sets, **$4.75**

CELERY SETS

Consists of tray and SIX salt dips. 1 set in pkg.

L6265—Tray 11x5¼, dips 3¾x2, enamel decorated gold outlined, ivory band edge, scattered pink and blue floral and foliage sprays, inner gold band. Temp. Out

L6266—Tray 11¼x5¼, dips 3¾x2¼, gold band edge and hdls., pink and green conventional floral wreath. Temp. Out

L6264—Tray 11½x5¼, dips 3⅞, pink and blue flowers with green foliage, gold edge and inner line. 2 sets in pkg. Set, **75c** (Total $1.50)

L6267—Tray 11¼x5⅛, dips 3¾x2¼, gold traced pink floral and foliage border with gold ornamented oriental medallions, beaded gold edge and inner band. Set, T. O.

REAL CHINA 42 Pc. DINNER SETS

Medium weight china, colors and decorations that are equal to any ever produced in this country or Europe.

L6732—42 pc. set, fine white dec. china. Art floral border, green and blue conventional sprays, green stripe, gold line edges and handles.
Composition as follows:
6 tea cups & saucers
6 plates 7½ in.
6 plates 8½ in.
6 indv. butters 3 in.
6 fruit dishes 5¼ in.
1 salad 9 in.
1 platter 12 in.
1 bowl 6 in.
1 sugar & creamer
1 set in carton, about 25lbs. Set, **$6.00**

L6733—42 pc. set, decorated white china. Enameled pink and blue floral decor. with green foliage and gold ornaments, small floral wreath border, maroon edges, gold lined knobs and handles
Composition as follows:
6 tea cups & saucers
6 plates 7½ in.
6 plates 8½ in.
6 indv. butters 3 in.
6 fruit dishes 5¼ in.
1 salad 10 in.
1 platter 12 in.
1 bowl 7 in.
1 sugar & creamer
1 set in carton, about 25 lbs. Set, **$6.75**

L6734—42 pc. set, decorated white china, vine border, dainty small pink flowers with light green foliage, gold ornamented edge, gold line inner border and handles.
Composition as follows:
6 tea cups & saucers
6 tea or breakfast plates 7½ in.
6 dinner plates 9½ in.
6 indv. butters 3 in.
6 fruit dishes 5¼ in.
1 salad 10 in.
1 platter 12 in.
1 bowl 7 in.
1 sugar & creamer
1 set in a carton, about 25 lbs. Set, **$8.25**

See Our Big New Line of

REAL CHINA CUPS AND SAUCERS

ON PAGE 366

In variety and price-lowness unequaled anywhere else in America.

WE HAVE THE GOODS

1917 Butler Bros. catalog.

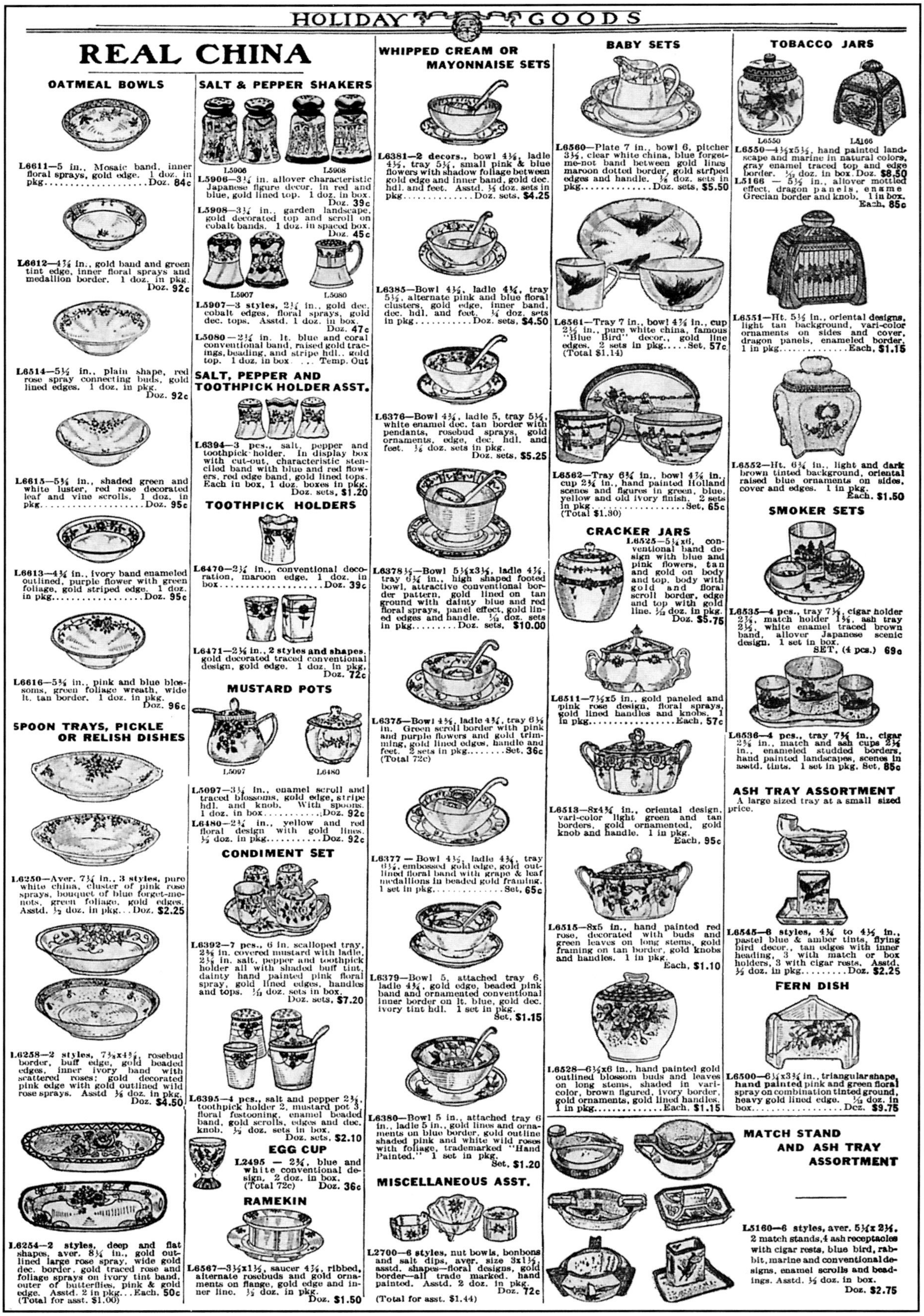

HOLIDAY GOODS

REAL CHINA

OATMEAL BOWLS

L6611—5 in., Mosaic band, inner floral sprays, gold edge. 1 doz. in pkg....................Doz. 84c

L6612—4⅞ in., gold band and green tint edge, inner floral sprays and medallion border. 1 doz. in pkg. Doz. 92c

L6514—5½ in., plain shape, red rose spray connecting buds, gold lined edges. 1 doz. in pkg. Doz. 92c

L6615—5⅝ in., shaded green and white luster, red rose decorated leaf and vine scrolls. 1 doz. in pkg....................Doz. 95c

L6613—4¾ in., ivory band enameled outlined, purple flower with green foliage, gold striped edge. 1 doz. in pkg..................Doz. 95c

L6616—5⅝ in., pink and blue blossoms, green foliage wreath, wide lt. tan border. 1 doz. in pkg. Doz. 96c

SPOON TRAYS, PICKLE OR RELISH DISHES

L6250—Aver. 7¼ in., 3 styles, pure white china, cluster of pink rose sprays, bouquet of blue forget-me-nots, green foliage, gold edges. Asstd. ½ doz. in pkg...Doz. $2.25

L6258—2 styles, 7⅜x4⅝, rosebud border, buff edge, gold beaded edges, inner ivory band with scattered roses; gold decorated pink edge with gold outlined wild rose sprays. Asstd ⅙ doz. in pkg. Doz. $4.50

L6254—2 styles, deep and flat shapes, aver. 8¼ in., gold outlined large rose spray, wide gold dec. border, gold traced rose and foliage sprays on ivory tint band, outer of butterflies, pink & gold edge. Asstd. 2 in pkg...Each, 50c (Total for asst. $1.00)

SALT & PEPPER SHAKERS

L5906 L5908

L5906—3¼ in. allover characteristic Japanese figure decor. in red and blue, gold lined top. 1 doz. in box. Doz. 39c

L5908—3¼ in., garden landscape, gold decorated top and scroll on cobalt bands. 1 doz. in spaced box. Doz. 45c

L5907 L5080

L5907—3 styles, 2¼ in., gold dec. cobalt edges, floral sprays, gold dec. tops. Asstd. 1 doz. in box. Doz. 47c

L5080—2¼ in. lt. blue and coral conventional band, raised gold tracings, beading, and stripe hdl., gold top. 1 doz. in box ... Temp. Out

SALT, PEPPER AND TOOTHPICK HOLDER ASST.

L6394—3 pcs., salt, pepper and toothpick holder. In display box with cut-out, characteristic stenciled band with blue and red flowers, red edge band, gold lined tops. Each in box, 1 doz. boxes in pkg. Doz. sets, $1.20

TOOTHPICK HOLDERS

L6470—2¼ in., conventional decoration, maroon edge. 1 doz. in box....................Doz. 39c

L6471—2⅜ in., 2 styles and shapes, gold decorated traced conventional design, gold edge. 1 doz. in pkg. Doz. 72c

MUSTARD POTS

L5097 L6480

L5097—3¼ in., enamel scroll and traced blossoms, gold edge, stripe hdl. and knob. With spoons. 1 doz. in box............Doz. 92c

L6480—2¼ in., yellow and red floral design with gold lines. ½ doz. in pkg...........Doz. 92c

CONDIMENT SET

L6392—7 pcs., 6 in. scalloped tray, 2⅝ in. covered mustard with ladle, 2⅛ in. salt, pepper and toothpick holder all with shaded buff tint, dainty hand painted pink floral spray, gold lined edges, handles and tops. ⅓ doz. sets in box. Doz. sets, $7.20

L6395—4 pcs., salt and pepper 2⅜, toothpick holder 2, mustard pot 3, floral festooning, enamel beaded band, gold scrolls, edges and dec. knob. ½ doz. sets in box. Doz. sets, $2.10

EGG CUP

L2495 — 2¾, blue and white conventional design, 2 doz. in box. (Total 72c) Doz. 36c

RAMEKIN

L6567—3½x1½, saucer 4⅞, ribbed, alternate rosebuds and gold ornaments on flange, gold edge and inner line. ½ doz. in pkg. Doz. $1.50

WHIPPED CREAM OR MAYONNAISE SETS

L6381—2 decors., bowl 4⅛, ladle 4½, tray 5¼, small pink & blue flowers with shadow foliage between gold edge and inner band, gold dec. hdl. and feet. Asstd. ⅙ doz. sets in pkg...............Doz. sets, $4.25

L6385—Bowl 4½, ladle 4¼, tray 5½, alternate pink and blue floral clusters, gold edge, inner band, dec. hdl. and feet. ¼ doz. sets in pkg...........Doz. sets, $4.50

L6376—Bowl 4¾, ladle 5, tray 5⅛, white enamel dec. tan border with pendants, rosebud sprays, gold ornaments, edge, dec. hdl. and feet. ⅙ doz. sets in pkg. Doz. sets, $5.25

L6378½—Bowl 5⅛x3⅛, ladle 4⅞, tray 6¾ in., high shaped footed bowl, attractive conventional border pattern, gold lined on tan ground with dainty blue and red floral sprays, panel effect, gold lined edges and handle. ⅓ doz. sets in pkg.........Doz. sets, $10.00

L6375—Bowl 4⅝, ladle 4¾, tray 6⅛ in. Green scroll border with pink and purple flowers and gold trimming, gold lined edges, handle and feet. 2 sets in pkg........Set, 36c (Total 72c)

L6377 — Bowl 4½, ladle 4¾, tray 6½, embossed gold edge, gold outlined floral band with grape & leaf medallions in beaded gold framing. 1 set in pkg...............Set, 65c

L6379—Bowl 5, attached tray 6, ladle 4¾, gold edge, beaded pink band and ornamented conventional inner border on lt. blue, gold dec. ivory tint hdl. 1 set in pkg. Set, $1.15

L6380—Bowl 5 in., attached tray 6 in., ladle 5 in., gold lines and ornaments on blue border, gold outline shaded pink and white wild roses with foliage, trademarked "Hand Painted." 1 set in pkg. Set, $1.20

MISCELLANEOUS ASST.

L2700—6 styles, nut bowls, bonbons and salt dips, aver. size 3x1½, asstd. shapes—floral designs, gold border—all trade marked. hand painted. Asstd. 2 doz. in pkg. Doz. 72c (Total for asst. $1.44)

BABY SETS

L6560—Plate 7 in., bowl 6, pitcher 3½, clear white china, blue forget-me-not band between gold lines maroon dotted border, gold striped edges and handle. ⅙ doz. sets in pkg..............Doz. sets, $5.50

L6561—Tray 7 in., bowl 4⅞ in., cup 2½ in., pure white china, famous "Blue Bird" decor., gold line edges. 2 sets in pkg.....Set, 57c (Total $1.14)

L6562—Tray 6¾ in., bowl 4⅞ in., cup 2¾ in., hand painted Holland scenes and figures in green, blue, yellow and old ivory finish. 2 sets in pkg...................Set, 65c (Total $1.30)

CRACKER JARS

L6525—5¼x6, conventional band design with blue and pink flowers, tan and gold on body and top, body with gold and floral scroll border, edge and top with gold line. ⅓ doz. in pkg. Doz. $5.75

L6511—7½x5 in., gold paneled and pink rose design, floral sprays, gold lined handles and knobs. 1 in pkg..................Each, 57c

L6513—8x4¾ in., oriental design, vari-color light green and tan borders, gold ornamented, gold knob and handle. 1 in pkg. Each, 95c

L6515—8x5 in., hand painted red rose, decorated with buds and green leaves on long stems, gold framing on tan border, gold knobs and handles. 1 in pkg. Each, $1.10

L6528—6½x6 in., hand painted gold outlined blossom buds and leaves on long stems, shaded in vari-color, brown figured, ivory border, gold ornaments, gold lined handles. 1 in pkg..............Each, $1.15

TOBACCO JARS

L6550 L5166

L6550—4½x5½, hand painted landscape and marine in natural colors, gray enamel traced top and edge border. ⅓ doz. in box. Doz. $8.50

L5166 — 5½ in., allover mottled effect, dragon panels, ename Grecian border and knob. 1 in box. Each, 85c

L6551—Ht. 5½ in., oriental designs, light tan background, vari-color ornaments on sides and cover, dragon panels, enameled border. 1 in pkg..............Each, $1.15

L6552—Ht. 6¾ in., light and dark brown tinted background, oriental raised blue ornaments on sides, cover and edges. 1 in pkg. Each. $1.50

SMOKER SETS

L6535—4 pcs., tray 7⅛, cigar holder 2⅞, match holder 1⅝, ash tray 2½, white enamel traced brown band, allover Japanese scenic design. 1 set in box. SET, (4 pcs.) 69c

L6536—4 pcs., tray 7⅝ in., cigar 2⅝ in., match and ash cups 2⅛ in., enameled studded borders, hand painted landscapes, scenes in asstd. tints. 1 set in pkg. Set, 85c

ASH TRAY ASSORTMENT

A large sized tray at a small sized price.

L6545—6 styles, 4¼ to 4½ in., pastel blue & amber tints, flying bird decor., tan edges with inner heading, 3 with match or box holders, 3 with cigar rests. Asstd. ½ doz. in pkg.........Doz. $2.25

FERN DISH

L6500—6¼x3¾ in., triangular shape, hand painted pink and green floral spray on combination tinted ground, heavy gold lined edge. ⅓ doz. in box..................Dcz. $9.75

MATCH STAND AND ASH TRAY ASSORTMENT

L5160—6 styles, aver. 5¼x2⅛, 2 match stands, 4 ash receptacles with cigar rests, blue bird, rabbit, marine and conventional designs, enamel scrolls and beadings. Asstd. ½ doz. in box. Doz. $2.75

1917 Butler Bros. catalog.

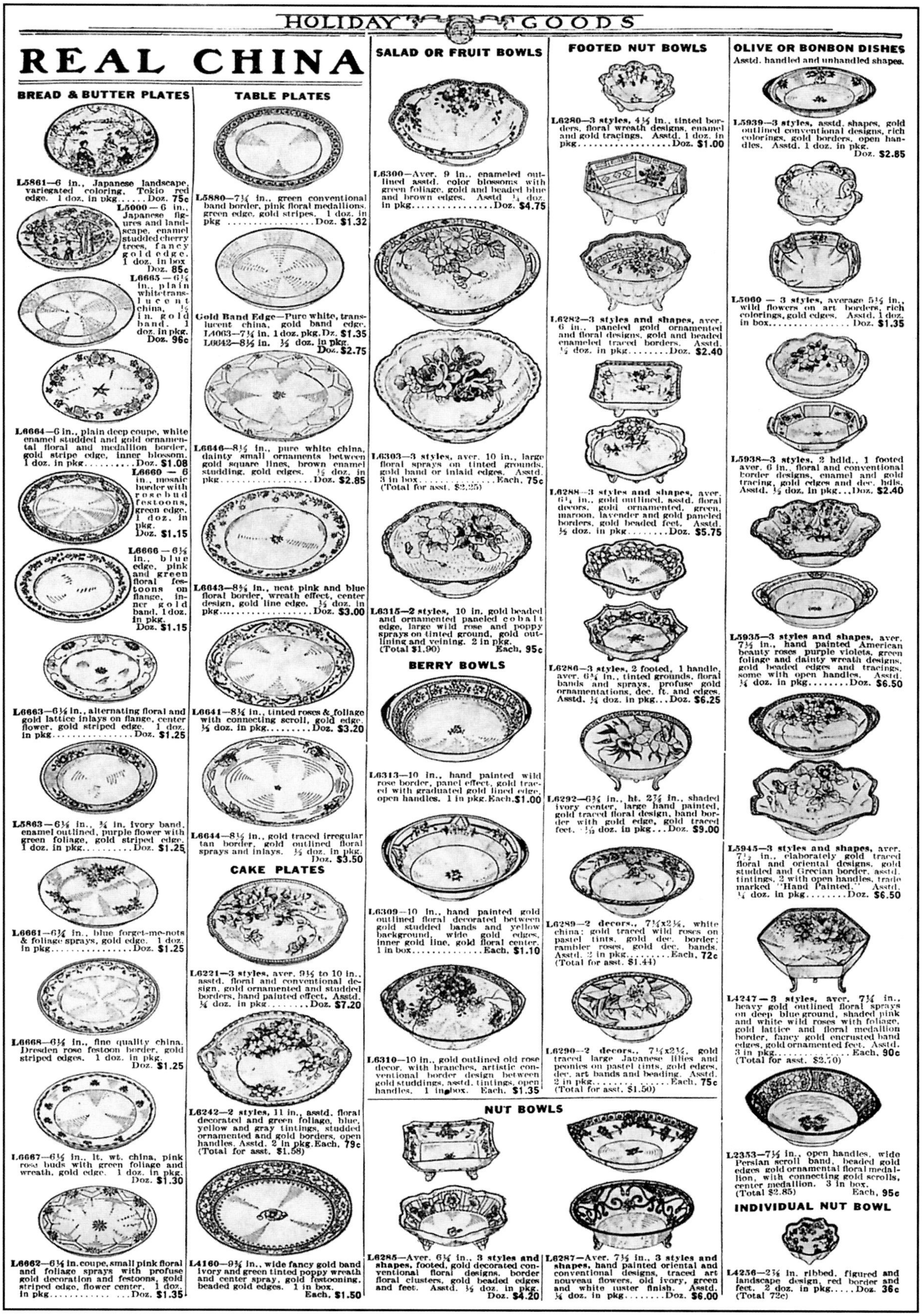

HOLIDAY GOODS

REAL CHINA

BREAD & BUTTER PLATES

L5861—6 in., Japanese landscape, variegated coloring, Tokio red edge. 1 doz. in pkg......Doz. **75c**

L5000—6 in., Japanese figures and landscape, enamel studded cherry trees, fancy gold edge. 1 doz. in box Doz. **85c**

L6665—6½ in., plain white translucent china, ½ in. gold band. 1 doz. in pkg. Doz. **96c**

L6664—6 in., plain deep coupe, white enamel studded and gold ornamental floral and medallion border, gold stripe edge, inner blossom. 1 doz. in pkg..........Doz. **$1.08**

L6660—6 in., mosaic border with rosebud festoons, green edge. 1 doz. in pkg. Doz. **$1.15**

L6666—6½ in., blue edge, pink and green floral festoons on flange, inner gold band. 1 doz. in pkg. Doz. **$1.15**

L6663—6½ in., alternating floral and gold lattice inlays on flange, center flower, gold striped edge. 1 doz. in pkg................Doz. **$1.25**

L5863—6½ in., ¾ in. ivory band, enamel outlined, purple flower with green foliage, gold striped edge. 1 doz. in pkg..........Doz. **$1.25**

L6661—6¼ in., blue forget-me-nots & foliage sprays, gold edge. 1 doz. in pkg................Doz. **$1.25**

L6668—6½ in., fine quality china, Dresden rose festoon border, gold striped edges. 1 doz. in pkg. Doz. **$1.25**

L6667—6½ in., lt. wt. china, pink rose buds with green foliage and wreath, gold edge. 1 doz. in pkg. Doz. **$1.30**

L6662—6¼ in. coupe, small pink floral and foliage sprays with profuse gold decoration and festoons, gold striped edge, flower center. 1 doz. in pkg...............Doz. **$1.35**

TABLE PLATES

L5880—7¼ in., green conventional band border, pink floral medallions, green edge, gold stripes. 1 doz. in pkg ....Doz. **$1.32**

Gold Band Edge—Pure white, translucent china, gold band edge.
L4063—7¼ in. 1 doz. pkg. Dz. **$1.35**
L6642—8½ in. ½ doz. in pkg. Doz. **$2.75**

L6646—8½ in., pure white china, dainty small ornaments between gold square lines, brown enamel studding, gold edges. ½ doz. in pkg.................Doz. **$2.85**

L6643—8½ in., neat pink and blue floral border, wreath effect, center design, gold line edge. ½ doz. in pkg.................Doz. **$3.00**

L6641—8¼ in., tinted roses & foliage with connecting scroll, gold edge. ½ doz. in pkg.........Doz. **$3.20**

L6644—8½ in., gold traced irregular tan border, gold outlined floral sprays and inlays. ½ doz. in pkg. Doz. **$3.50**

CAKE PLATES

L6221—3 styles, aver. 9½ to 10 in., asstd. floral and conventional design, gold ornamented and studded borders, hand painted effect. Asstd. ¼ doz. in pkg........Doz. **$7.20**

L6242—2 styles, 11 in., asstd. floral decorated and green foliage, blue, yellow and gray tintings, studded ornamented and gold borders, open handles. Asstd. 2 in pkg. Each. **79c** (Total for asst. $1.58)

L4160—9¾ in., wide fancy gold band ivory and green tinted poppy wreath and center spray, gold festooning, beaded gold edges. 1 in box. Each. **$1.50**

SALAD OR FRUIT BOWLS

L6300—Aver. 9 in., enameled outlined asstd. color blossoms with green foliage, gold and beaded blue and brown edges. Asstd ¼ doz. in pkg................Doz. **$4.75**

L6303—3 styles, aver. 10 in., large floral sprays on tinted grounds, gold band or inlaid edges. Asstd. 3 in box...............Each. **75c** (Total for asst. $2.25)

L6315—2 styles, 10 in. gold beaded and ornamented paneled cobalt edge, large wild rose and poppy sprays on tinted ground, gold outlining and veining. 2 in pkg. (Total $1.90) Each. **95c**

BERRY BOWLS

L6313—10 in., hand painted wild rose border, panel effect, gold traced with graduated gold lined edge, open handles. 1 in pkg. Each. **$1.00**

L6309—10 in., hand painted gold outlined floral decorated between gold studded bands and yellow background, wide gold edges, inner gold line, gold floral center. 1 in box..............Each. **$1.10**

L6310—10 in., gold outlined old rose decor. with branches, artistic conventional border design between gold studdings, asstd. tintings, open handles. 1 in box. Each. **$1.35**

FOOTED NUT BOWLS

L6280—3 styles, 4½ in., tinted borders, floral wreath designs, enamel and gold tracings. Asstd. 1 doz. in pkg...................Doz. **$1.00**

L6282—3 styles and shapes, aver. 6 in., paneled gold ornamented and floral designs, gold and beaded enameled traced borders. Asstd. ½ doz. in pkg........Doz. **$2.40**

L6288—3 styles and shapes, aver. 6¼ in., gold outlined, asstd. floral decors, gold ornamented, green, maroon, lavender and gold paneled borders, gold beaded feet. Asstd. ½ doz. in pkg........Doz. **$5.75**

L6286—3 styles, 2 footed, 1 handle, aver. 6¾ in., tinted grounds, floral bands and sprays, profuse gold ornamentations, dec. ft. and edges. Asstd. ¼ doz. in pkg...Doz. **$6.25**

L6292—6¾ in., ht. 2¾ in., shaded ivory center, large hand painted, gold traced floral design, band border with gold edge, gold traced feet. 1/12 doz. in pkg...Doz. **$9.00**

L6289—2 decors., 7¼x2⅛, white china; gold traced wild roses on pastel tints, gold dec. border; rambler roses, gold dec. bands. Asstd. 2 in pkg.........Each. **72c** (Total for asst. $1.44)

L6290—2 decors., 7¼x2½, gold traced large Japanese lilies and peonies on pastel tints, gold edges, dec. art bands and beading. Asstd. 2 in pkg............Each. **75c** (Total for asst. $1.50)

NUT BOWLS

L6285—Aver. 6¼ in., **3 styles and shapes**, footed, gold decorated conventional floral designs, border floral clusters, gold beaded edges and feet. Asstd. ½ doz. in pkg. Doz. **$4.20**

L6287—Aver. 7½ in., **3 styles and shapes**, hand painted oriental and conventional designs, traced art nouveau flowers, old ivory, green and white luster finish. Asstd. ¼ doz. in pkg........Doz. **$6.00**

OLIVE OR BONBON DISHES

Asstd. handled and unhandled shapes.

L5939—3 styles, asstd. shapes, gold outlined conventional designs, rich colorings, gold borders, open handles. Asstd. 1 doz. in pkg. Doz. **$2.85**

L5060 — 3 styles, average 5½ in., wild flowers on art borders, rich colorings, gold edges. Asstd. 1 doz. in box...............Doz. **$1.35**

L5938—3 styles, 2 hdld., 1 footed aver. 6 in., floral and conventional border designs, enamel and gold tracing, gold edges and dec. hdls. Asstd. ½ doz. in pkg...Doz. **$2.40**

L5935—3 styles and shapes, aver. 7½ in., hand painted American beauty roses purple violets, green foliage and dainty wreath designs, gold beaded edges and tracings, some with open handles. Asstd. ¼ doz. in pkg........Doz. **$6.50**

L5945—3 styles and shapes, aver. 7½ in., elaborately gold traced floral and oriental designs, gold studded and Grecian border, asstd. tintings, 2 with open handles, trade marked "Hand Painted." Asstd. ¼ doz. in pkg........Doz. **$6.50**

L4247 — 3 styles, aver. 7¼ in., heavy gold outlined floral sprays on deep blue ground, shaded pink and white wild roses with foliage, gold lattice and floral medallion border, fancy gold encrusted band edges, gold ornamented feet. Asstd. 3 in pkg...............Each. **90c** (Total for asst. $2.70)

L2353—7½ in., open handles, wide Persian scroll band, beaded gold edges gold ornamental floral medallion, with connecting gold scrolls, center medallion. 3 in box. (Total $2.85) Each. **95c**

INDIVIDUAL NUT BOWL

L4256—2¾ in. ribbed, figured and landscape design, red border and feet. 2 doz. in pkg.....Doz. **36c** (Total 72c)

1917 Butler Bros. catalog.

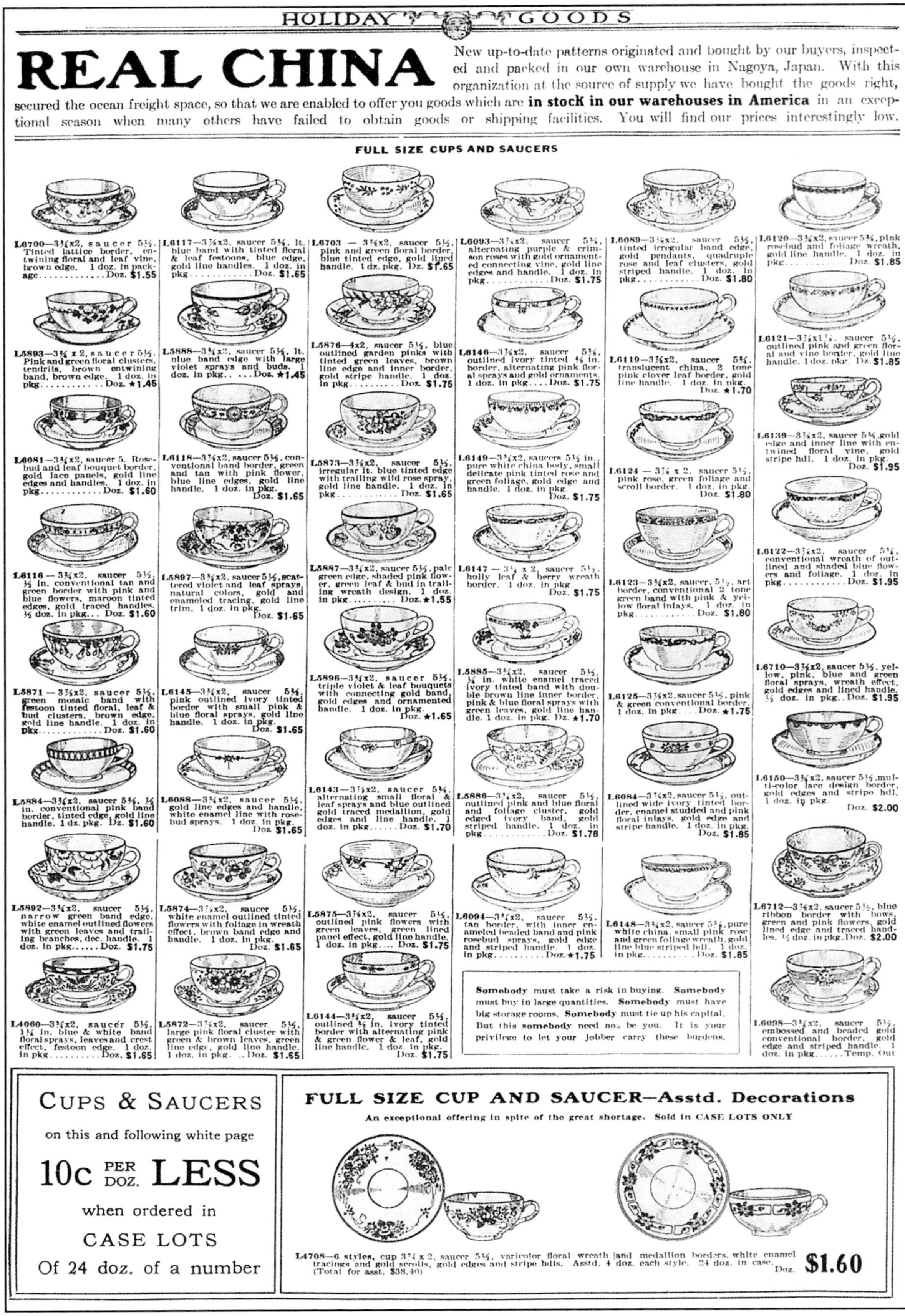

HOLIDAY GOODS

REAL CHINA

New up-to-date patterns originated and bought by our buyers, inspected and packed in our own warehouse in Nagoya, Japan. With this organization at the source of supply we have bought the goods right, secured the ocean freight space, so that we are enabled to offer you goods which are **in stock in our warehouses in America** in an exceptional season when many others have failed to obtain goods or shipping facilities. You will find our prices interestingly low.

FULL SIZE CUPS AND SAUCERS

L6700—3¾x2, saucer 5½. Tinted lattice border, entwining floral and leaf vine, brown edge. 1 doz. in package.......Doz. **$1.55**

L5893—3¾ x 2, saucer 5½. Pink and green floral clusters, tendrils, brown entwining band, brown edge. 1 doz. in pkg.......Doz. **★1.45**

L6081—3¾x2, saucer 5. Rosebud and leaf bouquet border, gold lace panels, gold line edges and handles. 1 doz. in pkg.......Doz. **$1.60**

L6116—3¾x2, saucer 5½. ½ in. conventional tan and green border with pink and blue flowers, maroon tinted edges, gold traced handles. ½ doz. in pkg... Doz. **$1.60**

L5871—3⅞x2, saucer 5½. green mosaic band with festoon tinted floral, leaf & bud clusters, brown edge, gold line handle. 1 doz. in pkg.......Doz. **$1.60**

L5884—3¾x2, saucer 5¼. ½ in. conventional pink band border, tinted edge, gold line handle. 1 dz. pkg. Dz. **$1.60**

L5892—3¾x2, saucer 5½. narrow green band edge, white enamel outlined flowers with green leaves and trailing branches, dec. handle. 1 doz. in pkg......Doz. **$1.75**

L4060—3¾x2, saucer 5½. 1¼ in. blue & white band floral sprays, leaves and crest effect, festoon edge. 1 doz. in pkg.......Doz. **$1.65**

L6117—3⅞x2, saucer 5⅜. lt. blue band with tinted floral & leaf festoons, blue edge, gold line handles. 1 doz. in pkg.......Doz. **$1.65**

L5888—3¾x2, saucer 5¼. lt. blue band edge with large violet sprays and buds. 1 doz. in pkg.. ...Doz. **★1.45**

L6118—3⅞x2, saucer 5½, conventional band border, green and tan with pink flower, blue line edges, gold line handle. 1 doz. in pkg. Doz. **$1.65**

L5897—3¾x2, saucer 5½, scattered violet and leaf sprays, natural colors, gold and enameled tracing, gold line trim. 1 doz. in pkg. Doz. **$1.65**

L6145—3¾x2, saucer 5¾. pink outlined ivory tinted border with small pink & blue floral sprays, gold line handle. 1 doz. in pkg. Doz. **$1.65**

L6088—3¾x2, saucer 5½. gold line edges and handle, white enamel line with rosebud sprays. 1 doz. in pkg. Doz **$1.65**

L5874—3¾x2, saucer 5½. white enamel outlined tinted flowers with foliage in wreath effect, brown band edge and handle. 1 doz. in pkg. Doz. **$1.65**

L5872—3¾x2, saucer 5½. large pink floral cluster with green & brown leaves, green line edge, gold line handle. 1 doz. in pkg. ..Doz. **$1.65**

L6703 — 3⅞x2, saucer 5½. pink and green floral border, blue tinted edge, gold lined handle. 1 dz. pkg. Dz. **$1.65**

L5876—4x2, saucer 5½, blue outlined garden pinks with tinted green leaves, brown line edge and inner border, gold stripe handle. 1 doz. in pkg.......Doz. **$1.75**

L5873—3⅞x2, saucer 5½. irregular lt. blue tinted edge with trailing wild rose spray, gold line handle. 1 doz. in pkg.......Doz. **$1.65**

L5887—3¾x2, saucer 5½, pale green edge, shaded pink flower, green leaf & bud in trailing wreath design. 1 doz. in pkg....... Doz. **★1.55**

L5896—3¾x2, saucer 5½. triple violet & leaf bouquets with connecting gold band, gold edges and ornamented handle. 1 doz. in pkg. Doz. **★1.65**

L6143—3⅞x2, saucer 5¾. alternating small floral & leaf sprays and blue outlined gold traced medallion, gold edges and line handle. 1 doz. in pkg......Doz. **$1.70**

L5875—3⅞x2, saucer 5½. outlined pink flowers with green leaves, green lined panel effect, gold line handle. 1 doz. in pkg.... Doz. **$1.75**

L6144—3¾x2, saucer 5½. outlined ⅜ in. ivory tinted border with alternating pink & green flower & leaf, gold line handle. 1 doz. in pkg. Doz. **$1.75**

L6093—3⅞x2, saucer 5¾. alternating purple & crimson roses with gold ornamented connecting vine, gold line edges and handle. 1 doz. in pkg.......Doz. **$1.75**

L6146—3⅞x2, saucer 5⅜. outlined ivory tinted ⅝ in. border, alternating pink floral sprays and gold ornaments. 1 doz. in pkg....Doz. **$1.75**

L6149—3¾x2, saucers 5½ in., pure white china body, small delicate pink tinted rose and green foliage, gold edge and handle. 1 doz. in pkg. Doz. **$1.75**

L6147 — 3¾ x 2, saucer 5½. holly leaf & berry wreath border. 1 doz. in pkg. Doz. **$1.75**

L5885—3¾x2, saucer 5½. ¼ in. white enamel traced ivory tinted band with double brown line inner border, pink & blue floral sprays with green leaves, gold line handle. 1 doz. in pkg. Dz. **★1.70**

L5886—3¾x2, saucer 5½. outlined pink and blue floral and foliage cluster, gold edged ivory band, gold striped handle. 1 doz. in pkg.......Doz. **$1.78**

L6094—3¾x2, saucer 5½. tan border, with inner enameled beaded band and pink rosebud sprays, gold edge and striped handle. 1 doz. in pkg.......Doz. **★1.75**

L6089—3⅞x2, saucer 5½. tinted irregular band edge, gold pendants, quadruple rose and leaf clusters, gold striped handle. 1 doz. in pkg.......Doz. **$1.80**

L6119—3⅞x2, saucer 5¾. translucent china, 2 tone pink clover leaf border, gold line handle. 1 doz. in pkg. Doz. **★1.70**

L6124 — 3¾ x 2, saucer 5½. pink rose, green foliage and scroll border. 1 doz. in pkg. Doz. **$1.80**

L6123—3¾x2, saucer, 5½, art border, conventional 2 tone green band with pink & yellow floral inlays. 1 doz. in pkg.......Doz. **$1.80**

L6125—3¾x2, saucer 5½, pink & green conventional border. 1 doz. in pkg....Doz. **★1.75**

L6084—3¾x2, saucer 5½, outlined wide ivory tinted border, enamel studded and pink floral inlays, gold edge and stripe handle. 1 doz. in pkg. Doz. **$1.85**

L6148—3¾x2, saucer 5½, pure white china, small pink rose and green foliage wreath, gold line blue striped hdl. 1 doz. in pkg.......Doz. **$1.85**

L6120—3¾x2, saucer 5¾, pink rosebud and foliage wreath, gold line handle. 1 doz. in pkg.......Doz. **$1.85**

L6121—3⅞x1⅞. saucer 5½. outlined pink and green floral and vine border, gold line handle. 1 doz. pkg. Dz. **$1.85**

L6139—3⅞x2, saucer 5¾, gold edge and inner line with entwined floral vine, gold stripe hdl. 1 doz. in pkg. Doz. **$1.95**

L6122—3⅞x2, saucer 5¼. conventional wreath of outlined and shaded blue flowers and foliage. 1 doz. in pkg.......Doz. **$1.95**

L6710—3¾x2, saucer 5½. yellow, pink, blue and green floral sprays, wreath effect, gold edges and lined handle. ½ doz. in pkg.. Doz. **$1.95**

L6150—3¾x2, saucer 5½, multi-color lace design border, gold edges and stripe hdl. 1 doz. in pkg. Doz. **$2.00**

L6712—3¾x2, saucer 5½, blue ribbon border with bows, green and pink flowers, gold lined edge and traced handles. ½ doz. in pkg. Doz. **$2.00**

L6098—3¾x2, saucer 5½. embossed and beaded gold conventional border, gold edge and striped handle. 1 doz. in pkg......Temp. Out

Somebody must take a risk in buying. **Somebody** must buy in large quantities. **Somebody** must have big storage rooms. **Somebody** must tie up his capital. But this **somebody** need not be you. It is your privilege to let your jobber carry these burdens.

CUPS & SAUCERS

on this and following white page

10c PER DOZ. LESS

when ordered in

CASE LOTS

Of 24 doz. of a number

FULL SIZE CUP AND SAUCER—Asstd. Decorations

An exceptional offering in spite of the great shortage. Sold in CASE LOTS ONLY

L4708—6 styles, cup 3¾ x 2, saucer 5¼. varicolor floral wreath and medallion borders, white enamel tracings and gold scrolls, gold edges and stripe hdls. Asstd. 4 doz. each style. 24 doz. in case. (Total for asst. $38.40) Doz. **$1.60**

1917 Butler Bros. catalog.

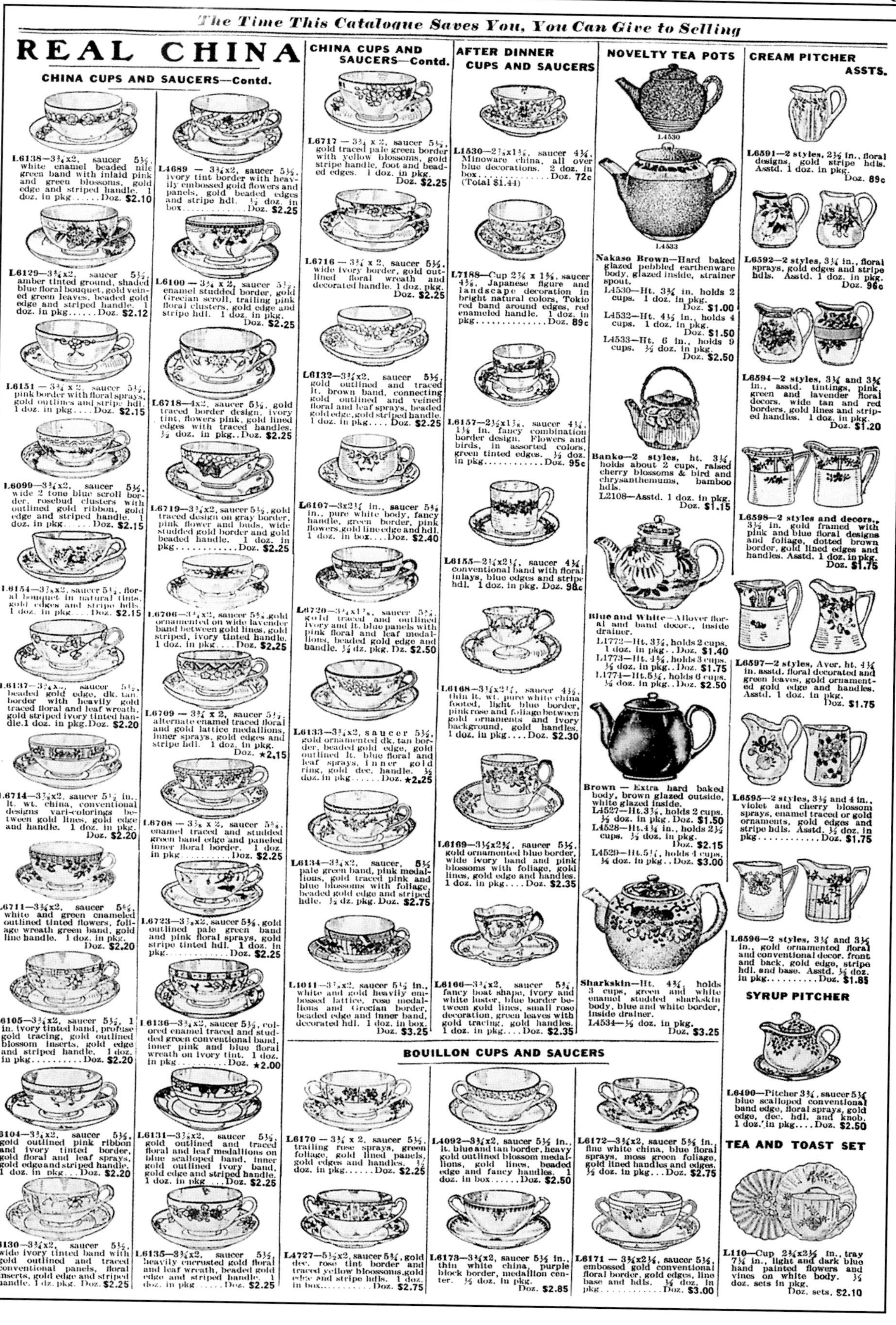

The Time This Catalogue Saves You, You Can Give to Selling

REAL CHINA

CHINA CUPS AND SAUCERS—Contd.

L6138—3¾x2, saucer 5½, white enamel beaded nile green band with inlaid pink and green blossoms, gold edge and striped handle. 1 doz. in pkg......Doz. **$2.10**

L6129—3¾x2, saucer 5½, amber tinted ground, shaded blue floral bouquet, gold veined green leaves, beaded gold edge and striped handle. 1 doz. in pkg......Doz. **$2.12**

L6151—3¾ x 2, saucer 5½, pink border with floral sprays, gold outlines and stripe hdl. 1 doz. in pkg....Doz. **$2.15**

L6099—3¾x2, saucer 5½, wide 2 tone blue scroll border, rosebud clusters with outlined gold ribbon, gold edge and striped handle. 1 doz. in pkg......Doz. **$2.15**

L6154—3⅞x2, saucer 5½, floral bouquet in natural tints, gold edges and stripe hdls. 1 doz. in pkg....Doz. **$2.15**

L6137—3¾x2, saucer 5½, beaded gold edge, dk. tan border with heavily gold traced floral and leaf wreath, gold striped ivory tinted handle. 1 doz. in pkg. Doz. **$2.20**

L6714—3⅞x2, saucer 5½ in., lt. wt. china, conventional designs vari-colorings between gold lines, gold edge and handle. 1 doz. in pkg. Doz. **$2.20**

L6711—3¾x2, saucer 5⅝, white and green enameled outlined tinted flowers, foliage wreath green band, gold line handle. 1 doz. in pkg. Doz. **$2.20**

L6105—3¾x2, saucer 5½, 1 in. ivory tinted band, profuse gold tracing, gold outlined blossom inserts, gold edge and striped handle. 1 doz. in pkg..........Doz. **$2.20**

L6104—3¾x2, saucer 5½, gold outlined pink ribbon and ivory tinted border, gold floral and leaf sprays, gold edge and striped handle. 1 doz. in pkg...Doz. **$2.20**

L6130—3¾x2, saucer 5½, wide ivory tinted band with gold outlined and traced conventional panels, floral inserts, gold edge and striped handle. 1 dz. pkg. Doz. **$2.25**

L4689—3¾x2, saucer 5½, ivory tint border with heavily embossed gold flowers and panels, gold beaded edges and stripe hdl. ½ doz. in box.............Doz. **$2.25**

L6100—3¾ x 2, saucer 5½, enamel studded border, gold Grecian scroll, trailing pink floral clusters, gold edge and stripe hdl. 1 doz. in pkg. Doz. **$2.25**

L6718—4x2, saucer 5½, gold traced border design, ivory tint, flowers pink, gold lined edges with traced handles. ½ doz. in pkg..Doz. **$2.25**

L6719—3¾x2, saucer 5½, gold traced design on gray border, pink flower and buds, wide studded gold border and gold beaded handle. 1 doz. in pkg............Doz. **$2.25**

L6706—3¾x2, saucer 5⅝, gold ornamented on wide lavender band between gold lines, gold striped, ivory tinted handle. 1 doz. in pkg....Doz. **$2.25**

L6709—3¾ x 2, saucer 5½, alternate enamel traced floral and gold lattice medallions, inner sprays, gold edges and stripe hdl. 1 doz. in pkg. Doz. **★2.15**

L6708—3⅞ x 2, saucer 5⅝, enamel traced and studded green band edge and paneled inner floral border. 1 doz. in pkg..........Doz. **$2.25**

L6723—3⅞x2, saucer 5⅝, gold outlined pale green band and pink floral sprays, gold stripe tinted hdl. 1 doz. in pkg............Doz. **$2.25**

L6136—3¾x2, saucer 5½, colored enamel traced and studded green conventional band, inner pink and blue floral wreath on ivory tint. 1 doz. in pkg..........Doz. **★2.00**

L6131—3⅞x2, saucer 5½, gold outlined and traced floral and leaf medallions on blue scalloped band, inner gold outlined ivory band, gold edge and striped handle. 1 doz. in pkg ...Doz. **$2.25**

L6135—3¾x2, saucer 5½, heavily encrusted gold floral and leaf wreath, beaded gold edge and striped handle. 1 doz. in pkg......Doz. **$2.25**

CHINA CUPS AND SAUCERS—Contd.

L6717—3¾ x 2, saucer 5½, gold traced pale green border with yellow blossoms, gold stripe handle, foot and beaded edges. 1 doz. in pkg. Doz. **$2.25**

L6716—3¾ x 2, saucer 5½, wide ivory border, gold outlined floral wreath and decorated handle. 1 doz. pkg. Doz. **$2.25**

L6132—3¾x2, saucer 5½, gold outlined and traced lt. brown band, connecting gold outlined and veined floral and leaf sprays, beaded gold edge, gold striped handle. 1 doz. in pkg.... Doz. **$2.25**

L6107—3x2¼ in., saucer 5⅜ in., pure white body, fancy handle, green border, pink flowers, gold line edge and hdl. 1 doz. in box...Doz. **$2.40**

L6720—3¾x1⅞, saucer 5⅜, gold traced and outlined ivory and lt. blue panels with pink floral and leaf medallions, beaded gold edge and handle. ½ dz. pkg. Dz. **$2.50**

L6133—3¾x2, saucer 5½, gold ornamented dk. tan border, beaded gold edge, gold outlined lt. blue floral and leaf sprays, inner gold ring, gold dec. handle. ½ doz. in pkg......Doz. **★2.25**

L6134—3¾x2, saucer, 5½ pale green band, pink medallions, gold traced pink and blue blossoms with foliage, beaded gold edge and striped hdle. ½ dz. pkg. Doz. **$2.75**

L1041—3⅞x2, saucer 5½ in., white and gold heavily embossed lattice, rose medallions and Grecian border, beaded edge and inner band, decorated hdl. 1 doz. in box. Doz. **$3.25**

AFTER DINNER CUPS AND SAUCERS

L1530—2⅞x1⅝, saucer 4¼, Minoware china, all over blue decorations. 2 doz. in box..............Doz. **72c** (Total $1.44)

L7188—Cup 2⅞ x 1⅝, saucer 4⅝, Japanese figure and landscape decoration in bright natural colors, Tokio red band around edges, red enameled handle. 1 doz. in pkg..............Doz. **89c**

L6157—2½x1⅞, saucer 4¼, 1⅛ in. fancy combination border design. Flowers and birds, in assorted colors, green tinted edges. ½ doz. in pkg...........Doz. **95c**

L6155—2¼x2¼, saucer 4¼, conventional band with floral inlays, blue edges and stripe hdl. 1 doz. in pkg. Doz. **98c**

L6168—3¼x2¼, saucer 4½, thin lt. wt. pure white china footed, light blue border, pink rose and foliage between gold ornaments and ivory background, gold handles. 1 doz. in pkg....Doz. **$2.30**

L6169—3½x2¾, saucer 5½, gold ornamented blue border, wide ivory band and pink blossoms with foliage, gold lines, gold edge and handles. 1 doz. in pkg....Doz. **$2.35**

L6166—3¾x2, saucer 5¾, fancy boat shape, ivory and white luster, blue border between gold lines, small rose decoration, green leaves with gold tracing, gold handles. 1 doz. in pkg....Doz. **$2.35**

NOVELTY TEA POTS

L4530

L4533

Nakaso Brown—Hard baked glazed pebbled earthenware body, glazed inside, strainer spout.

L4530—Ht. 3¾ in. holds 2 cups. 1 doz. in pkg. Doz. **$1.00**

L4532—Ht. 4½ in., holds 4 cups. 1 doz. in pkg. Doz. **$1.50**

L4533—Ht. 6 in., holds 9 cups. ½ doz. in pkg. Doz. **$2.50**

Banko—2 styles, ht. 3¼, holds about 2 cups, raised cherry blossoms & bird and chrysanthemums, bamboo hdls.

L2108—Asstd. 1 doz. in pkg. Doz. **$1.15**

Blue and White—Allover floral and band decor., inside drainer.

L1772—Ht. 3⅞, holds 2 cups. 1 doz. in pkg..Doz. **$1.40**

L1773—Ht. 4⅝, holds 3 cups. ½ doz. in pkg..Doz. **$1.75**

L1774—Ht. 5¼, holds 6 cups. ½ doz. in pkg..Doz. **$2.50**

Brown—Extra hard baked body, brown glazed outside, white glazed inside.

L4527—Ht. 3⅞, holds 2 cups. ½ doz. in pkg. Doz. **$1.50**

L4528—Ht. 4¼ in., holds 2½ cups. ½ doz. in pkg. Doz. **$2.15**

L4529—Ht. 5¼, holds 4 cups. ¼ doz. in pkg..Doz. **$3.00**

Sharkskin—Ht. 4¾, holds 3 cups, green and white enamel studded sharkskin body, blue and white border, inside drainer.

L4534—½ doz. in pkg. Doz. **$3.25**

CREAM PITCHER ASSTS.

L6591—2 styles, 2½ in., floral designs, gold stripe hdls. Asstd. 1 doz. in pkg. Doz. **89c**

L6592—2 styles, 3¼ in., floral sprays, gold edges and stripe hdls. Asstd. 1 doz. in pkg. Doz. **96c**

L6594—2 styles, 3¼ and 3¾ in., asstd. tintings, pink, green and lavender floral decors. wide tan and red borders, gold lines and striped handles. 1 doz. in pkg. Doz. **$1.20**

L6598—2 styles and decors., 3½ in. gold framed with pink and blue floral designs and foliage, dotted brown border, gold lined edges and handles. Asstd. 1 doz. in pkg. Doz. **$1.75**

L6597—2 styles, Aver. ht. 4¼ in. asstd. floral decorated and green leaves, gold ornamented gold edge and handles. Asstd. 1 doz. in pkg. Doz. **$1.75**

L6595—2 styles, 3½ and 4 in., violet and cherry blossom sprays, enamel traced or gold ornaments, gold edges and stripe hdls. Asstd. ½ doz. in pkg............Doz. **$1.75**

L6596—2 styles, 3¼ and 3½ in., gold ornamented floral and conventional decor. front and back, gold edge, stripe hdl. and base. Asstd. ½ doz. in pkg..........Doz. **$1.85**

SYRUP PITCHER

L6490—Pitcher 3¾, saucer 5¼ blue scalloped conventional band edge, floral sprays, gold edge, dec. hdl. and knob. 1 doz. in pkg....Doz. **$2.50**

TEA AND TOAST SET

L110—Cup 2¾x2½ in., tray 7¼ in., light and dark blue hand painted flowers and vines on white body. ½ doz. sets in pkg. Doz. sets, **$2.10**

BOUILLON CUPS AND SAUCERS

L6170—3¾ x 2, saucer 5½, trailing rose sprays, green foliage, gold lined panels, gold edges and handles. ½ doz. in pkg......Doz. **$2.25**

L4092—3¾x2, saucer 5½ in., lt. blue and tan border, heavy gold outlined blossom medallions, gold lines, beaded edge and fancy handles. 1 doz. in box......Doz. **$2.50**

L6172—3¾x2, saucer 5⅝ in., fine white china, blue floral sprays, moss green foliage, gold lined handles and edges. ½ doz. in pkg...Doz. **$2.75**

L4727—5½x2, saucer 5¾, gold dec. rose tint border and traced yellow bloossoms, gold edge and stripe hdls. 1 doz. in box...........Doz. **$2.75**

L6173—3¾x2, saucer 5½ in., thin white china, purple block border, medallion center. ½ doz. in pkg. Doz. **$2.85**

L6171—3¾x2⅛, saucer 5½, embossed gold conventional floral border, gold edges, line base and hdls. ½ doz. in pkg............Doz. **$3.00**

1917 Butler Bros. catalog.

Reproductions, Fakes, and Fantasies

Fake Nippon pieces are still a big problem for Nippon collectors and dealers. Many of the newest pieces are direct copies of original patterns and old molds. Most of the new wares are unmarked under the glaze and merely have a sticker on them giving the country of origin which is generally China. This sticker can be removed, and then the seller claims that the piece is unmarked Nippon. Genuine Nippon era pieces were manufactured during the years of 1891 and 1921, and the fakes have only been made since the late 1970s.

Collectors should refer to the Fifth and Sixth Series of the *Collector's Encyclopedia of Nippon Porcelain* for over 80 photos of these items. Another good reference is the International Nippon Collectors Club website, *http://www.nipponcollectorsclub.com*, for pictures and information on these pieces.

Collectors need to get to know what genuine pieces look and feel like so that they can avoid the reproductions. The new items are rougher to the touch, are usually a little heavier, and the gold is different in color.

Fakes are items that were never made originally, either in mold shape or pattern. Reproductions match some of the genuine patterns and mold forms. Fantasies are items never made during the Nippon era, such as an oyster plate or a porcelain kerosene lamp.

Some of the pieces are marked, and these fake marks can be found in the Fifth and Sixth Series. A new fake mark similar to one originally used by the Pickard Co. during World War I is the newest one to have surfaced. No such genuine Nippon mark exists.

This mark is based on an authentic Pickard China mark, circa 1906. No such Nippon mark exists.

Typical prices for the items shown in the following photos are tea sets, $60.00; sugar shakers, $5.00-7.50; hatpin holders, $5.00 – 13.50; egg cup, $2.50; ladle, $5.00; and tureen $12.00. They are quite inexpensive to purchase from the wholesaler, but the retail price the collector has to pay is usually quite substantial.

Sugar shaker, 5" tall.

Coffeepot, raised gold decoration, 7½" tall.

Left: Covered box, 5½" dia.; middle: pitcher, 7" tall; right: hatpin holder, 3½" tall.

Covered box, 6" long, has artist's signature written in gold.

Hatpin holder, 5" tall.

Hatpin holder, 5½" tall.

Hatpin holder, 4" tall.

Hatpin holder, raised gold decoration, 6" tall.

Hatpin holder with raised gold decoration, 6" tall.

Vase, 4" tall.

Ring holder, 3¾" wide.

Vanity organizer, 6" long, 4" tall.

Wallpocket, 9" long.

Hatpin holder, 5" tall.

Wallpocket, 5" long, cobalt and gold trimmed.

Wallpocket, 8½" long, raised gold beading.

Basket vase, 12½" tall.

Vase, 9" tall.

Vase, 9" tall.

Wallpocket, 5¾" long.

Vase, 4¼" tall.

Vase, 4¼" tall.

Vase, 4" tall.

Egg cup, 2½" tall.

Egg cup, 2½" tall.

Wallpocket, 8¾" tall.

Shaving mug with raised gold trim, 3½" tall.

Covered jar, raised gold decoration, 6" tall.

Small vase, 4¼" tall.

Vase, raised gold, 8¼" tall.

Covered dish, tray 11" long.

Cheese keeper, 7½" long, 4" high.

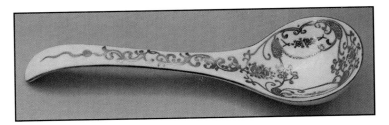

Ladle, 11" long.

Vase, 4¼" tall.

Tea set, teapot 7¼" tall.

Figurine, 5" tall.

Figurine, 5" tall.

Fake rising sun mark placed on bottom of both figurines.

Nippon Backstamps

1. Baby Bud Nippon; incised on doll.

2. Bara hand painted Nippon.

3. The Carpathia M Nippon.

4. Cherry blossom hand painted Nippon; found in blue, green, and magenta colors.

5. Cherry blossom in a circle hand painted Nippon.

6. Chikusa hand painted Nippon.

7. China E-OH hand painted Nippon; found in blue and green colors.

8. Crown (pointed), hand painted Nippon; found in green and blue colors.

9. Crown Nippon (pointed) made in Nippon; found in green and blue colors.

10. Crown (square), hand painted Nippon; found in green and green with red colors.

11. Chubby LW & Co. Nippon; found on dolls. (Louis Wolf & Co.)

12. D Nippon.

13. Dolly sticker found on Nippon's Dolly dolls; sold by Morimura Bros.

14. Double T Diamond Nippon.

15. Double T Diamond in circle Nippon.

16. Dowsie Nippon.

17. EE Nippon.

18. Elite B hand painted Nippon.

19. FY 401 Nippon; found on dolls.

20. FY 405 Nippon; found on dolls.

21. G in a circle hand painted Nippon.

22. Gloria L.W. & Co. hand painted Nippon (Louis Wolf Co., Boston, Mass. & N.Y.C.).

23. Hand painted Nippon.

24. Hand painted Nippon.

25. Hand painted Nippon.

26. Hand painted Nippon.

27. Hand painted Nippon.

28. Hand painted Nippon with symbol.

29. Hand painted Nippon with symbol.

30. Hand painted Nippon with symbol.

31. Hand painted Nippon with symbol.

32. Hand painted Nippon with symbol.

33. Hand painted Nippon with symbol.

34. Hand painted Nippon with symbol.

35. Hand painted Nippon with symbol.

36. Horsman No. 1 Nippon; found on dolls.

37. IC Nippon.

38. Imperial Nippon; found in blue and green.

39. J.M.D.S. Nippon.

40. The Jonroth Studio hand painted Nippon.

41. Kid Doll M.W. & Co. Nippon.

42. Kinjo Nippon.

43. Kinjo China hand painted Nippon.

44. L & Co Nippon.

45. LEH hand painted Nippon.

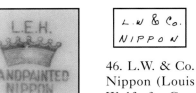

46. L.W. & Co. Nippon (Louis Wolf & Co., Boston, Mass & N.Y.C.).

47. M-in-wreath, hand painted (M stands for importer, Morimura Bros.); found in green, blue, magenta, and gold colors. Mark used since 1911.

48. M-in-wreath hand painted Nippon, D.M. Read Co. (M stands for importer, Morimura Bros.

49. M.B. (Morimura Bros.) Baby Darling sticker; found on dolls.

50. M. M. hand painted Nippon.

51. Made in Nippon.

52. Maple leaf Nippon; found in green, blue, and magenta, dates back to 1891.

53. Morimura Bros. sticker; found on Nippon items.

54. Mt. Fujiyama hand painted Nippon.

55. Nippon; found in blue, gold, and also incised into items.

56. Nippon 84.

57. Nippon 144.

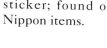

58. Nippon 221.

59. Nippon with symbol.

60. Nippon with symbol.

61. Nippon with symbol.

63. Nippon with symbol.

64. Nippon with symbol.

65. Nippon M incised on doll (note N is written backwards); #12 denotes size of doll; M is Morimura Bros.

62. Nippon with symbol.

66. Noritake M-in-wreath Nippon; M is Morimura Bros., found in green, blue, and magenta.

67. Noritake Nippon; found in green, blue, and magenta colors.

68. Noritake Nippon; found in green, blue, and magenta colors. Mark dates from 1911, used on blank pieces (undecorated) of Nippon.

69. O.A.C. Hand painted Nippon (Okura Art China, branch of Noritake Co.).

70. Oriental china Nippon.

71. Pagoda hand painted Nippon.

72. Patent No. 30441 Nippon.

73. Paulownia flowers and leaves hand painted Nippon (crest used by Empress of Japan, kiri no mon); found in a green/red color.

74. Paulownia flowers and leaves, hand painted Nippon (crest used by Empress of Japan, kiri no mon).

75. Pickard etched china, Noritake Nippon; Pickard mark is in black; Noritake; Nippon mark is blue in color.

76. W.A. Pickard hand painted china Nippon.

77. W.A. Pickard hand painted china, Noritake Nippon; Pickard mark printed in black, Noritake Nippon in magents.

78. Queue San Baby sticker; found on Nippon dolls.

79. RC Nippon; RC stands for Royal Crockery (fine china).

80. RC hand painted Nippon (combination of both red and green colors). RC stands for Royal Crockery (fine china). Mark used since 1911.

81. RC Noritake Nippon hand painted; found in green and blue. RC stands for Royal Crockery (fine china). This mark has been in existence since 1911.

82. RC Noritake Nippon, registered in 1911. RC stands for Royal Crockery (fine china).

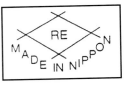

83. RE Nippon.

84. Rising Sun Nippon; mark used since 1911.

85. Royal dragon Nippon.

86. Royal dragon Nippon studio hand painted.

87. Royal Kaga Nippon.

88. Royal Kinran Nippon; found in blue, gold colors, made for domestic market in Japan since 1906.

89. Royal Kinran Crown Nippon; found in blue, gold, and green colors, made for domestic market in Japan since 1906.

90. Royal Moriye Nippon; found in green and blue colors.

91. Royal Nishiki Nippon; made for domestic market in Japan since 1906.

92. Royal Statsuma Nippon (cross within a ring, crest of House of Satsuma); made for domestic market in Japan since 1906.

93. Royal Sometuke Nippon; made for domestic market in Japan since 1906.

94. Royal Sometuke Nippon Sicily.

95. RS Nippon; found on coralene pieces.

96. S & K hand painted Nippon; found in green, blue, and magenta colors.

97. S & K hand painted Nippon; found in green, blue, and magenta colors.

98. Shinzo Nippon.

99. Shofu Nagoya Nippon.

100. SNB Nippon.

101. SNB Nagoya Nippon.

102. Spicer Studio Akron Ohio Nippon.

104. Studio hand painted Nippon.

103. Spoke hand painted Nippon; mark in existence as early as 1911.

105. Superior hand painted Nippon.

106. T Nippon hand painted (2 ho-o birds).

107. T hand painted Nippon.

108. T-in-wreath hand painted Nippon.

109. TN hand painted Nippon; mark is red and green.

110. T.S. hand painted Nippon.

111. TS hand painted Nippon.

112. Teacup, Made in Nippon.

113. Torri hand painted Nippon.

114. Tree crest hand painted Nippon (crest of Morimura family); also called Spider Mark.

115. Tree crest (also called Spider Mark) and maple leaf hand painted Nippon.

116. V Nippon, Scranton, PA.

117. The Yamato hand painted Nippon.

118. The Yamato Nippon.

119. C.G.N. hand painted Nippon; found in green.

120. F Nippon 03601 600; found incised on dolls, found in green.

121. F Nippon No. 76012 601; found incised on dolls.

122. F Nippon No. 76018 30/3; found incised on dolls.

123. FY Nippon No. 76018 403.

124. FY Nippon; found incised on dolls.

125. FY Nippon 301; found incised on dolls.

126. FY Nippon 402; found incised on dolls.

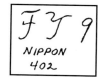

127. FY 9 Nippon 402; found incised on dolls.

128. FY Nippon 404; found incised on dolls.

129. FY Nippon 406; found incised on dolls.

130. FY Nippon 464; found incised on dolls.

131. FY Nippon No. 17604 604; found incised on dolls.

132. FY Nippon No. 70018 004; found incised on dolls.

133. FY Nippon (variation of mark) No. 70018 403; found incised on dolls.

134. FY Nippon No. 70018 406; found incised on dolls.

135. FY Nippon (variation of mark) No. 70018 406; found incised on dolls.

136. FY Nippon No. 76018; found incised on dolls, found in green.

137. Jollikid Nippon sticker (red and white), found on girl dolls; blue and white sticker found on boy dolls.

138. Ladykin Nippon sticker (red & gold); found on dolls.

139. Nippon (notice reversal of first N); found incised on items.

140. Nippon D13495; found in green.

141. Nippon E; found incised on dolls.

142. Nippon O; found incised on dolls.

143. Nippon 5; found incised on dolls.

144. Nippon 97; found incised on dolls.

145. Nippon 98; found incised of dolls.

146. Nippon 99; found incised on dolls.

147. Nippon 101; found incised on dolls.

148. Nippon 102; found incised on dolls.

149. Nippon 105; found incised on dolls.

150. Nippon 123; found incised on dolls.

151. Nippon 144 with symbol; found incised on dolls.

152. RE Nippon.

153. RE made in Nippon; found incised on dolls.

154. RE Nippon A9; found incised on dolls.

155. RE Nippon B8; found incised on dolls.

156. RE Nippon O 2; found incised on dolls.

157. Royal Hinode Nippon; found in blue.

158. Sonny sticker (gold, red, white, and blue); found on dolls.

159. Maruta Royal Blue Nippon.

160. Hand Painted Coronation Ware Nippon.

161. ATA Imperial Nippon.

162. Baby Doll, M.W. & Co. Nippon sticker; found on dolls.

163. BE, 4 Nippon.

164. Cherry blossom Nippon, similar to No. 4.

165. Cherry blossom (double) Nippon.

166. Louis Wolf & Co. Nippon.

167. C.O.N. Hand Painted Nippon.

168. FY Nippon 405; found on dolls.

169. FY Nippon 505; found on dolls.

170. FY Nippon 601; found on dolls.

171. FY Nippon 602; found on dolls.

172. FY Nippon 1602; found on dolls.

173. FY Nippon 603 No. 76018; found on dolls.

174. Happifat Nippon sticker; found on dolls.

175. Horsman Nippon, B9; found on dolls.

176. Horsman Nippon, B9; found on dolls.

177. James Studio China logo; used in conjuction with Crown Nippon mark.

178. JPL Hand Painted Nippon.

183. M Nippon F24.

179. Kenilworth Studios Nippon.

180. Komaru symbol, Hand Painted Nippon; since 1912.

181. Komaru symbol, Hand Painted Nippon No. 16034. Note: Japanese characters are fictitious.

182. M Nippon 10; found on dolls.

184. Manikin Nippon sticker; found on dolls.

185. Meiyo China Y-in-circle Nippon.

186. Nippon 3; found on dolls.

187. Nippon A3.

188. Nippon 144.

189. Nippon with symbol.

190. Nippon with symbol.

191. Nippon with symbol.

192. Nippon with symbol.

193. Nippon with symbol.

194. Nippon with symbol.

195. Nippon with symbol.

196. Nippon with symbol.

197. Hand painted Nippon with symbol.

198. Nippon with symbol, H in diamond, 14B, P.4.

199. Noritake M-in-wreath Nippon; M is Morimura Bros.; found in green, blue, and magenta; Derby indicates pattern.

200. Noritake M-in-wreath Nippon; M is Morimura Bros.; Sahara indicates pattern.

201. Noritake M-in-wreath Nippon; M is Morimura Bros.; The Kiva indicates pattern.

202. Noritake M-in-wreath Nippon; M is Morimura Bros.; The Metz indicates pattern.

203. Noritake M-in-wreath Nippon; M is Morimura Bros. Registered in Japan in 1912.

204. Noritake M-in-wreath Hand Painted Nippon; M is Morimura Bros.; Marguerite indicates pattern.

205. Noritake M-in-wreath Hand Painted Nippon; M is Morimura Bros.; Sedan indicates pattern. First dinner set made in Noritake factory 1914.

206. Noritake M-in-wreath Hand Painted Nippon; M is Morimura Bros.; The Vitry indicates pattern.

207. NPMC Nippon Hand Painted.

208. RC Noritake Nippon; Waverly indicates pattern.

209. RE Nippon 1120; found on dolls.

210. RE Nippon B 9; found on dolls.

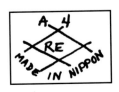

211. RE Nippon A4; found on dolls.

213. RE Made in Nippon A5; found on dolls.

214. RE Made in Nippon B9; found on dolls.

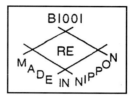

215. RE Made in Nippon B1001; found on dolls.

216. Royal Kuyu Nippon.

217. S in circle Nippon.

218. Sendai Hand Painted Nippon.

219. Stouffer Hand Painted Nippon.

220. Tanega Hand Painted Nippon.

221. Torii Nippon; similar to No. 113.

222. Nagoya N & Co. Nippon.

223. Old Blue Nippon Hand Painted.

---

* These marks were used during the Nippon era but may have also been used after 1921.

224.* RC Noritake mark, used for domestic market in Japan by Noritake Co. since 1908. The RC stands for Royal Crockery (fine china). The symbol design is called Yajirobe (toy of balance). It symbolizes the balance in management.

225.* RC Noritake mark, used for domestic market in Japan by Noritake Co. since 1912. The RC stands for Royal Crockery (fine china). The symbol design is called Yajirobe (toy of balance). It symbolizes the balance in management.

226. * RC Nippontoki Nagoya mark, for export since 1911. The RC stands for Royal Crockery (fine china).

227. * Made in Japan mark, used by Noritake Co., registered in London in 1908.

232. Coalportia Nippon.

228.* Noritaké, made in Japan, for export to England, registered in 1908 by Noritake Co.

229.* Noritaké, registered in London in 1908 by Noritake Co.

230.* Noritaké, made in Japan mark, registered in London in 1908.

231.* RC Japan; Noritake Co. started using the mark in 1914. It was used on items sent to India and Southeast Asia. RC stands for Royal Crockery (fine china).

233. FY Nippon 302; found incised on dolls.

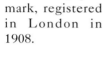

234. FY Nippon 303; found incised on dolls.

235. FY Nippon 501; found incised on dolls.

236. No. 700 Nippon HO6; found incised on dolls.

237. RE Made in Nippon C8; found incised on dolls.

238. RE Nippon M18; found incised on dolls.

239. SK Hand Painted Made in Nippon.

240. Patent No. 17705 Royal Kinjo.

241. RS Japan; found on coralene pieces.

242. U.S. Patent 912171; found on coralene pieces.

243. U.S. Patent 912171; found on coralene pieces.

244. Kinran U.S. Patent 912171; found on coralene pieces.

244. Kinran U.S. Patent 912971; found on coralene pieces.

245. Patent applied for No. 38257; found on coralene pieces.

246. Kinran Patent No. 16137; found on coralene pieces.

247. FY Nippon 401; found on dolls.

248. FY Nippon 409; found on dolls.

249. FY Nippon 15/4; found on dolls.

250. ESO hand-painted Nippon.

251. Miyako Nippon.

252. Royal Fuji Nippon.

253. RC Noritake, Nippon Toki Kaisha, circa 1912.

254. Komaru Nippon, circa 1906.

255. Noritake Howo, circa 1916.

256. Chikaramachi, made in Japan, circa 1912.

257. Noritake M, Japan, circa 1916.

258. Kokura, Japan, circa 1920.

259. FY Nippon No. 76018, 402; found incised on dolls.

260. FY Nippon, 11148; found incised on dolls.

261. L & Co. Nippon.

262. Yanagi Nippon, Louis Wolf & Co.

263. SK Hand Painted Nippon.

264. FY Nippon 106; found on dolls.

265. FY Nippon 203; found on dolls.

266. FY Nippon 304; found on dolls.

267. FY Nippon 1604; found on dolls.

268. Scrolled FY No. 76018 Nippon 30/3; found on dolls.

269. Scrolled FY NO 76018 Nippon 30/6; found on dolls.

270. Scrolled FY NO 76018 Nippon 30/8; found on dolls.

271. Scrolled FY NO 76018 Nippon 20/0; found on dolls.

272. Scrolled FY No 76018 103 Nippon; found on dolls.

273. Scrolled FY NO 70018 Nippon 301; found on dolls.

274. Scrolled FY NO 76018 Nippon 405; found on dolls.

275. Scrolled FY NO 76018 Nippon 502; found on dolls.

276. Scrolled FY NO 76018 Nippon 601; found on dolls.

277. Scrolled FY NO 76018 Nippon 603; found on dolls.

278. Scrolled FY NO 76018 Nippon 902; found on dolls.

279. Scrolled FY NO 76016 Nippon 2001; found on dolls.

280. BE in diamond, Nippon; found on dolls.

281. RE Nippon A1; found on dolls.

282. RE Nippon O2; found on dolls.

283. RE Made in Nippon A10; found on dolls.

284. RE Nippon M20; found on dolls.

285. BE Nippon B10; found on dolls.

286. Horsman Nippon NO1; found on dolls.

287. Horsman Nippon B.6; found on dolls.

288. Horsman Nippon NO-11; found on dolls.

289. JW Nippon 603; found on dolls.

290. H in diamond, Nippon 14B P.4.; found on dolls.

291. HS in an oval, Nippon 12A; found on dolls.

292. HS in an oval, Nippon 14C; found on dolls.

293. M in blossom Nippon 18; found on dolls.

294. M in blossom Nippon; found on dolls.

295. KKS in star, Nippon 3003 P.47; found on dolls.

296. KKS in star, Nippon 4003 P.53; found on dolls.

297. M in blossom, Nippon 4; found on dolls.

298. M in blossom, Nippon E20; found on dolls.

299. M Nippon 12; found on dolls.

300. M in circle, Nippon E24; found on dolls.

301. M in circle, Nippon W10; found on dolls.

302. Patent No. 30441 Nippon; found incised on dolls.

303. H Nippon; found incised on dolls.

304. 2 Nippon; found incised on dolls.

305. 3 Nippon; found incised on dolls.

306. Nippon 20; found incised on dolls.

307. Nippon 21; found incised on dolls.

308. Nippon 22; found incised on dolls.

309. Nippon 23; found incised on dolls.

310. Nippon 24; found incised on dolls.

311. NO. 32 N i p p o n; found incised on dolls.

312. Nippon 50; found incised on dolls.

313. Nippon 77; found incised on dolls.

314. Nippon 80; found incised on dolls.

315. Nippon 81; found incised on dolls.

316. Nippon 82; found incised on dolls.

317. Nippon 86; found incised on dolls.

318. Nippon 88; found incised on dolls.

319. Nippon 89; found incised on dolls.

320. A 3 Nippon; found incised on dolls.

321. A 13 Nippon; found incised on dolls.

322. Nippon B1; found incised on dolls.

323. Nippon B5; found incised on dolls.

324. Nippon B10; found incised on dolls.

325. Nippon B11; found incised on dolls.

326. C 02 Nippon; found incised on dolls.

327. X Nippon; found incised on dolls.

328. Patent Nippon; found incised on dolls.

329. Nippon D; found incised on dolls.

330. Nippon 87; found incised on dolls.

331. 93 Nippon; found incised on dolls.

332. Nippon 96; found incised on dolls.

333. 103 Nippon; found incised on dolls.

334. Nippon 113; found incised on dolls.

335. Nippon 122; found incised on dolls.

336. 222 Nippon; found incised on dolls.

337. Sticker found on Crinoline ballerina dolls.

338. Sticker found on Pixie doll.

339. Sticker found on Sweetie doll; Louis Wolf & Co.

340. Sticker found on Baby Belle doll; Morimura Bros.

341. Sticker found on Cutie doll; Louis Wolf & Co.

342. Sticker found on Kewpie doll.

343. Sticker found on the feet of Nippon Kewpie doll.

344. M & C Nagoya Nippon.

345. Orange Blossom, made in Nippon.

346. Noritake, Nippon.

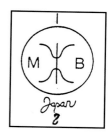

347. 1 MB (Morimura Bros.), Japan 8; found on dolls.

348. A9, RE Nippon; found on dolls.

349. No. 9 Horsman, Nippon; found on dolls.

350. No. 4, Horsman Nippon; found on dolls.

351. Royal Toya Nippon.

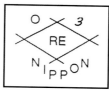

352. 03, RE in a diamond Nippon; found on dolls.

353. 14A, HS in an oval, Nippon.

354. M Nippon; found on dolls.

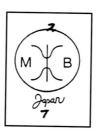

355. 2 MB (Morimura Bros.) Japan 7; found on dolls.

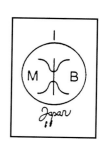

356. 1 MB (Morimura Bros.) Japan 11; found on dolls.

81

Cobalt

Plate 4257. Floral vase, 10½" tall, green mark #47, $1,000.00 – 1,200.00.

Plate 4258. Floral vase, 10¼" tall, blue mark #52, $1,100.00 – 1,300.00.

Plate 4259. Floral vase, 5½" tall, blue mark #52, $650.00 – 800.00.

Plate 4260. Floral vase, 8¾" tall, blue mark #524, $1,000.00 – 1,200.00.

Plate 4261. Floral vase, 11¾" tall, mark #230, $900.00 – 1,050.00.

Plate 4262. Floral vase, 8½" tall, unmarked, $500.00 – 600.00.

Plate 4263. Floral vase, 4" tall, unmarked, $325.00 – 400.00.

Plate 4264. Floral vase, 5¼" tall, blue mark #52, $650.00 – 800.00.

Plate 4265. Floral vase, 6" tall, blue mark #47, $350.00 – 425.00.

Plate 4266. Floral vase, 5½" tall, green mark #52, $400.00 – 500.00.

Plate 4267. Covered bolted urn, 13½" tall, mark #52 $2,500.00 – 3,000.00.

Plate 4268. Floral vase, 8¼" tall, blue mark #52, $900.00 – 1,050.00.

Plate 4269. Floral vase, 8¾" tall, blue mark #52, $400.00 – 500.00.

Plate 4270. Scenic vase, 7½" tall, blue mark #47, $600.00 – 700.00.

Plate 4271. Scenic vase, 7" tall, blue mark #52, $600.00 – 700.00.

Plate 4273. Pair of floral vases, 8" tall, unmarked, $600.00 – 700.00 each.

Plate 4272. Pair of scenic and floral covered urns, 7" tall, unmarked. $600.00 – 700.00 each.

Plate 4274. Scenic vase, 6½" tall, mark #230, $600.00 – 700.00.

Plate 4275. Scenic vase, 7" tall, blue mark #52, $900.00 – 1,050.00.

Plate 4276. Scenic vase, 9" tall, green mark #52, $900.00 – 1,050.00.

Plate 4277. Floral small pitcher, 5" tall, blue mark #52, $275.00 – 350.00.

Plate 4279. Floral ferner, 6½" tall, unmarked, $600.00 – 700.00.

Plate 4278. Wall plaque, 12½" wide, blue mark #52, $1,400.00 – 1,700.00.

Plate 4280. Floral plate, 9" wide, blue mark #52, $600.00 – 700.00.

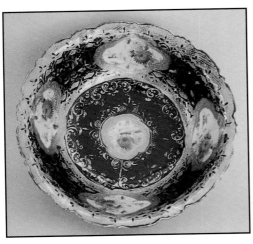

Plate 4281. Floral bowl, 10" wide, blue mark #52, $800.00 – 950.00.

Plate 4282. Floral bowl, 7½" wide, unmarked, $500.00 – 600.00.

Plate 4284. Floral teapot, creamer, and sugar bowl, teapot is 5" tall, blue mark #52, $1,200.00 – 1,500.00.

Plate 4283. Floral cracker jar, 8" tall, unmarked, $1,000.00 – 1,200.00.

Plate 4285. Floral rose bowl, 4" tall, unmarked, $600.00 – 700.00.

Plate 4286. Floral syrup, 5¼" tall, unmarked, $500.00 – 600.00.

Plate 4287. Floral tray, 10" long, blue mark #52, $700.00 – 850.00.

Plate 4288. Floral whip cream set, under-plate is 6¾" wide, mark scratched off, $400.00 – 500.00.

Plate 4289. Scenic cake set, serving plate is 10" wide, individual plates are 8" wide, blue mark #52, $1,200.00 – 1,500.00.

Plate 4290. Floral bowl, 9¾" wide, unmarked, $650.00 – 800.00.

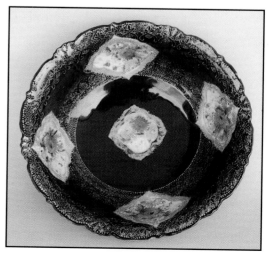

Plate 4291. Floral bowl, 10" wide, blue mark #52, $600.00 – 700.00.

Plate 4292. Scenic tray, 12½" long, blue mark #52, $600.00 – 750.00.

Plate 4293. Floral humidor, 8¼" tall, mark #70, $600.00 – 725.00.

Plate 4294. Scenic cake dish, 10¾" wide, green mark #47, $425.00 – 500.00.

Plate 4295. Scenic bowl, 10¼" wide, blue mark #52, $425.00 – 500.00.

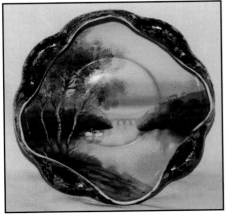

Plate 4296. Scenic bowl, 9¾" wide, green mark #47, $425.00 – 500.00.

Plate 4297. Floral cracker jar, 7½" tall, mark #52, $1,000.00 – 1,200.00.

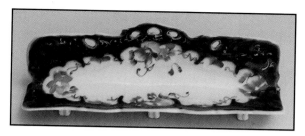

Plate 4298. Floral pen tray, 7¾" long, mark #97, $225.00 – 275.00.

Plate 4299. Floral pitcher, 7½" tall, mark #52, $425.00 – 525.00.

Plate 4300. Floral pitcher, 6½" tall, green mark #50, $500.00 – 625.00.

Plate 4303. Floral pitcher, 5" tall, blue mark #52, $275.00 – 350.00.

Plate 4301. Floral tankard, 15½" tall, mark #70, $1,100.00 – 1,300.00.

Plate 4302. Floral tankard, 16" tall, unmarked, $1,200.00 – 1,500.00.

Plate 4304. Cobalt and floral tankard, 12" tall, unmarked, $800.00 – 1,000.00.

Plate 4305. Floral pancake server, 8¾" wide, unmarked, $450.00 – 575.00.

Plate 4306. Floral potpourri jar, 5½" tall, unmarked, $225.00 – 300.00.

Plate 4307. Floral tea strainer, 1½" tall, green mark #47, $325.00 – 375.00.

Plate 4308. Cake set, large plate is 11" wide, six small ones are 6½" wide, $600.00 – 725.00.

Plate 4309. Scenic bowl, 9½" wide, green mark #52, $700.00 – 850.00.

Plate 4310. Scenic plate, 8½" wide, blue mark #47, $150.00 – 200.00.

Plate 4311. Scenic dinner plate, 10" wide, blue mark #52, $250.00 – 300.00.

Plate 4312. Ferner, 5¾" wide, blue mark #52, $300.00 – 375.00.

Plate 4313. Plate, 7½" wide, green mark #47, $500.00 – 600.00.

Plate 4314. Cake plate, 10½" wide, blue mark #52, $700.00 – 850.00.

Plate 4315. Scenic bowl set, large bowl is 10" wide, blue mark #52, $1,000.00 – 1,200.00.

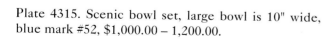

Plate 4316. Cobalt and gold bouillon cups, blue mark #52, $1,600.00 – 1,900.00 per set.

Plate 4317. Scenic plate, 7½" wide, blue mark #52, $800.00 – 950.00.

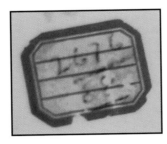

Plate 4319. Original sticker found on bowl shown in Plate 4320.

Plate 4318. Scenic bowl, 11¼" wide, mark #228, $800.00 – 950.00.

Plate 4320. Floral bowl, 11½" wide, mark #89, $500.00 – 650.00.

Plate 4321. Floral chocolate set, pot is 13¼" tall, unmarked, $1,300.00 – 1,600.00.

Plate 4322. Floral cologne bottle, 6¼" tall, blue mark #52, $300.00 – 375.00.

Plate 4323. Floral mustache cup, blue mark #52, $350.00 – 425.00.

Plate 4324. Cobalt and gold relish dish, 7½" long, blue mark #52, $300.00 – 400.00.

Plate 4325. Cobalt and gold tea pot, 6½" tall, blue mark #52, $300.00 – 400.00.

Plate 4326. Cobalt and gold rose bowl, 6" wide, blue mark #52, $300.00 – 400.00.

Plate 4327. Cobalt and gold compote, 3½" tall, blue mark #52, $350.00 – 425.00.

Plate 4328. Cobalt and gold bowl, 8" wide, blue mark #52, $300.00 – 400.00.

Plate 4329. Scenic hatpin holder, 4¾" tall, mark #44, $200.00 – 265.00.

Plate 4330. Floral nappy, 7" wide, unmarked, $225.00 – 275.00.

Plate 4331. Floral nappy, 4½" wide, mark scratched off, $135.00 – 170.00.

Plate 4332. Scenic sugar shaker, 4½" tall, blue mark #52, $225.00 – 300.00.

Plate 4333. Floral bowl, 10½" wide, green mark #47, $400.00 – 500.00.

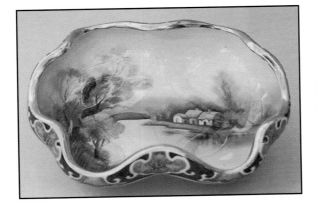

Plate 4334. Scenic bowl, 8¾" long, green mark #47, $325.00 – 400.00.

Plate 4335. Scenic bowl, 8¼" wide, green mark #47, $325.00 – 300.00.

Plate 4336. Set of six cobalt and silver overlay demitasse cups, mark #80, $850.00 – 1,000.00 per set.

Portraits

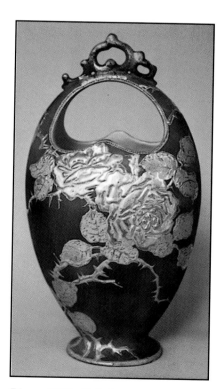

Plate 4337. Cobalt and gold overlay vase, 18" tall, green mark #47, $2,500.00 – 2,800.00.

Plate 4338. Cobalt and gold overlay basket vase, 9½" tall, blue mark #52, $800.00 – 950.00.

Plate 4339. Cobalt vase, 7½" tall, green mark #52, $1,300.00 – 1,600.00.

Plate 4340. Cobalt vase, 12½" tall, blue mark #52, $1,800.00 – 2,000.00.

Plate 4341. Cobalt vase, 4¼" tall, green mark #52, $1,100.00 – 1,300.00.

Plate 4342. Cobalt vase, 6½" tall, green mark #52, $1,250.00 – 1,450.00.

Plate 4344. Vase, 7½" tall, green mark #52, $1,000.00 – 1,200.00.

Plate 4343. Cobalt vase, 4¾" tall, green mark #52, $600.00 – 750.00.

Plate 4345. Salt and pepper shakers, 2¼" tall, unmarked, $325.00 – 425.00.

Plate 4346. Close-up of portrait shown in Plate 4347.

Plate 4347. Cracker jar, 6½" tall, green mark #47, $1,000.00 – 1,200.00.

Plate 4348. Moriage vase, 10" tall, blue mark #52, $2,200.00 – 2,600.00.

Plate 4349. Vase, 14½" tall, green mark #47, $2,600.00 – 3,000.00.

Plate 4350. Chocolate set, pot is 10" tall, unmarked, $2,000.00 – 2,400.00.

Plate 4352. Covered box, Admiral Togo, 2½" wide, unmarked, $250.00 – 325.00.

Plate 4351. Humidor, 5½" tall, green mark #47, $1,500.00 – 1,800.00.

Plate 4353. Tankard, "The Cardinal," 14" tall, mark #52, $3,500.00 – 4,000.00.

Plate 4354. Reverse side of Plate 4353.

Plate 4355. Portrait mug, "The Cardinal," 5¼" tall, green mark #52, $800.00 – 950.00.

Plate 4356. Bowl, 7¾" long, green mark #52, $800.00 – 900.00.

Plate 4357. Pair of portrait vases, showing front and back views, 6" tall, blue mark #52, $1,000.00 – 1,200.00 each.

Plate 4358. Pair of portrait vases, showing front and back views, 6" tall, blue mark #52, $1,000.00 – 1,200.00 each.

Plate 4359. Powder box, 4" wide, mark #52, $600.00 – 725.00.

Plate 4360. Vase, 5½" tall, unmarked, $750.00 – 900.00.

Tapestry

Plate 4361. Floral vase, 9 " tall, blue mark #52, $1,500.00 – 1,750.00.

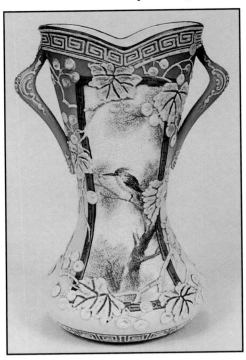

Plate 4362. Floral vase, 10" tall, blue mark #52, $1,600.00 – 1,850.00.

Plate 4363. Floral ewer, 7½" tall, $1,300.00 – 1,500.00.

Plate 4364. Scenic vase, 6" tall unmarked, $1,000.00 – 1,200.00.

Plate 4365. Scenic humidor, 6½" tall, green #47, $1,600.00 – 1,900.00.

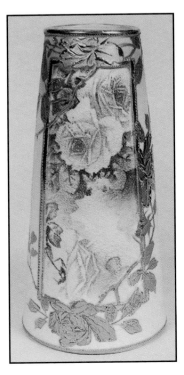

Plate 4366. Floral vase, 9½" tall, blue mark #52, $1,100.00 – 1,300.00.

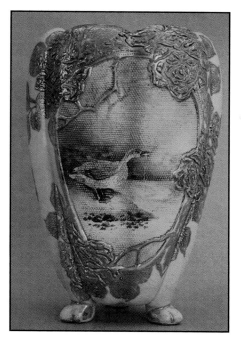

Plate 4367. Tapestry and gold overlay scenic vase, 8½" tall, blue mark #52, $1,100.00 – 1,300.00.

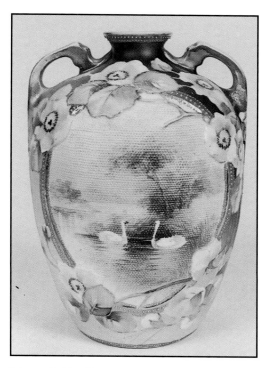

Plate 4368. Vase, 8" tall, blue mark #52, $1,300.00 – 1,500.00.

Plate 4369. Left: Vase (similar to Plate 2987), 8" tall, blue mark #52, $1,100.00 – 1,300.00. Right: Ewer, 10¾" tall, blue mark #52, $1,800.00 – 2,100.00.

Plate 4370. Vase, 8" tall, mark indistinguishable, $1,000.00 – 1,200.00.

Plate 4371. Vase, 9¾" tall, blue mark #52, $1,100.00 – 1,300.00.

Coralene

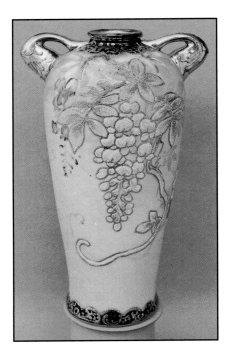

Plate 4372. Vase, 8½" tall, mark #242, $1,000.00 – 1,200.00.

Plate 4373. Vase, 8¼" tall, mark removed, $1,100.00 – 1,300.00.

Plate 4374. Vase, 7" tall, mark #242, $1,000.00 – 1,200.00.

Plate 4375. Vase, 6¼" tall, mark #244, $900.00 – 1,100.00.

Plate 4376. Vase, 10½" tall, mark #242, $1,400.00 – 1,700.00.

Plate 4377. Vase, 10" tall, mark #242, $1,200.00 – 1,400.00.

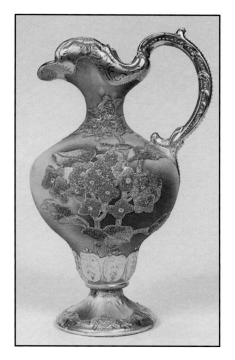

Plate 4378. Ewer, 9½" tall, mark #245, $2,000.00 – 2,400.00.

Plate 4379. Vase, 6" tall, mark #242, $800.00 – 900.00.

Plate 4380. Vase, 12" tall, mark #241, $900.00 – 1,000.00.

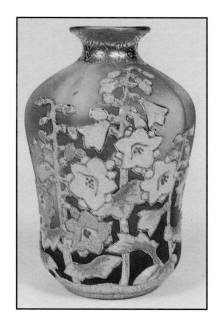

Plate 4381. Vase, 6¾" tall, mark #242, $800.00 – 950.00.

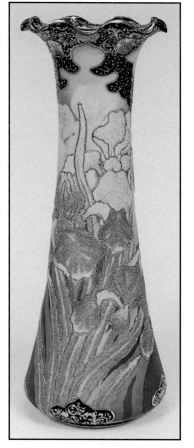

Plate 4382. Vase, 18" tall, mark #242, $4,000.00 – 5,200.00.

Plate 4383. Vase, 6½" tall, mark #242, $800.00 – 950.00.

Plate 4384. Vase, 7" tall, mark #243, $800.00 – 950.00.

Plate 4385. Vase, 5½" tall, mark #244, $900.00 – 1,100.00.

Plate 4387. Pair of vases, 7" tall, mark #246, $700.00 – 850.00 each.

Plate 4388. Vase, 7" tall, mark #246, $700.00 – 850.00.

Plate 4386. Vase, 11" tall, mark #242, $1,200.00 – 1,400.00.

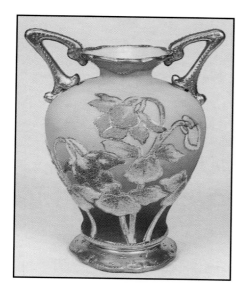

Plate 4389. Vase, 6½" tall, mark #245, $850.00 – 1,000.00.

Plate 4390. Vase, 8¼" tall, mark #245, $1,100.00 – 1,300.00.

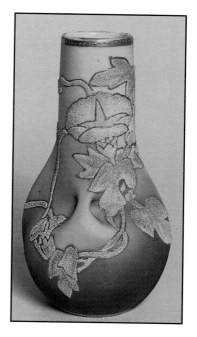

Plate 4391. Vase, 8½" vase, mark #242, $1,000.00 – 1,200.00.

Plate 4392. Vase, 8¾" tall, mark #242, $1,100.00 – 1,300.00.

Plate 4393. Tankard, 13¼" tall, mark #245, $2,500.00 – 3,000.00.

Plate 4394. Left: Vase, 9" tall, mark #242, $1,100.00 – 1,300.00. Right: Vase, 9" tall, mark #242, $1,100.00 – 1,300.00.

Plate 4395. Pitcher, 4¾" tall, mark #242, $600.00 – 700.00.

Plate 4396. Vase, 6" tall, mark #246, $900.00 – 1,050.00.

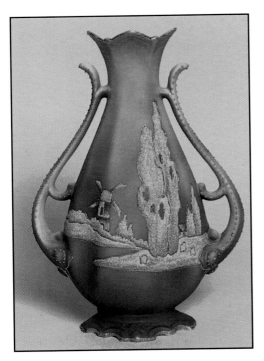

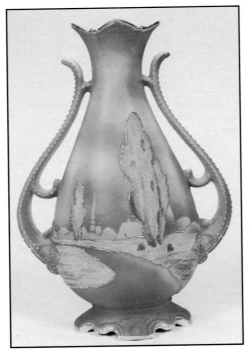

Plate 4397. Vase, 12" tall, mark #244, $1,300.00 – 1,500.00.

Plate 4398. Vase, 12" tall, mark #242, $1,300.00 – 1,500.00.

Plate 4399. Vase, 9" tall, mark #242, $1,050.00 – 1,200.00.

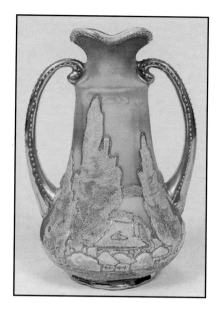

Plate 4400. Vase, 6¼" tall, mark #242, $900.00 – 1,000.00.

Plate 4401. Vase, 7" tall, mark #241, $800.00 – 900.00.

Plate 4402. Vase, 4¾" tall, mark #241, $550.00 – 650.00.

Plate 4403. Hatpin holder, 4" tall, mark #242, $500.00 – 625.00.

Plate 4404. Demitasse set, 8" tall, mark #242, $2,100.00 – 2,400.00.

Plate 4405. Wall plaque, 9½" wide, mark #242, $1,100.00 – 1,300.00.

Plate 4406. Chamberstick, 6½" long, mark #242, $1,000.00 – 1,150.00.

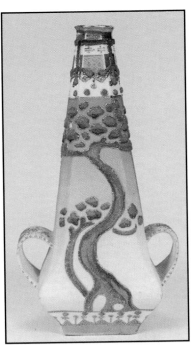

Plate 4407. Vase, 9¼" tall, mark #244, $900.00 – 1,050.00.

Plate 4408. Wall plaque, 7½" wide, mark #242, $900.00 – 1,050.00.

Plate 4409. Hair receiver, 4½" wide, mark #242, $500.00 – 625.00.

Wedgwood

Plate 4410. Flowergate vase, 7½" long, 4¼" tall, green mark #47, $500.00 – 600.00.

Plate 4411. Trinket box, 4" long, green mark #47, $175.00 – 225.00.

Plate 4412. Plate, 7¼" wide, mark scratched off, $150.00 – 200.00.

Plate 4414. Lavender bowl, 11¾" long, green mark #47, $900.00 – 1,050.00.

Plate 4413. Humidor with match holder and striker, similar to Plate 1304, 7" tall, green mark #37, $2,500.00 – 2,800.00.

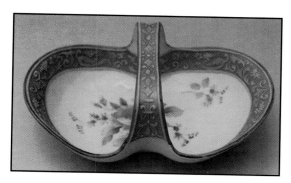

Plate 4416. Basket dish, 7½" long, green mark #47, $250.00 – 325.00.

Plate 4415. Vase/lamp base (factory drilled for lamp base), 10" tall, green mark #47, $900.00 – 1,050.00.

Plate 4417. Bowl, 10¾" long, green mark #47, $650.00 – 800.00.

Heavily Beaded

Plate 4418. Bowl, 7¾" long, blue mark #52, $450.00 – 550.00.

Plate 4419. Vase, 5½" tall, green mark #52, $775.00 – 900.00.

Plate 4420. Vase, 8¼", green mark #52, $500.00 – 600.00.

Plate 4421. Vase, 10¾" tall, blue mark #52, $1,100.00 – 1,300.00.

Plate 4423. Bowl, 11" wide, unmarked, $600.00 – 750.00.

Plate 4422. Bowl, 9½" wide, mark #89, $600.00 – 750.00.

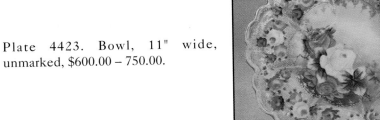

Plate 4426. Sandwich tray, 11¼" wide, blue mark #52, $600.00 – 750.00.

Plate 4424. Cracker/biscuit jar, 6¾" tall, blue mark #52, $1,100.00 – 1,300.00.

Plate 4425. Candlestick, 6¼" tall, mark #89, $350.00 – 450.00.

Cloisonné, Pattern Stamped & Figural

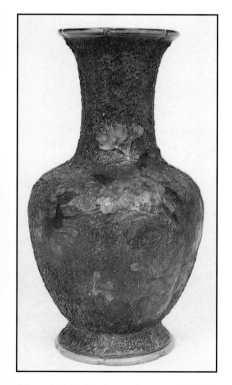

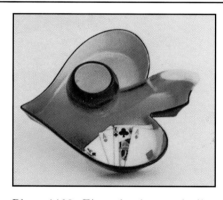

Plate 4429. Figural ashtray, similar to Plate 1543, 5¼" wide, green mark #47, $350.00 – 450.00.

Plate 4427. Cloisonné vase, 10" tall, green mark #47, $700.00 – 800.00.

Plate 4428. Pattern stamped vase, 9½" tall, green mark #47, $300.00 – 400.00.

Plate 4430. Cloisonné ferner, 5½" wide, green mark #47, $450.00 – 550.00.

Plate 4431. Figural bowl, 7" long, mark #47, $250.00 – 325.00.

Plate 4433. Vase, 8" tall, green mark #47, $800.00 – 900.00.

Plate 4434. Ferner, 7¼" wide, green mark #47, $400.00 – 500.00.

Molded in Relief

Plate 4432. Vase, 9½" tall, blue mark #52, $1,200.00 – 1,400.00.

Plate 4435. Ferner (similar to Plate 564), 8½" tall, blue mark #52, $900.00 – 1,100.00.

Plate 4436. Humidor (same as Plate 544 but with original lid), 6½" tall, green mark #47, $2,500.00 – 3,000.00.

Royal Kinjo

Plate 4437. Vase, 9½" tall, mark #240, $600.00 – 700.00.

Plate 4438. Vase, 10" tall, mark #240, $600.00 – 700.00.

Plate 4439. Moriage vase, 9½" tall, mark #240, $1,800.00 – 2,200.00.

Plate 4440. Wall plaque, 10" wide, mark #240, $1,000.00 – 1,200.00.

Souvenir & Advertising

Plate 4441. Souvenir tray, Capitol at Washington, DC, 11½" long, mark #31, $75.00 – 120.00.

Plate 4442. Souvenir cracker jar, "Business Section from Waterfront, Seattle Washington," 8" tall, mark #100, $550.00 – 650.00.

Plate 4443. Advertising covered box, 3" wide, mark #47, $135.00 – 165.00.

Plate 4445. Mark inside lid of box in Plate 4443.

Plate 4444. Advertising trinket box, 2¼" tall, compliments of Morimura Bros., mark #80, $250.00 – 350.00.

Plate 4446. Mark inside top of trinket box shown in Plate 4444.

Plate 4447. Souvenir powder box, 3" wide, blue mark #84, $135.00 – 165.00.

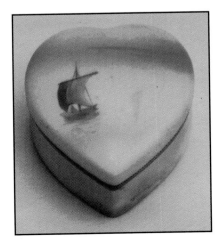

Plate 4448. Advertising trinket box, 3" wide, "Compliments of Eastern Outfitting Co.," green mark #47, $135.00 – 165.00.

Plate 4449. Inside lid of box shown in Plate 4448.

Moriage

Plate 4450. Vase, 9½" tall, blue mark #52, $950.00 – 1,100.00.

Plate 4451. Vase, 14" tall, blue mark #52, $1,600.00 – 1,800.00.

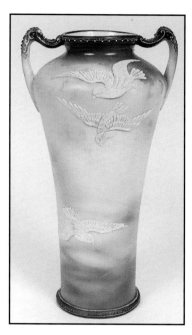

Plate 4452. Vase, 12" tall, blue mark #52, $850.00 – 950.00.

Plate 4453. Vase, 3" tall, blue mark #52, $950.00 – 1,100.00.

Plate 4454. Vase, 8" tall, blue mark #52, $1,100.00 – 1,300.00.

Plate 4455. Vase, 9½" tall, blue mark #52, $1,200.00 – 1,350.00.

Plate 4456. Vase, 14" tall, green mark #52, $1,800.00 – 2,200.00.

Plate 4457. Vase, 8½" tall, green mark #52, $950.00 – 1,150.00.

Plate 4458. Vase, 10" tall, blue mark #52, $1,000.00 – 1,200.00.

Plate 4459. Vase, 6¼" tall, mark #24, $600.00 – 700.00.

Plate 4460. Covered urn, 9¼" tall, blue mark #52, $1,100.00 – 1,300.00.

Plate 4461. Vase, 7" tall, green mark #52, $600.00 – 700.00.

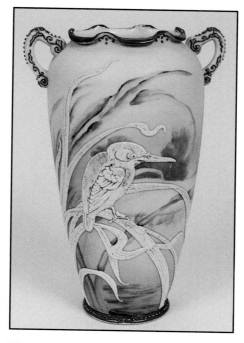

Plate 4462. Vase, 11" tall, blue mark #52, $1,300.00 – 1,500.00.

Plate 4463. Vase, 13" tall, blue mark #52, $1,400.00 – 1,600.00.

Plate 4464. Vase, 4½" tall, unmarked, $900.00 – 1,000.00.

Plate 4466. Ewer, 11¼" tall, blue mark #52, $1,300.00 – 1,600.00.

Plate 4465. Vase, 7¾" tall, blue mark #52, $900.00 – 1,000.00.

Plate 4467. Vase, 10" tall, blue mark #52, $800.00 – 925.00.

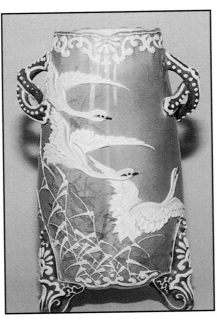

Plate 4468. Vase, 9" tall, unmarked, $900.00 – 1,050.00.

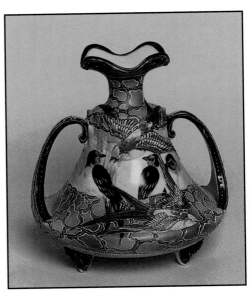

Plate 4469. Vase, 8½" tall, blue mark #52, $900.00 – 1,050.00.

Plate 4470. Vase, 4½" tall, green mark #24, $325.00 – 400.00.

Plate 4472. Pitcher, 5" tall, green mark #47, $250.00 – 300.00.

Plate 4471. Tankard, 16" tall, unmarked, $1,200.00 – 1,400.00.

Plate 4473. Left: Vase, 3½" tall, green mark #47, $150.00 – 200.00. Right: Vase, 5" tall, green mark #47, $200.00 – 250.00.

Plate 4474. Tankard, 10" tall, unmarked, $900.00 – 1,100.00.

Plate 4475. Pair of vases, 6½" tall, green mark #47, $350.00 – 450.00 each.

Plate 4477. Close-up of handle of vase shown in Plate 4476.

Plate 4476. Vase, 6½" tall, green mark #47, $350.00 – 450.00.

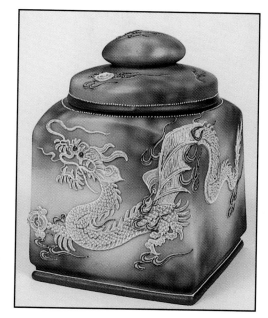

Plate 4478. Humidor, 6¾" tall, green mark #47, $700.00 – 850.00.

Plate 4479. Vase, 5" tall, blue mark #52, $250.00 – 300.00.

Plate 4480. Vase, 9" tall, unmarked, $850.00 – 950.00.

Plate 4482. Vase, 8¼" tall, unmarked, $800.00 – 900.00.

Plate 4481. Covered urn, 19½" tall, unmarked, $1,800.00 – 2,300.00.

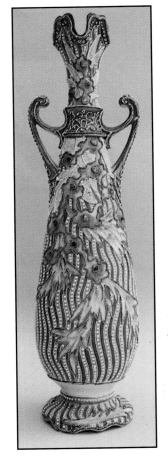

Plate 4483. Vase, 12" tall, unmarked, $1,000.00 – 1,150.00.

Plate 4484. Vase, 15" tall, unmarked, $1,400.00 – 1,600.00.

Plate 4485. Vase, 11¼" tall, blue mark #52, $800.00 – 900.00.

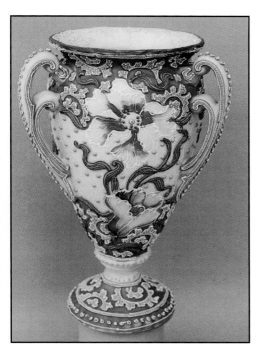

Plate 4486. Vase, 8¼" tall, unmarked, $750.00 – 850.00.

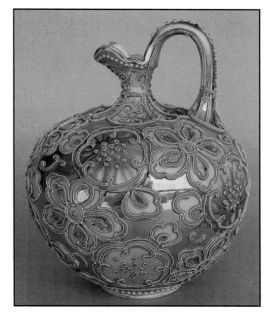

Plate 4487. Ewer, 7½" tall, unmarked, $700.00 – 800.00.

Plate 4488. Vase, 4¼" tall, unmarked, $350.00 – 425.00.

Plate 4489. Vase, 5½" tall, unmarked, $500.00 – 600.00.

Plate 4490. Vase, 7" tall, unmarked, $600.00 – 700.00.

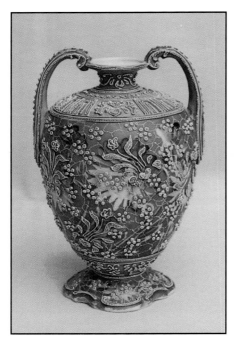

Plate 4491. Vase, 9" tall, unmarked, $850.00 – 950.00.

Plate 4492. Vase, 8" tall, blue mark #90, $800.00 – 900.00.

Plate 4493. Vase, 9" tall, blue mark #52, $850.00 – 950.00.

Plate 4494. Vase, 8½" tall, blue mark #47, $800.00 – 900.00.

Plate 4495. Vase, 8½" tall, blue mark #52, $800.00 – 900.00.

Plate 4496. Vase, 10½" tall, blue mark #52, $1,200.00 – 1,500.00.

Plate 4497. Vase, 8¾" tall, blue mark #52, $800.00 – 900.00.

Plate 4498. Vase, 9" tall, blue mark #52, $1,000.00 – 1,200.00.

Plate 4499. Vase, 6½" tall, unmarked, $600.00 – 700.00.

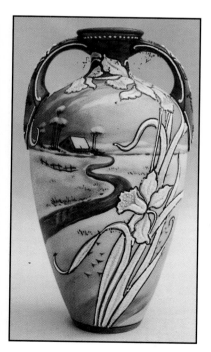

Plate 4500. Vase, 8" tall, blue mark #52, $750.00 – 850.00.

Plate 4501. Humidor, 6½" tall, blue mark #52, $1,050.00 – 1,200.00.

Plate 4502. Humidor, 8½" tall, unmarked, $800.00 – 950.00.

Plate 4503. Vase, 5" tall, green mark #52, $425.00 – 500.00.

Plate 4504. Humidor, 7" tall unmarked, $850.00 – 1,000.00.

Plate 4505. Pitcher, 10¼" tall, blue mark #52, $900.00 – 1,100.00.

Plate 4506. Ewer, 9½" tall, unmarked, $850.00 – 950.00.

Plate 4507. Ferner, 7¾" wide, green mark #47, $375.00 – 450.00.

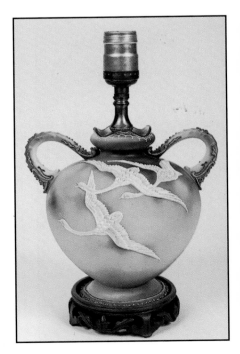

Plate 4508. Vase/lamp, 6½" tall, $650.00 – 750.00.

Plate 4510. Ferner, decorated with grasshoppers, 9" wide, blue mark #52, $800.00 – 950.00.

Plate 4509. Chocolate pot, 9½" tall, unmarked, $400.00 – 500.00.

Plate 4512. Vase, 5" tall, unmarked, $350.00 – 425.00.

Plate 4511. Snack set and creamer and sugar bowl, unmarked; snack set, $200.00 – 250.00, creamer and sugar bowl, $300.00 – 375.00.

Plate 4513. Cracker/biscuit jar, 7½" tall, unmarked, $550.00 – 650.00.

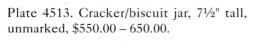

Plate 4514. Chocolate pot, 9¼" tall, unmarked, $550.00 – 650.00.

Plate 4515. Chocolate set, basketweave design, six cups and saucers, green mark #47, $2,400.00 – 2,800.00.

Plate 4516. Wall plaque, 8" wide, blue mark #52, $300.00 – 400.00.

Plate 4517. Wall plaque, 8½" wide, blue mark #52, $300.00 – 400.00.

Plate 4518. Wall plaque, 8" wide, blue mark #52, $300.00 – 400.00.

Plate 4519. Wall plaque, 9" wide, blue mark #52, $300.00 – 400.00.

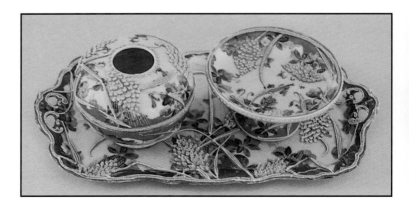

Plate 4520. Dresser set, tray 11¼" long, unmarked, $900.00 – 1,100.00.

Plate 4521. Hair receiver, 3" tall, unmarked, $200.00 – 275.00.

Plate 4524. Mug, 5½" tall, unmarked, $350.00 – 450.00.

Plate 4522. Candlestick, 11" tall, mark #52, $300.00 – 375.00.

Plate 4523. Bowl, 6" wide, mark #52, $200.00 – 250.00.

Plate 4525. Ashtray, 5" wide, unmarked, $200.00 – 250.00.

Hunt Scene

Plate 4526. Humidor, 8¼" tall, blue mark #52, $1,500.00 – 1,800.00.

Plate 4527. Humidor, 8¼" tall, blue mark #52, $1,500.00 – 1,800.00.

Plate 4528. Wall plaque, 9¼" wide, blue mark #52, $700.00 – 850.00.

Plate 4529. Wine jug, 11" tall, blue mark #52, $1,600.00 – 1,800.00.

Plate 4530. Pair of vases, 6¼" tall, green mark #47, $700.00 – 850.00 each.

Arrival of the Coach Scene & Egyptian Design

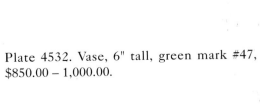

Plate 4531. Cigarette box, 4½" long, green mark #47, $500.00 – 600.00.

Plate 4532. Vase, 6" tall, green mark #47, $850.00 – 1,000.00.

Plate 4533. Ink blotter, 4" long, green mark #47, $350.00 – 450.00.

Plate 4534. Stamp box, 2¾" wide, green mark #47, $175.00 – 225.00.

Galle Scene

Plate 4535. Vase, 5¼" tall, green mark #47, $400.00 – 500.00.

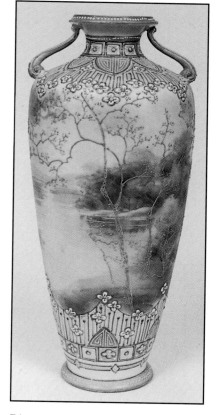

Plate 4536. Vase, 14" tall, blue mark #52, $1,500.00 – 1,750.00.

Plate 4537. Humidor, 5½" tall, green mark #47, $1,900.00 – 2,300.00.

Plate 4538. Cigarette holder, 3½" tall, blue mark #52, $250.00 – 325.00.

Plate 4539. Tray, 11" long, blue mark #52, $600.00 – 750.00.

American Indian Design

Plate 4540. Pitcher, 4¾" tall, mark scratched off, $135.00 – 175.00.

Plate 4541. Vase, 12" tall, blue mark #38, $650.00 – 800.00.

Plate 4542. Matchbox holder, 2¾" tall, green mark #47, $225.00 – 275.00.

Plate 4543. Vase, 8½" tall, mark #47, $750.00 – 950.00.

Plate 4544. Vase, 14" tall, green mark #47, $1,100.00 – 1,300.00.

Man on a Camel Scene

Plate 4545. Vase, 9¾" tall, blue mark #52, $800.00 – 950.00.

Plate 4546. Vase, 14" tall, green mark #47, $1,500.00 – 1,800.00.

Plate 4547. Bowl, 6½" wide, mark #84, $110.00 – 150.00.

Plate 4548. Vase, 10" tall, green mark #47, $850.00 – 950.00.

Plate 4549. Vase, 6" tall, green mark #47, $600.00 – 700.00.

Gouda Design

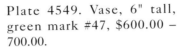

Plate 4551. Ferner, 5½" tall, mark #47, $400.00 – 500.00.

Plate 4552. Humidor, 5" tall, green mark #47, $550.00 – 650.00.

Plate 4550. Humidor, 5" tall, green mark #47, $500.00 – 600.00.

Plate 4553. Basket dish, 7¾" long, mark #47, $225.00 – 300.00.

Plate 4554. Bouillon cup and underplate, 6" wide, green mark #47, $250.00 – 325.00.

Woodland Scene

Plate 4555. Compote, 6" tall, green mark #47, $400.00 – 500.00.

Plate 4556. Vase, 8¼" tall, green mark #47, $1,100.00 – 1,300.00.

Plate 4557. Wall plaque, 11¼" wide, blue mark #52, $800.00 – 950.00.

Plate 4558. Mustard jar, 3" tall, green mark #47, $300.00 – 350.00.

Plate 4559. Condensed milk container, 6" tall, green mark #47, $1,800.00 – 2,200.00.

Plate 4560. Vase, 8½" tall, green mark #47, $1,200.00 – 1,500.00.

Plate 4561. Vase, 8½" tall, green mark #47, $1,200.00 – 1,500.00.

Plate 4563. Shaving mug, 4" tall, blue mark #52, $500.00 – 650.00.

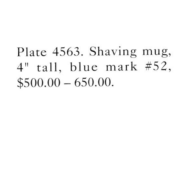

Plate 4562. Vase, 8½" tall, blue mark #47, $1,100.00 – 1,300.00.

Plate 4564. Ewer, 7" tall, blue mark #52, $800.00 – 900.00.

Airplane Scene

Plate 4565. Powder jar, 3½" wide, green mark #47, $600.00 – 700.00.

Plate 4566. Ashtray, 5" wide, green mark #47, $600.00 – 700.00.

Plate 4567. Loving cup, 4" tall, green mark #47, $600.00 – 700.00.

Wall Plaques

Plate 4568. Mirror image of Plate 357, 10" wide, blue mark #47, $550.00 – 650.00.

Plate 4569. Rectangular, 8" x 10", green mark #47, $2,400.00 – 3,000.00.

Plate 4570. 11" wide, green mark #47, $500.00 – 600.00.

Plate 4571. 10" wide, green mark #47, $500.00 – 600.00.

Plate 4572. 8" wide, green mark #47, $750.00 – 900.00.

Plate 4573. Similar to Plate 890, 8¾" wide, green mark #47, $500.00 – 600.00.

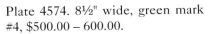

Plate 4574. 8½" wide, green mark #4, $500.00 – 600.00.

Plate 4575. Charger, 14" wide, mark #254, $600.00 – 700.00.

Plate 4576. 9" wide, green mark #47, $350.00 – 450.00.

Plate 4577. 10" wide, green mark #47, $350.00 – 450.00.

Plate 4578. 9" wide, green mark #47, $350.00 – 450.00.

Plate 4579. 10" wide, green mark #47, $250.00 – 350.00.

Plate 4580. 10" wide, green mark #47, $300.00 – 400.00.

Plate 4581. 10" wide, mark #17, $300.00 – 400.00.

Plate 4582. 10" wide, green mark #47, $300.00 – 400.00.

Plate 4583. 10" wide, green mark #47, $350.00 – 450.00.

Plate 4584. 10¼" wide, green mark #47, $350.00 – 450.00.

Plate 4585. 9" wide, green mark #47, $300.00 – 400.00.

Plate 4586. 9" wide, green mark #47, $300.00 – 400.00.

Plate 4587. 9" wide, green mark #47, $300.00 – 400.00.

Plate 4588. 10¼" wide, green mark #47, $350.00 – 450.00.

Plate 4589. 8" wide, green mark #47, $300.00 – 400.00.

Plate 4590. 10" wide, green mark #47, $300.00 – 400.00.

Plate 4591. 10" wide, green mark #47, $450.00 – 550.00.

Plate 4592. 10" wide, green mark #47, $600.00 – 700.00.

Plate 4593. 9" wide, unmarked, $300.00 – 400.00.

Plate 4594. 10" wide, blue mark #52, $300.00 – 400.00.

Plate 4595. 10" wide, blue mark #52, $400.00 – 500.00.

Plate 4596. 8¾" wide, green mark #99, $250.00 – 325.00.

Plate 4597. 10" wide, green mark #52, $400.00 – 500.00.

Plate 4598. 12" wide, green mark #47, $750.00 – 1,000.00.

Plate 4599. 11" wide, green mark #47, $400.00 – 500.00.

Plate 4600. 10" wide, green mark #47, $350.00 – 450.00.

Plate 4601. 10" wide, green mark #47, $300.00 – 400.00.

Plate 4602. 11" wide, green mark #47, $400.00 – 500.00.

Plate 4603. 11" wide, blue mark #52, $400.00 – 500.00.

Plate 4604. 9½" wide, blue mark #52, $300.00 – 400.00.

Plate 4605. 8½" wide, blue mark #52, $275.00 – 350.00.

Plate 4606. 10" wide, green mark #47, $300.00 – 400.00.

Plate 4607. 9½" wide, blue mark #47, $300.00 – 400.00.

Plate 4608. 9½" wide, green mark #47, $300.00 – 400.00.

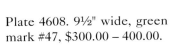

Urns & Vases

Plate 4610. Pair of covered urns, 10" tall, green mark #52, $1,200.00 – 1,400.00 each.

Plate 4609. 11" wide, blue mark #52, $400.00 – 500.00.

Plate 4611. Covered urn, 10" tall, blue mark #52, $1,200.00 – 1,400.00.

Plate 4612. Bolted urn, 12" tall, blue mark #52, $750.00 – 850.00.

Plate 4613. Bolted urn, 14" tall, mark #47, $1,100.00 – 1,300.00.

Plate 4614. Bolted urn, 8½" tall, green mark #47, $700.00 – 800.00.

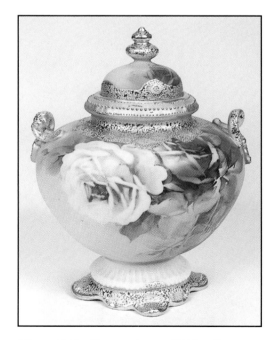

Plate 4615. Covered urn, 7¾" tall, green mark #52, $1,000.00 – 1,200.00.

Plate 4616. Bolted urn, 9" tall, blue mark #47, $500.00 – 600.00.

Plate 4617. Bolted urn, 12" tall, blue mark #52, $900.00 – 1,100.00.

Plate 4618. Bolted urn, 16½" tall, blue mark #52, $1,200.00 – 1,400.00.

Plate 4619. Bolted urn, 18½" tall, blue mark #52, $1,400.00 – 1,600.00.

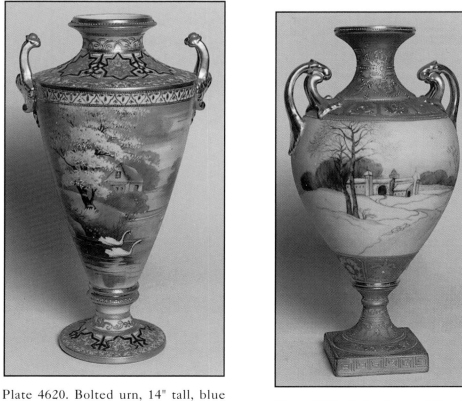

Plate 4620. Bolted urn, 14" tall, blue mark #47, $1,100.00 – 1,300.00.

Plate 4621. Bolted urn, 13" tall, blue mark #47, $1,200.00 – 1,400.00.

Plate 4622. Vase, 18" tall, blue mark #52, $1,100.00 – 1,300.00.

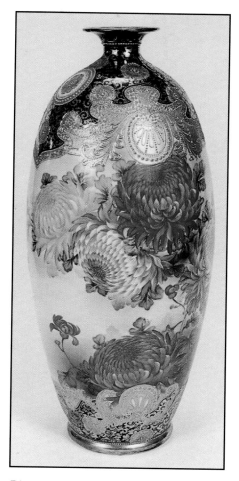

Plate 4623. Vase, 24" tall, blue mark #52, $4,500.00 – 5,500.00.

Plate 4624. Vase, 18" tall, blue mark #52, $1,300.00 – 1,600.00.

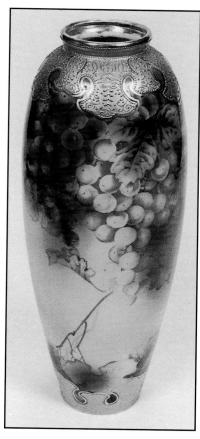

Plate 4625. Vase, 18" tall, blue mark #52, $1,300.00 – 1,600.00.

Plate 4626. Pair of bolted urns, 8" tall, green mark #47, $700.00 – 800.00 each.

Plate 4627. Bolted urn, 12" tall, mark #52, $900.00 – 1,050.00.

Plate 4630. Pair of vases, 9¼" tall, green mark #47, $275.00 – 350.00 each.

Plate 4629. Vase, 15" tall, blue mark #52, $1,200.00 – 1,400.00.

Plate 4628. Left: Vase, 18¼" tall, blue mark #52, $1,500.00 – 1,800.00. Right: Vase, 18¼" tall, blue mark #52, $1,500.00 – 1,800.00.

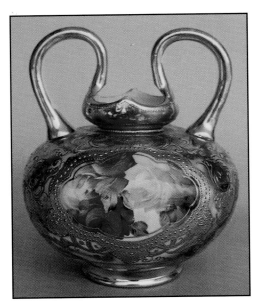

Plate 4632. Vase, 6½" tall, green mark #47, $250.00 – 325.00.

Plate 4631. Vase, 7½" tall, unmarked, $500.00 – 600.00.

Plate 4633. Vase, 8" tall, green mark #47, $450.00 – 550.00.

Plate 4634. Vase, 8½" tall, green mark #52, $400.00 – 500.00.

Plate 4635. Vase, 8½" tall, blue mark #52, $350.00 – 425.00.

Plate 4636. Vase, 17½" tall, blue mark #52, $1,400.00 – 1,600.00.

Plate 4637. Vase, 9½" tall, blue mark #52, $400.00 – 500.00.

Plate 4638. Vase, 9¾" tall, green mark #47, $400.00 – 500.00.

Plate 4639. Vase, 10" tall, green mark #47, $350.00 – 450.00.

Plate 4640. Vase, 8¼" tall, green mark #47, $225.00 – 275.00.

Plate 4641. Vase, 10" tall, green mark #47, $400.00 – 500.00.

Plate 4642. Vase, 10" tall, green mark #47, $500.00 – 575.00.

Plate 4643. Vase, 6" tall, green mark #47, $225.00 – 275.00.

Plate 4644. Pair of bolted urns, 6" tall, mark #230, $225.00 – 275.00 each.

Plate 4645. Vase, 13" tall, mark #52, $900.00 – 1,050.00.

Plate 4646. Vase, 10¼" tall, blue mark #52, $400.00 – 500.00.

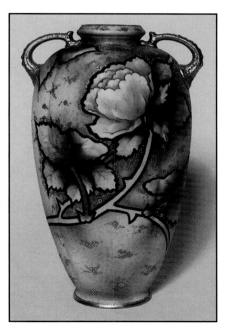

Plate 4647. Vase, 10¼" tall, unmarked, $400.00 – 500.00.

Plate 4648. Vase, 10" tall, green mark #52, $400.00 – 500.00.

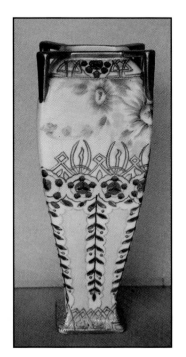

Plate 4649. Vase, 12" tall, green mark #47, $400.00 – 500.00.

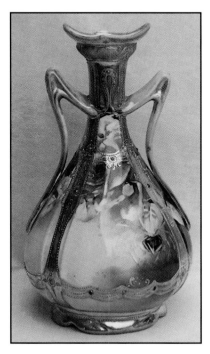

Plate 4650. Vase, 12" tall, blue mark #52, $700.00 – 850.00.

Plate 4651. Vase, 10¾" tall, green mark #47, $400.00 – 500.00.

Plate 4652. Vase, 9¾" tall, unmarked, $400.00 – 500.00.

Plate 4653. Vase, 13" tall, green mark #47, $550.00 – 700.00.

Plate 4654. Vase, 8½" tall, mark #45, $400.00 – 500.00.

Plate 4655. Vase, 11½" tall, mark #7, $400.00 – 500.00.

Plate 4656. Vase, 9¼" tall, green mark #47, $450.00 – 550.00.

Plate 4657. Vase, 12" tall, mark #91, $450.00 – 550.00.

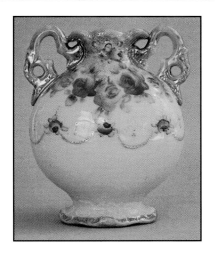

Plate 4658. Vase, 5¼" tall, blue mark #52, $150.00 – 200.00.

Plate 4659. Vase, 10¾" tall, mark #47, $400.00 – 500.00.

Plate 4660. Vase, 11½" tall, mark #47, $500.00 – 600.00.

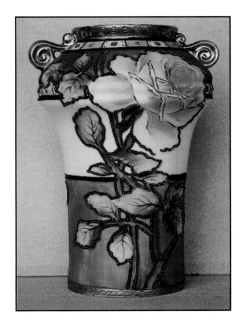

Plate 4661. Vase, 7¼" tall, mark #17, $300.00 – 400.00.

Plate 4662. Vase, 5" tall, mark #70, $300.00 – 400.00.

Plate 4663. Vase, 9" tall, green mark #47, $400.00 – 500.00.

151

Plate 4664. Vase, 8" tall, green mark #52, $400.00 – 500.00.

Plate 4665. Vase, 12¼" tall, green mark #47, $450.00 – 550.00.

Plate 4666. Vase, 9¾" tall, green mark #47, $400.00 – 500.00.

Plate 4667. Vase, 6" tall, green mark #47, $200.00 – 250.00.

Plate 4668. Vase, 7¼" tall, unmarked, $600.00 – 700.00.

Plate 4669. Vase, 7" tall, blue mark #38, $200.00 – 250.00.

Plate 4670. Vase, 11¾" tall, mark #88, $500.00 – 600.00.

Plate 4671. Vase, 6" tall, green mark #47, $225.00 – 260.00.

Plate 4672. Vase, 12" tall, green mark #47, $600.00 – 750.00.

Plate 4674. Vase. 6¼" tall, green mark #47, $250.00 – 310.00.

Plate 4673. Vase, 10½" tall, green mark #47, $400.00 – 500.00.

Plate 4675. Vase, 6" tall, green mark #47, $200.00 – 250.00.

Plate 4676. Vase, 9½" tall, green mark #47, $350.00 – 450.00.

Plate 4677. Vase, 8" tall, green mark #47, $350.00 – 450.00.

Plate 4678. Vase, 12½" tall, green mark #52, $1,000.00 – 1,200.00.

Plate 4679. Vase, 13½" tall, blue mark #52, $1,400.00 – 1,700.00.

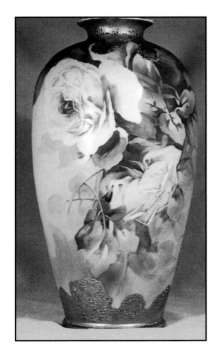

Plate 4680. Vase, 11½" tall, blue mark #52, $900.00 – 1,100.00.

Plate 4681. Vase, 10" tall, blue mark #52, $750.00 – 850.00.

Plate 4682. Vase, 14½" tall, blue mark #52, $1,200.00 – 1,400.00.

Plate 4683. Vase, 10" tall, blue mark #52, $600.00 – 700.00.

Plate 4684. Vase, 16½" tall, blue mark #52, $1,300.00 – 1,600.00.

Plate 4685. Vase, 14" tall, blue mark #52, $700.00 – 900.00.

Plate 4686. Vase, 10" tall, green mark #47, $450.00 – 550.00.

Plate 4687. Left: Vase, 15½" tall, blue mark #52, $1,200.00 – 1,500.00. Right: Vase, 15½" tall, blue mark #52, $1,200.00 – 1,500.00.

Plate 4688. Ewer, 7¼" tall, blue mark #52, $550.00 – 650.00.

Plate 4689. Ewer, 10½" tall, unmarked, $700.00 – 800.00.

Plate 4690. Vase, 13¾" tall, mark #110, $500.00 – 600.00.

Plate 4691. Vase, 8" tall, mark #47, $300.00 – 375.00.

Plate 4692. Vase, 7¼" tall, green mark #47, $275.00 – 335.00.

Plate 4693. Vase, 11¼" tall, green mark #47, $450.00 – 550.00.

Plate 4694. Vase, 8½" tall, blue mark #52, $400.00 – 500.00.

Plate 4695. Vase, 7½" tall, blue mark #47, $350.00 – 425.00.

Plate 4696. Vase, 8½" tall, blue mark #47, $400.00 – 500.00.

Plate 4697. Left: Vase, 5" tall, green mark #7, $150.00 – 200.00. Right: Vase, 5" tall, green mark #47, $150.00 – 200.00.

Plate 4698. Left: Vase, 6" tall, green mark #47, $150.00 – 200.00. Right: Vase, 5" tall, blue mark #218, $150.00 – 200.00.

Plate 4699. Vase, 12" tall, mark #47, $800.00 – 950.00.

Plate 4701. Vase, 3½" tall, green mark #47, $100.00 – 150.00.

Plate 4700. Left: Vase, 8¼" tall, green mark #47, $250.00 – 300.00. Right: Vase, 9" tall, blue mark #47, $300.00 – 375.00.

Plate 4702. Vase, 5½" tall, green mark #47, $150.00 – 200.00.

Plate 4703. Vase, 6" tall, green mark #47, $175.00 – 225.00.

Plate 4704. Vase, 7" tall, green mark #47, $250.00 – 300.00.

Plate 4705. Bottle vase, 8½" tall, blue mark #47, $350.00 – 450.00.

Plate 4706. Vase, 11½" tall, green mark #47, $400.00 – 500.00.

Plate 4707. Vase, 8½" tall, green mark #47, $300.00 – 400.00.

Plate 4708. Vase, 6½" tall, green mark #47, $200.00 – 250.00.

Plate 4709. Vase, 10¼" tall, green mark #47, $400.00 – 500.00.

Plate 4710. Vase, 13" tall, green mark #47, $700.00 – 800.00.

Plate 4711. Vase, 11¼" tall, green mark #47, $550.00 – 625.00.

Plate 4712. Vase, 10" tall, green mark #47, $400.00 – 500.00.

Plate 4713. Vase, 5¾" tall, green mark #47, $175.00 – 225.00.

Plate 4714. Vase, 8½" tall, green mark #47, $400.00 – 500.00.

Plate 4715. Vase, 6" tall, green mark #7, $200.00 – 225.00.

Plate 4716. Vase, 7" tall, blue mark #47, $400.00 – 500.00.

Plate 4717. Vase, 8" tall, green mark #47, $325.00 – 400.00.

Plate 4718. Vase, 7¾" tall, green mark #47, $325.00 – 400.00.

Plate 4719. Vase, 12¼" tall, green mark #47, $500.00 – 600.00.

Plate 4720. Left: Vase, 3" tall, blue mark #52, $100.00 – 135.00. Right: Vase, 3" tall, blue mark #52, $100.00 – 135.00.

Plate 4722. Left: Vase, 5¼" tall, blue mark #52, $135.00 – 165.00. Right: Vase, 5" tall, blue mark #52, $135.00 – 165.00.

Plate 4721. Vase, 6½" tall, green mark #47, $225.00 – 300.00.

Plate 4723. Vase, 5½" tall, blue mark #47, $150.00 – 200.00.

Plate 4724. Left: Vase, 6" tall, green mark #47, $150.00 – 200.00. Right: Vase, 4½" tall, green mark #47, $110.00 – 150.00.

Plate 4725. Vase, 4½" tall, green mark #47, $110.00 – 150.00.

Plate 4726. Vase, 8" tall, mark #47, $400.00 – 500.00.

Plate 4727. Vase, 9" tall, green mark #47, $400.00 – 500.00.

Plate 4728. Vase, 10" tall, mark #47, $450.00 – 550.00.

Plate 4729. Vase, 4½" tall, green mark #47, $300.00 – 350.00.

Plate 4730. Vase, 9" tall, mark #47, $400.00 – 500.00.

Plate 4731. Vase, 7¾" tall, green mark #47, $400.00 – 500.00.

Plate #4732. Pair of vases, 8" tall, green mark #47, $200.00 – 250.00 each.

Plate 4733. Vase, 8" tall, green mark #47, $165.00 – 235.00.

Plate 4734. Left: Vase, 3" tall, mark #230, $100.00 – 135.00. Right: Vase, 3¼" mark #25, $100.00 – 135.00.

Plate 4735. Vase, 6½" tall, green mark #47, $225.00 – 275.00.

Plate 4736. Pair of vases, 4½" tall, green mark #47, $100.00 – 135.00 each.

Plate 4737. Vase, 8½" tall, mark #47, $375.00 – 450.00.

Plate 4738. Vase, 16½"tall, mark #110, $1,600.00 – 2,200.00.

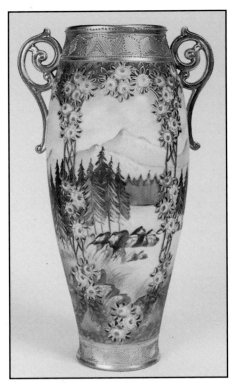

Plate 4739. Vase, 15" tall, green mark #47, $1,200.00 – 1,400.00.

Plate 4740. Vase, 9" tall, mark #38, $375.00 – 450.00.

Plate 4741. Vase, 10" tall, mark #91, $500.00 – 600.00.

Plate 4742. Vase, 10¾" tall, mark #88, $400.00 – 500.00.

Plate 4743. Vase, 8½" tall, green mark #47, $400.00 – 500.00.

Plate 4744. Vase, 11½" tall, green mark #47, $300.00 – 400.00.

Plate 4745. Ewer, 7¼" tall, green mark #47, $400.00 – 500.00.

Plate 4746. Vase, 11½" tall, blue mark #52, $800.00 – 900.00.

Plate 4747. Vase, 12" tall, green mark #47, $1,600.00 – 1,800.00.

Plate 4749. Pair of vases, 12" tall, mark #4, $300.00 – 400.00 each.

Plate 4748. Vase, 10" tall, blue mark #52, $1,000.00 – 1,300.00.

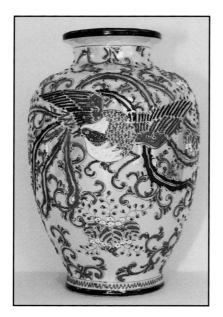

Plate 4750. Vase, 12" tall, mark #32, $400.00 – 500.00.

Plate 4751. Vase, 12" tall, mark #91, $400.00 – 500.00.

Plate 4752. Vase, 7" tall, green mark #47, $350.00 – 425.00.

Plate 4753. Vase, 8" tall, green mark #47, $700.00 – 800.00.

Plate 4754. Vase, 8½" tall, blue mark #52, $900.00 – 1,100.00.

Plate 4756. Left: Vase, 6" tall, green mark #47, $175.00 – 225.00. Middle: Vase, 5¼" tall, green mark #47, $150.00 – 200.00. Right: Vase, 4½" tall, green mark #47, $135.00 – 175.00.

Plate 4755. Vase, 8" tall, blue mark #52, $1,000.00 – 1,200.00.

Plate 4757. Vase, 8¼" tall, green mark #47, $400.00 – 500.00.

Plate 4759. Vase, 12" tall, green mark #47, $600.00 – 700.00.

Plate 4758. Vase, 14" tall, green mark #47, $800.00 – 950.00.

Plate 4760. Vase, 6¾" tall, green mark #47, $225.00 – 275.00.

Plate 4761. Vase, 3¾" tall, green mark #47, $75.00 – 115.00.

Plate 4762. Vase, 6½" tall, green mark #47, $225.00 – 275.00.

Plate 4764. Vase, 9½" tall, mark #52, $400.00 – 500.00.

Plate 4763. Vase, 9½" tall, green mark #47, $400.00 – 500.00.

Plate 4766. Vase, 7½" tall, green mark #47, $375.00 – 450.00.

Plate 4765. Vase, 8¼" tall, green mark #47, $350.00 – 425.00.

Plate 4767. Vase, 5¼" tall, green mark #47, $150.00 – 200.00.

Plate 4769. Vase, 5¾" tall, blue mark #47, $500.00 – 600.00.

Plate 4768. Vase, 7¾" tall, blue mark #52, $700.00 – 800.00.

Plate 4772. Vase, 4" tall, blue mark #47, $75.00 – 100.00.

Plate 4771. Vase, 6" tall, green mark #47, $135.00 – 175.00.

Plate 4770. Vase, 7½" tall, green mark #47, $400.00 – 475.00.

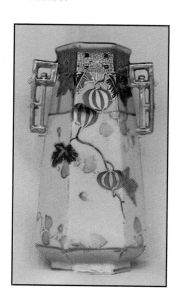

Plate 4773. Vase, 7¾" tall, blue mark #38, $275.00 – 350.00.

Plate 4774. Bolted urn, 7"
tall, mark #228, $300.00 –
350.00.

Plate 4775. Ewer, 7½" tall, mark
#89, $250.00 – 300.00.

Plate 4776. Ewer, 7½" tall, green mark #47,
$400.00 – 500.00.

Plate 4777. Ewer, 12½" tall, blue
mark #52, $700.00 – 850.00.

Plate 4778. Ewer, 12½" tall, blue
mark #52, $700.00 – 850.00.

Plate 4779. Tankard, 14" tall, blue
mark #52, $1,000.00 – 1,300.00.

Chocolate Sets

Plate 4780. Ewer, 11¼" tall, blue mark #52, $600.00 – 700.00.

Plate 4781. Includes four cups and saucers and creamer and sugar bowl; pot is 9" tall, green mark #47, $800.00 – 850.00.

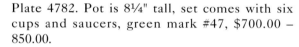

Plate 4782. Pot is 8¼" tall, set comes with six cups and saucers, green mark #47, $700.00 – 850.00.

Plate 4783. Pot is 8½" tall, set comes with six cups and saucers, green mark #47, $650.00 – 750.00.

Plate 4784. Includes six cups and saucers, green mark #47, $1,400.00 – 1,700.00.

Plate 4785. Includes six cups and saucers, blue mark #52, $1,400.00 – 1,700.00.

Plate 4786. Includes six cups and saucers, blue mark #52, $1,800.00 – 2,100.00.

Plate 4787. Pot is 9" tall, mark #103. Includes four cups and saucers. $300.00 – 400.00.

Plate 4788. Pot is 9" tall, set comes with four cups and saucers, green mark #47, $250.00 – 300.00.

Plate 4789. Pot is 9" tall, set includes six cups and saucers, green mark #47, $500.00 – 600.00.

Plate 4790. Pot is 9" tall, includes six cups and saucers, mark #92, $400.00 – 500.00.

Plate 4791. Pot is 10" tall, set includes six cups and saucers, mark #71, $500.00 – 600.00.

Plate 4792. Pot is 9½" tall, set includes two cups and saucers, green mark #47, $250.00 – 300.00.

Plate 4793. Pot is 9½" tall, set includes four cups and saucers, unmarked, $900.00 – 1,100.00.

Plate 4794. Includes four cups and saucers, blue mark #52, $1,700.00 – 2,000.00.

Plate 4795. Pot is 10" tall, set includes 12 cups and saucers, creamer and sugar bowl, green mark #47, $1,500.00 – 2,000.00.

Plate 4796. Chocolate pot, 10" tall, green mark #47, $350.00 – 450.00.

Plate 4797. Chocolate cup and saucer, cup is 2¾" tall, mark #6, $85.00 – 135.00.

Tea Sets & Miscellaneous

Plate 4798. Tea set, five cups and saucers, five luncheon plates, 7½" wide, mark #80, $750.00 – 1,000.00.

Plate 4799. Tray is 11" wide, teapot, 5½" tall, four cups and saucers, creamer and sugar bowl, mark #4, $600.00 – 725.00.

Plate 4800. Creamer or small pitcher, 3" tall, blue mark #52, $125.00 – 160.00.

Plate 4801. Demitasse cup and saucer, mark #6, $85.00 – 135.00.

Plate 4802. Mustache cup with under-plate, green mark #47, $200.00 – 275.00.

Plate 4803. Pot is 5¼" tall, set includes five cups and saucers, creamer and sugar bowl, blue mark #52, $1,700.00 – 2,000.00.

Plate 4804. Set includes six cups and saucers, creamer and sugar bowl, green mark #47, $1,400.00 – 1,700.00.

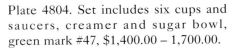

Plate 4805. Set includes six cups and saucers, creamer and sugar bowl, green mark #47, $500.00 – 600.00.

Demitasse Sets

Plate 4806. Pot is 6¾" tall, mark scratched off, $300.00 – 400.00.

Plate 4807. Tea cup and saucer, green mark #47, $30.00 – 45.00.

Plate 4808. Includes six cups and saucers, cups are in copper cup holders made by Manning Bowman, magenta mark #47, $1,000.00 – 1,200.00.

Plate 4809. Tea cup and saucer, blue mark #180, $30.00 – 45.00.

Plate 4810. Pot is 8¼" tall, set includes four cups and saucers, unmarked, $300.00 – 400.00.

Plate 4811. Demitasse pot, 6½" tall, mark #80, $175.00 – 225.00.

Miscellaneous

Plate 4812. Beverage set, tankard is 8½" tall, five mugs, 4¼" tall, green mark #47, $900.00 – 1,100.00.

Plate 4813. Mug, reverse side of Plate 4814.

Plate 4814. Mug, 5" tall, green mark #47, $300.00 – 400.00.

Plate 4815. Mug, 5½" tall, green mark #47, $300.00 – 400.00.

Plate 4816. Mug, 5" tall, green mark #47, $300.00 – 400.00.

Plate 4817. Mug, 5" tall, green mark #47, $300.00 – 400.00.

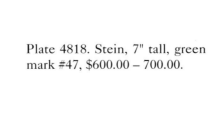

Plate 4818. Stein, 7" tall, green mark #47, $600.00 – 700.00.

Plate 4819. Stein, 7" tall, blue mark #47, $600.00 – 700.00.

Plate 4820. Mug, 7½" tall, mark #52, $300.00 – 400.00.

Plate 4821. Stein, 7" tall, green mark #47, $750.00 – 850.00.

Plate 4822. Pitcher, 6½" tall, blue mark #52, $500.00 – 600.00.

Plate 4824. Ewer/pitcher, 5" tall, blue mark #52, $150.00 – 200.00.

Plate 4825. Pitcher, 4¾" tall, mark #52, $200.00 – 250.00.

Plate 4823. Whiskey jug, 7¼" tall, blue mark #52, $750.00 – 850.00.

Smoking Items

Plate 4826. Humidor, 6½" tall, blue mark #47, $600.00 – 700.00.

Plate 4827. Humidor, 6" tall, green mark #47, $500.00 – 600.00.

Plate 4828. Humidor, 7" tall, blue mark #52, $500.00 – 600.00.

Plate 4829. Humidor, 5½" tall, green mark #47, $600.00 – 700.00.

Plate 4830. Humidor, 6" tall, green mark #47, $550.00 – 650.00.

Plate 4831. Humidor, 6" tall, unmarked, $400.00 – 500.00.

Plate 4832. Humidor, 7" tall, green mark #47, $650.00 – 750.00.

Plate 4833. Humidor, 5" tall, green mark #47, $700.00 – 850.00.

Plate 4834. Humidor, 4½" tall, green mark #47, $500.00 – 600.00.

Plate 4835. Humidor, 6½", green mark #47, $1,100.00 – 1,300.00.

Plate 4836. Humidor, 5½" tall, green mark #47, $450.00 – 500.00.

Plate 4837. Humidor, 5½" tall, mark #351, $500.00 – 600.00.

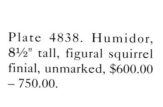

Plate 4838. Humidor, 8½" tall, figural squirrel finial, unmarked, $600.00 – 750.00.

Plate 4839. Matchbox holder and ashtray, 3" tall, unmarked, $150.00 – 200.00.

Plate 4840. Humidor, 8" tall, mark #52, $550.00 – 650.00.

Plate 4841. Ashtray, 5½" wide, green mark #47, $600.00 – 700.00.

Plate 4842. Cigarette holder and tray, tray is 11" long, mark #10, $350.00 – 450.00.

Plate 4843. Match holder, 3½" tall, mark #47, $200.00 – 250.00.

Plate 4844. Match holder, 3" tall, mark #47, $200.00 – 250.00.

Plate 4845. Smoke set, mark #47, $800.00 – 900.00.

Plate 4846. Match box holder, 3¼" tall, blue mark #47, $250.00 – 300.00.

Plate 4847. Ashtray, 4½" wide, mark #47, $450.00 – 550.00.

Plate 4848. Spitoon/ashtray, 3" wide, blue mark #52, $175.00 – 225.00.

Plate 4849. Ashtray, 7" wide, green mark #47, $300.00 – 400.00.

Plate 4850. Cigarette box, 4½" wide, blue mark #47, $400.00 – 475.00.

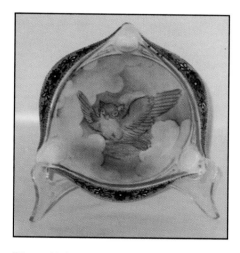

Plate 4851. Ashtray, 5½" wide, mark #17, $200.00 – 275.00.

Plate 4852. Smoke set, green mark #47, $800.00 – 950.00.

Plate 4853. Ashtray, 5½" wide, green mark #47, $200.00 – 275.00.

Plate 4854. Cigarette box, 4½" long, green mark #47, $350.00 – 450.00.

Desk & Toiletry Items

Plate 4855. Desk set, inkwell, blotter, calendar holder, stamp box, tray, green mark #47; inkwell, $325.00 – 400.00, blotter, $250.00 – 300.00, calendar holder, $250.00 – 300.00, stamp box, $200.00 – 275.00, tray, $100.00 – 125.00.

Plate 4856. Ink blotter, 4½" wide, green mark #47, $175.00 – 225.00.

Plate 4857. Inkwell, 2½" tall, green mark #47, $225.00 – 275.00.

Plate 4858. Top row: Powder box, 2½" wide, green mark #47, $40.00 – 60.00. Powder box, 2½" wide, green mark #47, $30.00 – 50.00. Powder box, 2½" wide, mark #68, $40.00 – 60.00. Bottom row: Powder box, 2½" wide, mark #84, $40.00 – 60.00. Powder box, 2½" wide, mark #84, $30.00 – 50.00. Powder box, 2½" wide, mark #84, $40.00 – 60.00.

Plate 4859. Left: Stamp box, 4" long, green mark #47, $90.00 – 135.00. Right: Stamp box, 3¾" long, green mark #47, $90.00 – 135.00.

Plate 4860. Ring holder, 3¾" wide, mark #52, $90.00 – 135.00.

Dresser Items

Plate 4861. Top row: Trinket box, 3¼" long,, green mark #47, $90.00 – 130.00 Trinket box, 3¼" long, green mark #47, $120.00 – 150.00. Trinket box, 3¼" long, mark #84, $80.00 – 110.00. Bottom row: Trinket box, 3¼" long, blue mark #47, $90.00 – 130.00. Trinket box, 3 _" long, green mark #47, $100.00 – 135.00. Trinket box, 3¼" long, green mark #47, $80.00 – 110.00.

Plate 4862. Trinket box, 1¾" dia., magenta mark #47, $50.00 – 75.00.

Plate 4863. Left: Trinket box, 3¾" tall, blue mark #52, $150.00 – 200.00. Middle: Trinket box, 3¾" long, green mark #47, $110.00 – 150.00. Right: Trinket box, 3¾" long, green mark #47, $100.00 – 130.00.

Plate 4864. Powder box, 2" tall, mark #47, $120.00 – 150.00.

Plate 4865. Dresser set, green mark #47, $1,000.00 – 1,200.00.

Plate 4866. Trinket box, 3½" wide, green mark #47, $90.00 – 130.00.

Plate 4867. Dresser set, tray is 11½" long, green mark #47, $950.00 – 1,050.00.

Plate 4868. Powder box, handwritten on it is "Minnie 1915," 3" wide, mark #84, $40.00 – 60.00.

Plate 4869. Dresser items: ring tree, powder jar, trinket box, trinket box, all are marked blue #52, ring tree, $100.00 – 125.00; powder jar, $80.00 – 110.00; trinket box, $100.00 – 130.00; trinket box, $110.00 – 140.00.

Plate 4870. Trinket box, 5" wide, blue mark #52, $150.00 – 200.00.

Plate 4871. Trinket box, 4½" wide, blue mark #52, $130.00 – 160.00.

Plate 4872. Left: Trinket box, 2½" wide, mark #84, $30.00 – 50.00. Right: Powder box, 3¾" wide, blue mark #52, $40.00 – 60.00.

Plate 4873. Trinket box, 3½" tall, mark #80, $75.00 – 120.00.

Plate 4874. Left to right: Hatpin holder, 4¾" tall, mark #47, $90.00 – 130.00. Hatpin holder, 5" tall, mark #80, $110.00 – 150.00. Hatpin holder, 4¾" tall, mark #47, $90.00 – 130.00. Hatpin holder, 4¾" tall, mark #47, $90.00 – 130.00.

Plate 4875. Trinket box, 4½" long, green mark #47, $140.00 – 180.00.

Plate 4876. Talcum powder flask, 5" tall, green mark #47, $140.00 – 180.00.

Plate 4877. Pair of trinket boxes, 2" tall, green mark #47, $45.00 – 65.00 each.

Plate 4878. Hair receiver and powder box, 3½" tall, green mark #47, $150.00 – 200.00.

Plate 4879. Hatpin holder, 4¾" tall, mark #84, $90.00 – 130.00.

Plate 4880. Dresser set, tray is 9" long, mark #84, $225.00 – 275.00.

Plate 4882. Nail buffer, 3¾" long, unmarked, $200.00 – 250.00.

Plate 4884. Dresser tray, mark #106, $85.00 – 115.00.

Plate 4881. Left to right: Ring tree, 3½" wide, blue mark #52, $100.00 – 130.00. Ring tree, 3" wide, green mark #47, $90.00 – 120.00. Ring tree, 3½" wide, blue mark #52, $100.00 – 130.00.

Plate 4883. Dresser tray, 11½" long, magenta mark #47, $140.00 – 180.00.

Plate 4885. Dresser tray, 11¾" long, green mark #47, $80.00 – 110.00.

Plate 4886. Trinket box, 3½" long, green mark #47, $90.00 – 130.00.

Other Pieces

Plate 4887. Ferner, 8" wide, green mark #47, $350.00 – 425.00.

Plate 4888. Hanging ferner, 4½" tall, green mark #47, $550.00 – 650.00.

Plate 4889. Ferner, 6" wide, green mark #47, $225.00 – 275.00.

Plate 4890. Ferner, 10½" wide, unmarked, $450.00 – 550.00.

Plate 4891. Ferner, 7½" wide, green mark #47, $300.00 – 375.00.

Plate 4892. Ferner, 7¼" wide, blue mark #52, $250.00 – 300.00.

Plate 4893. Ferner, 7½" wide, mark #39, $235.00 – 280.00.

Plate 4894. Ferner, has original insert, 3¼" tall, green mark #47, $450.00 – 550.00.

Plate 4895. Ferner, 8" wide, green mark #47, $200.00 – 250.00.

Plate 4896. Ferner, 10" wide, green mark #47, $600.00 – 700.00.

Plate 4897. Shaving mug, 3½" tall, unmarked, $175.00 – 225.00.

Plate 4898. Left to right: Shaving mug, 3¾" tall, mark #84, $175.00 – 225.00. Shaving mug, 3¾" tall, mark #84, $140.00 – 180.00. Shaving mug, 3¾" tall, mark #84, $140.00 – 180.00. Shaving mug, 3¾" tall, mark #84, $140.00 – 180.00.

Plate 4899. Cracker/biscuit jar, 8" tall, unmarked, $400.00 – 500.00.

Plate 4900. Cracker/biscuit jar, 7½" tall, unmarked, $400.00 – 500.00.

Plate 4901. Cracker/biscuit jar, 8½" tall, green mark #47, $600.00 – 700.00.

Plate 4902. Cracker/biscuit jar, 9½" wide, mark #80, $250.00 – 300.00.

Plate 4903. Cracker/biscuit jar, 6½" tall, green mark #47, $225.00 – 275.00.

Plate 4904. Cracker/biscuit jar, 8½" tall, green mark #47, $1,500.00 – 1,800.00.

Plate 4906. Salt dish, 3¾" long, green mark #47, $15.00 – 20.00.

Plate 4905. Nut set, master bowl is 6" wide, small ones are 2¾" wide, green mark #47, $150.00 – 200.00.

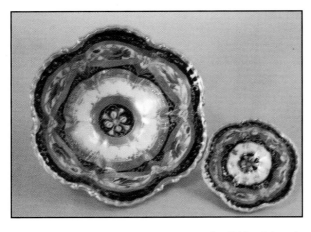

Plate 4907. Nut set, master bowl is 5¾" wide, six individual ones are 2¾" wide, mark #89, $225.00 – 275.00.

Plate 4908. Ten pedestalled nut dishes, 1½" tall, green mark #47, $200.00 – 265.00 set.

Plate 4910. Nut dishes, each 1½" wide, mark #25, $20.00 – 30.00 each.

Plate 4909. Nut set, master bowl is 5¾" wide, blue mark #52, $175.00 – 225.00.

Plate 4911. Small cake or serving plate, 7½" wide, magenta mark #47, $125.00 – 150.00.

Plate 4912. Cake plate, 10½" wide, blue mark #52, $550.00 – 650.00.

Plate 4913. Bread and butter set, large plate is 7½" wide, small ones are 4¾" wide, magenta mark #47, $150.00 – 200.00.

Plate 4914. Sandwich tray, 11½" wide, blue mark #52, $450.00 – 550.00.

Plate 4915. Cake set, serving plate is 10½" wide, green mark #47, $200.00 – 250.00.

Plate 4916. Cake plate, 9½" wide, blue mark #52, $175.00 – 235.00.

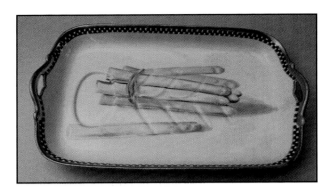

Plate 4917. Asparagus tray, 11¾" long, comes with six plates, one shown in Plate 4919, green mark #47, $250.00 – 300.00 set.

Plate 4918. Cake plate, 11" wide, blue mark #52, $175.00 – 225.00.

Plate 4919. Asparagus plate, 7½" wide, one of six in set, matches tray in Plate 4917, green mark #47, $250.00 – 300.00 set.

Plate 4920. Cake plate, 10½" wide, magenta mark #47, $90.00 – 125.00.

Plate 4921. Cake plate, 10¾" wide, mark #103, $175.00 – 225.00.

Plate 4922. Cake plate, 9½" wide, green mark #52, $150.00 – 200.00.

Plate 4923. Punch set, bowl is 16" wide, cups are 3" tall, blue mark #52, $3,700.00 – 4,500.00.

Plate 4924. Covered jar, 5½" tall, green mark #47, $300.00 – 400.00.

Plate 4925. Bowl, 10¼" wide, green mark #52, $350.00 – 450.00.

Plate 4926. Bowl, 11¼" wide, unmarked, $375.00 – 475.00.

Plate 4927. Bowl, 10¼" wide, blue mark #52, $350.00 – 450.00.

Plate 4928. Bowl, 10½" wide, blue mark #52, $350.00 – 450.00.

Plate 4929. Bowl set, large bowl is 9¼" wide, six small ones are 5" wide, blue mark #47, $375.00 – 475.00.

Plate 4930. Bowl set, large bowl is 9½" wide, small ones are 5½" wide, mark #81, $375.00 – 475.00.

Plate 4931. Bowl, 10½" wide, green mark #47, $140.00 – 185.00.

Plate 4932. Bowl, 7" wide, mark #52, $275.00 – 350.00.

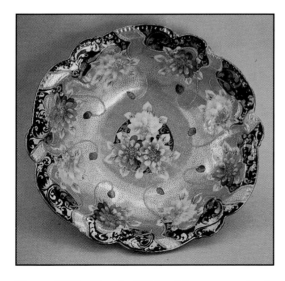

Plate 4934. Bowl, 10½" wide, unmarked, $350.00 – 450.00.

Plate 4933. Bowl, 9¾" wide, unmarked, $350.00 – 450.00.

Plate 4935. Bowl, 7¼" wide, green mark #47, $125.00 – 165.00.

Plate 4936. Bowl, 8½" wide, blue mark #52, $225.00 – 300.00.

Plate 4937. Bowl, 7¾" wide, green mark #47, $225.00 – 275.00.

Plate 4938. Bowl, 10½" wide, blue mark #52, $250.00 – 325.00.

Plate 4939. Bowl, 10¾" wide, green mark #47, $350.00 – 400.00.

Plate 4940. Bowl, 10½" wide, green mark #47, $350.00 – 400.00.

Plate 4941. Bowl, 9½" wide, green mark #47, $250.00 – 300.00.

Plate 4942. Bowl, 7¼" wide, green mark #47, $150.00 – 200.00.

Plate 4943. Bowl, 7½" wide, blue mark #52, $150.00 – 200.00.

Plate 4944. Bowl, 8½" wide, green mark #52 (leaf is missing), $150.00 – 200.00.

Plate 4945. Bowl, 10¼" wide, green mark #47, $250.00 – 300.00.

Plate 4946. Bowl, 7¼" long, blue mark #52, $150.00 – 200.00.

Plate 4947. Bowl, 7" wide, green mark #47, $150.00 – 200.00.

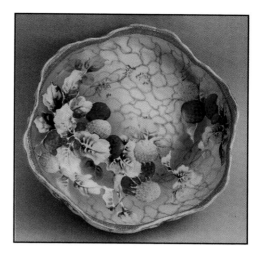

Plate 4948. Bowl, 8½" wide, blue mark #52, $175.00 – 225.00.

Plate 4949. Bowl, 7¼" long, blue mark #52, $175.00 – 225.00.

Plate 4950. Left: Bowl, 7½" wide, mark #81, $200.00 – 250.00. Right: Bowl, 6½" wide, mark #81, $175.00 – 225.00.

Plate 4951. Bowl, 8½" wide, green mark #47, $200.00 – 250.00.

Plate 4952. Left: Bowl, 6" wide, green mark #47, $100.00 – 150.00. Right: Bowl, 6" wide, green mark #47, $100.00 – 150.00.

Plate 4953. Bowl, 7" wide, blue mark #47, $135.00 – 175.00.

Plate 4954. Bowl, 4½" wide, green mark #43, $60.00 – 85.00.

Plate 4955. Bowl, 9½" wide, mark #80, $80.00 – 125.00.

Plate 4956. Bowl, 8" wide, mark #47, $90.00 – 140.00.

Plate 4957. Nappy, 7" wide, mark #84, $90.00 – 140.00.

Plate 4958. Left: Nappy, 5½" long, blue mark #52, $130.00 – 170.00. Right: Nappy, 6½" long, blue mark #52, $140.00 – 180.00.

Plate 4959. Basket dish, 7" long, magenta mark #47, $140.00 – 180.00.

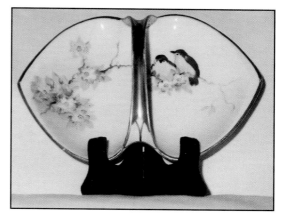

Plate 4960. Basket dish, 7" long, green mark #47, $140.00 – 180.00.

Plate 4961. Bowl, 7¾" long, mark #81, $150.00 – 200.00.

Plate 4962. Bowl, 7½" wide, mark #80, $150.00 – 200.00.

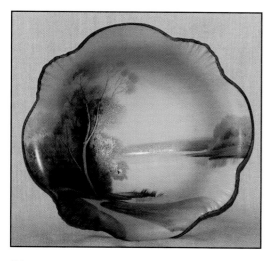

Plate 4963. Bowl, 8½" wide, green mark #47, $150.00 – 200.00.

Plate 4964. Bowl, 6" wide, green mark #47, $150.00 – 200.00.

Plate 4965. Salt and pepper shakers, 2¼" tall, green mark #47, $50.00 – 75.00.

Plate 4966. Salt and pepper shakers, 3½" tall, unmarked, $50.00 – 75.00.

Plate 4967. Creamer and sugar bowl, green mark #47, $100.00 – 150.00.

Plate 4968. Left: Creamer, 2½" tall, green mark #47, $30.00 – 45.00. Right: Creamer, 2½" tall, green mark #47, $30.00 – 45.00.

Plate 4969. Creamer and sugar bowl, green mark #47, $175.00 – 225.00.

Plate 4970. Creamer and sugar bowl, green mark #47, $175.00 – 225.00.

Plate 4971. Nappy, 6½" long, mark #47, $100.00 – 135.00.

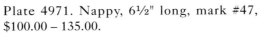

Plate 4972. Celery dish, 13¼" long, blue mark #52, $225.00 – 300.00.

Plate 4973. Pitcher, 3" tall, green mark #47, $50.00 – 70.00.

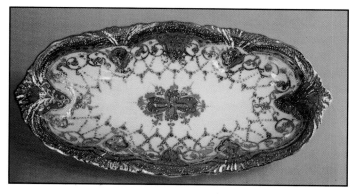

Plate 4974. Celery dish, 12" long, blue mark #52, $225.00 – 300.00.

Plate 4975. Compote, 5¾" wide, blue mark #52, $125.00 – 165.00.

Plate 4976. Celery dish, 11½" long, mark #82, $150.00 – 200.00.

Plate 4977. Tray, 13" long, green mark #52, $200.00 – 250.00.

Plate 4978. Toothpick holder, 3" tall, green mark #47, $100.00 – 135.00.

Plate 4979. Relish dish, 9" long, green mark #47, $90.00 – 135.00.

Plate 4980. Plate, 7¾" wide, mark #180, $30.00 – 50.00.

Plate 4981. Celery set, green mark #47, $200.00 – 250.00.

Plate 4982. Toothpick holder, 4¾" tall, green mark #47, $100.00 – 135.00.

Plate 4983. Toothpick holder, 3" tall, green mark #47, $100.00 – 135.00.

Plate 4984. Platter, 14" long, mark #81, $300.00 – 400.00.

Plate 4985. Toothpick holder, 2½" tall, mark #47, $75.00 – 110.00.

Plate 4986. Game platter, 17" long, blue mark #52, $800.00 – 900.00.

Plate 4987. Plate, 11" wide, green mark #47, $275.00 – 350.00.

Plate 4988. Fish plate, 9" wide, green mark #47, $200.00 – 265.00.

Plate 4989. Celery dish, 12" long, green mark #47, $200.00 – 250.00.

Plate 4990. Toothpick holder, 2" tall, mark #52, $110.00 – 160.00.

Plate 4991. Relish dish, 9½" long, mark #80, $150.00 – 200.00.

Plate 4992. Butter pat, 3¾" wide, mark #254, $15.00 – 25.00.

Plate 4993. Left to right: Small pitcher, 3" tall, green mark #52, $60.00 – 90.00. Toothpick holder, 2¼" tall, green mark #52, $60.00 – 90.00. Tooth-pick holder, 1¾" tall, green mark #52, $60.00 – 90.00. Trinket box, 1½" tall, blue mark #84, $50.00 – 70.00.

Plate 4994. Heart-shaped trinket dish, 4½" long, green mark #47, $50.00 – 70.00.

Plate 4995. Plate, 7½" wide, green mark #47, $50.00 – 70.00.

Plate 4996. Plate, 7½" wide, mark #81, $50.00 – 70.00.

Plate 4997. Plate, 9½" wide, blue mark #52, $150.00 – 200.00.

Plate 4998. Plate, 10" wide, mark #89, $150.00 – 200.00.

Plate 4999. Plate, 8¾" wide, mark #81, $50.00 – 70.00.

Plate 5000. Plate, 9½" wide, blue mark #52, $30.00 – 50.00.

Plate 5001. Slanted cheese dish, 8" long, blue mark #52, $250.00 – 300.00.

Plate 5002. Jam jar, mark #47, $125.00 – 160.00.

Plate 5003. Left: Bowl, 5½" wide, blue mark #52, $70.00 – 9.00. Right: Mayonnaise set, 4½" wide, blue mark #52, $100.00 – 135.00.

Plate 5005. Left and right: Creamer and sugar bowl, mark #10, $75.00 – 115.00. Middle: Toothpick holder, 2" tall, mark #10, $60.00 – 80.00.

Plate 5004. Bouillon cup and underplate, plate is 5½" wide, mark #81, $150.00 – 200.00.

Plate 5006. Pancake server, 8¾" wide, mark #80, $135.00 – 165.00.

Plate 5007. Sauce set, underplate is 7" long, green mark #47, $135.00 – 165.00.

Plate 5008. Mayonnaise set, mark #47, $135.00 – 165.00.

Plate 5009. Left: Mayonnaise set, bowl, 4½" wide, blue mark #84, $100.00 – 135.00. Right: Mayonnaise set, bowl, 4½" wide, blue mark #84, $100.00 – 135.00.

Plate 5010. Cheese and cracker dish, 8½" wide, mark #180, $75.00 – 110.00.

Plate 5011. Berry bowl and underplate, bowl is 5½" wide, blue mark #47, $110.00 – 140.00.

Plate 5012. Left to right: Sugar shaker, 4½" tall, blue mark #52, $250.00 – 300.00. Wall plaque, 8¼" wide, blue mark #52, $250.00 – 300.00. Egg cup, 2½" tall, blue mark #52, $160.00 – 210.00.

Dolls

Plate 5013. Doll, 4½" tall, incised with mark #55, $165.00 – 200.00.

Plate 5014. Left: Doll, 4⅝" tall, incised with mark #55, $100.00 – 125. Right: Doll, 4⅝" tall, incised with mark #51, $100.00 – 125.00.

Plate 5015. Left to right: Doll, 4" tall, mark #55 stamped on bottom of feet, $135.00 – 175.00. Doll, 4" tall, flange neck, bisque head, mark #55, $90.00 – 130.00. Doll, 2½" tall, flange neck, bisque head, mark #55, $90.00 – 130.00. Doll, 4½" tall, mark #55, $110.00 – 135.00.

Plate 5016. Doll, 5" tall, 7¼" tall with hat, incised with mark #55, $125.00 – 150.00.

Plate 5017. Doll, 5¼" tall, incised with mark #55, $135.00 – 160.00.

Plate 5018. Doll, 5" tall, mark #55, $135.00 – 160.00.

Plate 5019. Doll, 5½" tall, mark #55 stamped in ink, $100.00 – 135.00.

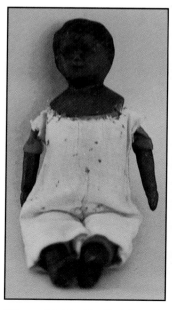

Plate 5020. Doll, 7" tall, mark #302, $150.00 – 185.00.

Plate 5021. Doll, Hiawatha, 4¼" tall, mark #55 stamped in ink on bottom of feet, $140.00 – 170.00.

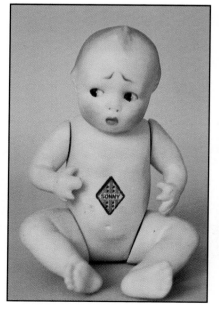

Plate 5022. Doll, Sonny, 6¾" tall, mark #55 plus Sonny sticker, #158, very rare doll, $200.00 – 250.00.

Plate 5023. Doll, Ladykin, 3½" tall, mark #55, $135.00 – 165.00.

Plate 5024. Doll, 6½" tall, mark #322, $140.00 – 170.00.

Plate 5025. Figural soldier, 4¾" tall, incised with mark #55, $175.00 – 225.00.

Plate 5026. Doll, 6¾" tall, crepe paper dress, mark #55, $135.00 – 160.00.

Plate 5027. Doll, 3½" tall, mark #139, $100.00 – 135.00.

Plate 5028. Doll, 5½" tall, cloth body, bisque head/shoulderplate, mark #55, $90.00 – 110.00.

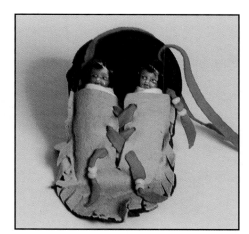

Plate 5029. Souvenir dolls in original felt holder, partially painted to look like Indians, mark #55, $135.00 – 160.00.

Plate 5030. Doll, 4½" tall, mark #55, $100.00 – 135.00.

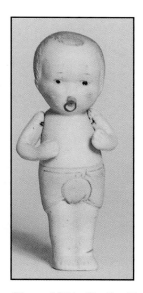

Plate 5031. Doll, 4" tall, incised with mark #55, $100.00 – 135.00.

Plate 5032. Doll, 4½" tall, mark #55, $140.00 – 170.00.

Plate 5033. Miniature cup and saucer, saucer is 1½" wide, written on saucer, "Lillie & Jackson Feb 10, 1903," saucer is marked Japan, $15.00 – 20.00.

Plate 5034. Doll in bathtub, tub is 3¼" long, doll is 2½" tall, both incised with mark #55, $110.00 – 140.00.

Plate 5035. Pair of dolls, 7½" tall, flange necks, cloth bodies, bisque arms and legs, mark #55, $125.00 – 160.00 each.

Plate 5036. Doll, 5" tall, bisque head, composition body, mark #324, $90.00 – 110.00.

Plate 5037. Doll, 6½" tall, five-piece composition body, painted eyes, open mouth, mark #142, $120.00 – 150.00.

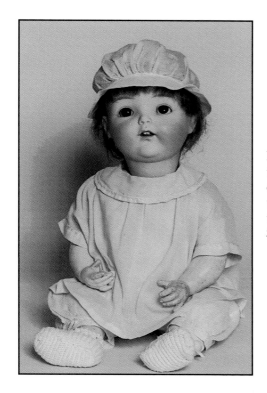

Plate 5038. Doll, 22" tall, brown sleep eyes, open mouth with two upper teeth, molded tongue, mark #350, $700.00 – 800.00.

Plate 5039. Doll, 11½" tall, blue set eyes, open – closed mouth with painted teeth, mark #323, $250.00 – 300.00.

Plate 5040. Doll, Hilda look-alike, 22" tall, oyster shell body, blue sleep eyes, open mouth with two upper teeth, molded tongue, original mohair wig, mark #285, $900.00 – 1,000.00.

Plate 5041. Doll, 17" tall, brown sleep eyes, open mouth with two upper teeth, composition body, mark #285, $550.00 – 600.00.

Plate 5042. Doll, 15" tall, oyster shell body, blue sleep eyes, open mouth with two upper teeth, mohair wig, mark #215, $400.00 – 450.00.

Plate 5043. Doll, bisque head, composition body, blue sleep eyes, open mouth with two upper teeth, mark #182, $200.00 – 250.00.

Plate 5044. Doll, 14" tall, composition body, open mouth with two upper teeth, brown sleep eyes, mark #355, $350.00 – 400.00.

Plate 5045. Doll, 17" tall, Hilda look-alike, blue eyes, open mouth with two upper teeth, mark #155, $600.00 – 700.00.

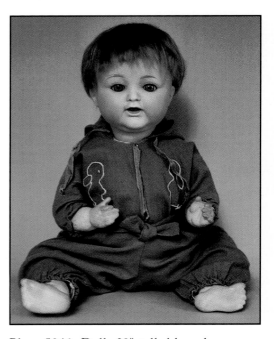

Plate 5046. Doll, 20" tall, blue sleep eyes, open mouth, molded tongue, oyster shell body, mark #348, $600.00 – 650.00.

Plate 5048. Doll, 15" tall, brown sleep eyes, molded celluloid tongue, mohair wig, mark #270, $325.00 – 375.00.

Plate 5047. Doll, Hilda look-alike, 20½" tall, brown sleep eyes, open mouth with two upper teeth, original mohair wig, mark #211, $800.00 – 900.00.

Plate 5049. Doll, 24" tall, brown sleep eyes, open mouth with four upper teeth, mark #168, $475.00 – 525.00.

Plate 5050. Doll, 24" tall, brown sleep eyes, open mouth with four upper teeth, ball jointed composition body, mark #215, $500.00 – 550.00.

Plate 5051. Doll, 24" tall, blue sleep eyes, open mouth with two upper teeth, mark #354, $450.00 – 500.00.

Plate 5052. Doll, 24" tall, composition body, brown sleep eyes, mark #20, $400.00 – 450.00.

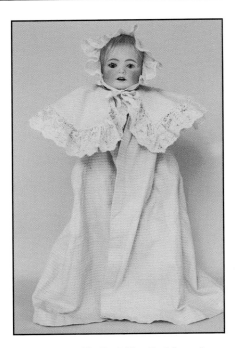

Plate 5053. Doll, 14" tall, blue sleep eyes, mark #353, $350.00 – 400.00.

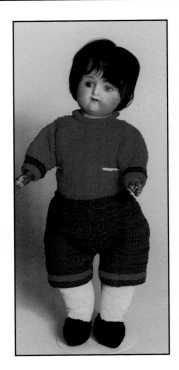

Plate 5054. Doll, 17½" tall, blue sleep eyes, open mouth with four upper teeth, cloth straw-stuffed body with leather hands, mark #352, $250.00 – 300.00.

Plate 5055. Doll, 29" tall, composition body, blue sleep eyes, open mouth with two upper teeth, mark #356, $500.00 – 600.00.

Plate 5056. Doll, 27" tall, blue sleep eyes, composition body, open mouth with four upper teeth, mark #347, $550.00 – 600.00.

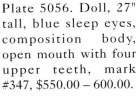

Glossary

American Indian design: A popular collectible on Nippon porcelain; these designs include the Indian in a canoe, Indian warrior, Indian hunting wild game, and the Indian maiden.

Apricot (ume): In Japan, stands for strength and nobility, also a symbol of good luck.

Art Deco: A style of decoration which hit its peak in Europe and America around 1925 although items were manufactured with this decor as early as 1910. The style was modernistic; geometric patterns were popular. Motifs used were shapes such as circles, rectangles, cylinders, and cones.

Art Nouveau: The name is derived from the French words meaning "new art." During the period of 1885 – 1925, artists tended to use bolder colors, and realism was rejected. Free-flowing designs were used, breaking away from the imitations of the past.

Artist signed: Items signed by the artist. Most signatures appear to be those of Western artists, probably painted during the heyday of hand painting chinaware at the turn of the century.

Azalea pattern: Pattern found on Nippon items, pink azaleas with green to gray leaves and gold rims. Nippon-marked pieces match the Noritake-marked Azalea pattern items. The Azalea pattern was originally offered by the Larkin Co. to its customers as premiums.

Backstamp: Mark found on Nippon porcelain items identifying the manufacturer, exporter or importer, and country of origin.

Bamboo tree: In Japan, symbolic of strength, faithfulness, and honesty, also a good luck symbol. The bamboo resists the storm, but it yields to it and rises again.

Beading: Generally a series of clay dots applied on Nippon porcelain, very often painted over in gold. Later Nippon pieces merely had dots of enameling.

Biscuit: Clay which has been fired but not glazed.

Bisque: Same as biscuit, term also used by collectors to describe a matte finish on an item.

Blank: Greenware or bisque items devoid of decoration.

Blown-out items: This term is used by collectors and dealers for items that have a molded relief pattern embossed on by the mold in which the article was shaped. It is not actually "blown-out" as the glass items are, but the pattern is raised from the item (see molded relief).

Bottger, Johann F.: A young German alchemist who supposedly discovered the value of kaolin in making porcelain. This discovery helped to revolutionize the china making industry in Europe beginning in the early 1700s.

Carp: Fish that symbolizes strength and perseverance.

Casting: The process of making reproductions by pouring slip into molds.

Cha no yu: Japanese tea ceremony.

Chargers: Archaic term for large platters or plates.

Cheese hard clay: Same as leather hard clay.

Cherry blossoms: National flower of Japan and emblem of the faithful warrior.

Ching-te-Chen: Ancient city in China where nearly a million people lived and worked with almost all devoted to the making of porcelain.

Chrysanthemum: Depicts health and longevity, the crest of the emperor of Japan. The chrysanthemum blooms late in the year and lives longer than other flowers.

Citron: Stands for wealth.

Cloisonné on porcelain: On Nippon porcelain wares it resembles the other cloisonné pieces except that it was produced on a porcelain body instead of metal. The decoration is divided into cells called cloisons. These cloisons were divided by strips of metal wire which kept the colors separated during the firing.

Cobalt oxide: Blue oxide imported to Japan after 1868 for decoration of wares. Gosu, a pebble found in Oriental riverbeds, had previously been used but was scarce and more expensive than the imported oxide. Cobalt oxide is the most powerful of all the coloring oxides for tinting.

Coralene items: Made by firing small colorless beads on the wares. Many are signed Kinran, US Patent, NBR 912171, February 9, 1909, Japan. Tiny glass beads had previously been applied to glass items in the shapes of birds, flowers, leaves, etc. and no doubt this was an attempt to copy it. Japanese coralene was patented by Alban L. Rock, an American living in Yokohama, Japan. The vitreous coating of beads gave the item a plush velvety look. The beads were permanently fired on and gave a luminescence to the design. The most popular design had been one of seaweed and coral, hence the name coralene was given to this type of design.

Crane: A symbol of good luck in Japan, also stands for marital fidelity and is an emblem of longevity.

Daffodil: A sign of spring to the Japanese.

Decalcomania: A process of transferring a wet paper print onto the surface of an item. It was made to resemble hand-painted work.

Deer: Stands for divine messenger.

Diaper pattern: Repetitive pattern of small design used on Nippon porcelain, often geometric or floral.

Dragons (ryu): A symbol of strength, goodness, and good fortune. The Japanese dragon has three claws and was thought to reside in the sky. Clouds, water, and lightning often accompany the dragon. The dragon is often portrayed in high relief using the slip trailing method of decor.

Drain mold: A mold used in making hollow ware. Liquid slip is poured into the mold until the desired thickness of the walls is achieved. The excess clay is poured out. When the item starts to shrink away from the mold, the mold is removed.

Drape mold: Also called flop-over mold. Used to make flat bottomed items. Moist clay is rolled out and draped over the mold. It is then pressed firmly into shape.

Dutch scenes: Popular on Nippon items, includes those of windmills, and men and women dressed in Dutch costumes.

Edo: Or Yedo, the largest city in Japan, later renamed Tokyo, meaning eastern capital.

Embossed design: See molded relief.

Enamel beading: Dots of enameling painted by the artist in gold or other colors and often made to resemble jewels, such as emeralds and rubies. Many times this raised beading will be found in brown or black colors.

Fairings: Items won or bought as souvenirs at fairs.

Feldspar: Most common rock found on earth.

Fern leaves: Symbolic of ample good fortune.

Fettles or mold marks: Ridges formed where sections of molds are joined at the seam. These fettles have to be removed before the item is decorated.

Finial: The top knob on a cover of an item, used to lift off the cover.

Firing: The cooking or baking of clay ware.

Flop-over mold: Same as drape mold.

Flux: An ingredient added to glaze to assist in making the item fire properly. It causes the glaze to melt at a specified temperature.

Glaze: Composed of silica, alumina, and flux, and is applied to porcelain pieces. During the firing process, the glaze joins with the clay item to form a glasslike surface. It seals the pores and makes the item impervious to liquids.

Gold trim: Has to be fired at lower temperatures or the gold would sink into the enameled decoration. If overfired, the gold becomes discolored.

Gouda ceramics: Originally made in Gouda, a province of south Holland. These items were copied on the Nippon wares and were patterned after the Art Nouveau style.

Gosu: Pebble found in Oriental riverbeds, a natural cobalt. It was used to color items until 1868 when oxidized cobalt was introduced into Japan.

Greenware: Clay which has been molded but not fired.

Hard paste porcelain: Paste meaning the body of substance, porcelain being made from clay using kaolin. This produces a hard translucent body when fired.

Ho-o bird: Sort of a bird of paradise who resides on earth and is associated with the empress of Japan. See also Phoenix bird.

Incised backstamp: The backstamp marking scratched into the surface of a clay item.

Incised decoration: A sharp tool or stick was used to produce the design right onto the body of the article while it was still in a state of soft clay.

Iris: The Japanese believe this flower wards off evil; associated with warriors because of its sword-like leaves.

Jasperware: See Wedgwood.

Jigger: A machine resembling a potter's wheel. Soft pliable clay is placed onto a convex revolving mold. As the wheel turns, a template is held against it, trimming off the excess clay on the outside. The revolving mold shapes the inside of the item and the template cuts the outside.

Jolley: A machine like a jigger only in reverse. The revolving mold is concave and the template forms the inside of the item. The template is lowered inside the revolving mold. The mold forms the outside surface while the template cuts the inside.

Jomon: Neolithic hunters and fishermen in Japan dating back to approximately 2500 B.C. Their pottery was hand formed and marked with an overall rope or cord pattern. It was made of unwashed clay, unglazed, and was baked in open fires.

Kaga: Province in Japan.

Kaolin: Highly refractory clay and one of the principal ingredients used in making porcelain. It is a pure white residual clay, a decomposition of granite.

Kao-ling: Chinese word meaning "the high hills," the word kaolin is derived from it.

Kiln: Oven in which pottery is fired.

Leather hard clay: Clay which is dry enough to hold its shape but still damp and moist, no longer in a plastic state, also called cheese hard.

Liquid slip: Clay in a liquid state.

Lobster: Symbol of long life.

Luster decoration: A metallic type of coloring decoration, gives an iridescent effect.

Matte finish: Also "mat" and "matt." A dull glaze having a low reflectance when fired.

McKinley Tariff Act of 1890: Chapter 1244, Section 6 states "That on and after the first day of March, eighteen hundred and ninety-one, all articles of foreign manufacture, such as are usually or ordinarily marked, stamped, branded, or labeled, and all packages containing such or other imported articles, shall, respectively, be plainly marked, stamped, branded, or labeled in legible English words, so as to indicate the country of their origin; and unless so marked, stamped, branded, or labeled, they shall not be admitted to entry."

Meiji period: Period of 1868 – 1912 in Japan when Emperor Mutsuhito reigned. It means "enlightened rule."

Middle East scenes: Designs used on Nippon pieces, featuring pyramids, deserts, palm trees, and riders on camels.

Model: The shape from which the mold is made.

Molded relief items: The pattern is embossed on the item by the mold in which the article is shaped. These items give the appearance that the pattern is caused by some type of upward pressure from the underside. Collectors often refer to these items as "blown-out."

Molds: Contain a cavity in which castings are made. They are generally made from plaster of Paris and are used for shaping clay objects. Both liquid and plastic clay may be used. The mold can also be made of clay or rubber, however, plaster was generally used as it absorbed moisture immediately from the clay. Raised ornamentation may also be formed directly in the mold.

Moriage: Refers to liquid clay (slip) relief decoration. On Nippon items this was usually done by "slip trailing" or hand rolling and shaping the clay on an item.

Morimura Brothers: Importers of Japanese wares in the United States and the sole importers of Noritake wares. The business was opened in New York City in 1876 and closed in 1941.

Mutsuhito: Emperor of Japan from 1868 to 1912. His reign was called the Meiji period which meant enlightened rule.

Nagoya: A large city in Japan, location of Noritake Co.

Slurry: Thick slip.

Solid casting mold: Used for shallow type items such as bowls and plates. In this type of mold, the thickness of the walls is determined by the mold and every piece is formed identically. The mold shapes both the inside and the outside of the piece and the thickness of the walls can be controlled. Solid casting can be done with either liquid or plastic clay.

Sometsuke style decoration: Items decorated with an underglaze of blue and white colors.

Sprigging: The application of small molded relief decoration to the surface of porcelain by use of liquid clay as in Jasperware.

Sprig mold: A one-piece mold used in making ornaments. Clay is fitted or poured into a mold which is incised with a design. Only one side is molded and the exposed side becomes the back of the finished item.

Taisho: Name of the period reigned over by Emperor Yoshihito in Japan from 1912 to 1926. It means "great peace."

Tapestry: A type of decor used on Nippon porcelain. A cloth was dipped into liquid slip and then stretched onto the porcelain item. During the bisque firing, the material burned off and left a textured look on the porcelain piece, resembling needlepoint in many cases. The item was then painted and fired again in the usual manner.

Template: Profile of the pattern being cut.

Throwing: The art of forming a clay object on a potter's wheel.

Tiger (tora): A symbol of longevity.

Transfer print: See Decalcomania.

Translucent: Not transparent, but clear enough to allow rays of light to pass through.

Ultraviolet lamp: Lamp used to detect cracks and hidden repairs in items.

Underglaze decoration: This type of decoration is applied on bisque china (fired once), then the item is glazed and fired again.

Victorian Age design: Decor used on some Nippon pieces, gaudy and extremely bold colors used.

Vitreous: Glass like.

Vitrify: To change into a glasslike substance due to the application of heat.

Wasters: Name given to pieces ruined or marred in the kiln.

Water lilies: Represent autumn in Japan.

Wedgwood: Term used to refer to Nippon pieces which attempt to imitate Josiah Wedgwood's Jasperware. The items usually have a light blue background. The Nippon pieces were generally produced with a slip trailing decor however, rather than the sprigging ornamentation made popular by Wedgwood. White clay slip was trailed onto the background color of the item by use of tubing or a cone-shaped device to form the pattern.

Yamato: District in central Japan.

Yayoi: People of the bronze and iron culture in Japan dating back to 300 – 100 B.C. They were basically an agricultural people. They made pottery using the potter's wheel.

Yedo: Or Edo, the largest city in Japan, renamed Tokyo, meaning eastern capital.

Yoshihito: Emperor of Japan from 1912 to 1926. He took the name of Taisho which meant "great peace."

Bibliography

Arnold, Edwin, Sir, *Japonica*, New York, NY, Charles Scribner's Sons, 1891.

Arnett, Ross, H. and Jacques, Richard, L., Jr., *Insect Life*, Englewood Cliffs, NJ, Prentice-Hall, Inc., 1985.

Bailey, Jill, *How Spiders Make Their Webs*, Tarrytown, NY, Marshall Cavendish Corp.

Berenbaum, May, R., *Bugs in the System*, Reading, MA, Addison-Wesley Publishing Co., 1995.

Blaney, William, *How Insects Live*, New York, NY, EP Dutton and Co., Inc.

Brackenbury, John, *Insects Life Cycles and the Seasons*, New York, NY, Sterling Publishing Co. Inc., 1994.

Butler Brothers catalogs, circa 1908-1921.

Caras, Roger, *A Celebration of Cats*, New York, NY, Simon and Schuster, 1986.

Caselli, Giovanni, *A Medieval Monk*, New York, NY, Peter Bedrick Books, 1986.

Dewey, Jennifer, Owings, *Spiders Near and Far*, New York, NY, Dutton Children's Books, Marshall Cavendish Corp., 1997.

Fischer-Nagel, Heiderose and Andrea, *The Life of the Butterfly*, Minneapolis, MN, Carolrhoda Books, Inc., 1987.

Fischer-Nagel, Heiderose and Andrea, *Life of the Honeybee*, Minneapolis, MN, Carolrhoda Books, Inc., 1986.

Fischer-Nagel, Heiserose and Andrea, *The Housefly*, Minneapolis, MN, Carolrhoda Books, Inc., 1990.

Franklyn, Julian, *Heraldry*, Cranbury, NJ, A.S. Barnes & Co., Inc., 1965.

Hillyard, Paul, *The Book of the Spider*, New York, NY, Random House, 1994.

Hutchins, Ross, E., *The Bug Clan*, New York, NY, Dodd, Mead and Co., 1973.

Lavies, Bianca, *Backyard Hunter, The Praying Mantis*, New York, NY, E.P. Dutton, 1990.

Limburg, Peter, *What's in the Names of Flowers*, NY, Coward, McCann.

Line, Les, *The Audubon Society Book of Insects*, Japan, Chanticleer Press, Inc., 1983.

Johnson, Sylvia, A., *Mantises*, Minneapolis, MN, Lerner Publications Co., 1984.

Macquity, Miranda, *Amazing Bugs*, New York, NY, DK Publishing Inc.

Mattock, John, *The Complete Book of Roses*, London, Ward Lock, 1994.

McClung, Robert, M., *Bees, Wasps and Hornets and How They Live*, New York, NY, Wm. Murrow & Co., Inc.

McGavin, George, C., Dr., *Insects*, San Diego, CA, Thunder Bay Press, 1995.

Mound, Lawrence, *Insect*, New York, NY, Alfred A. Knopf, 1990.

Norris, Desmond, *Catlore*, New York, NY, Crown Publishers, Inc., 1987.

Ormond, Richard, *Sir Edwin Landseer*, London, Rizzoli, NY in association with the Philadelphia Museum of Art and the Tate Gallery, 1981.

O'Toole, Christopher, *The Encyclopedia of Insects*, New York, NY, Facts on File, Inc., 1986.

Patent, Dorothy, Hinshaw, *Butterflies and Moths*, New York, NY Holiday House, 1979.

Patent, Dorothy, Hinshaw and Paul C. Shroeder, *Beetles and How They Live*, New York City, NY, Holiday House, 1978.

Preston-Mafham, Ken, *Grasshoppers and Mantids of the World*, New York, NY, Facts on File, Inc., 10016.

Preston-Mafham, Ken and Rod, *The Natural History of Spiders*, Ramsbury, Wiltshire, The Crowood Press, Ltd.

Seward, Diamond, *Monks and Wine*, New York City, NY, Crown Publishers, Inc., 1979.

Van Patten, Joan F., *Collector's Encyclopedia of Nippon Porcelain*, Paducah, KY, Collector Books, 1979.

Van Patten, Joan F., *Collector's Encyclopedia of Nippon Porcelain, Second Series*, Paducah, KY, Collector Books, 1982.

Van Patten, Joan F., *Collector's Encyclopedia of Nippon Porcelain, Third Series*, Paducah, KY, Collector Books, 1986.

Van Patten, Joan F., *Collector's Encyclopedia of Nippon Porcelain, Fourth Series*, Paducah, KY, Collector Books, 1997.

Van Patten, Joan F., *Collector's Encyclopedia of Nippon Porcelain, Fifth Series*, Paducah, KY, Collector Books, 1998.

Van Patten, Joan F., *Collector's Encyclopedia of Nippon Porcelain, Sixth Series*, Paducah, KY, Collector Books, 2000.

Van Patten, Joan F. and Linda Lau, *Nippon Dolls and Playthings*, Paducah, KY, Collector Books, 2000.

Wooten, Anthony, *Insects of the World*, New York, NY, Facts on File Publications.

Index

Numbers are Plate numbers where pieces can be seen in this book.

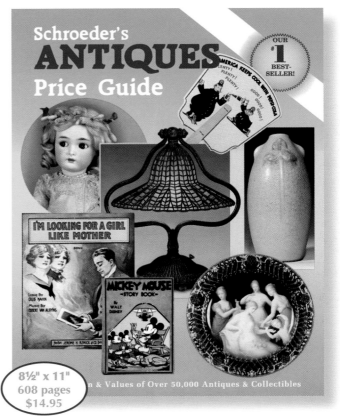